00376

KU-300-970

WITHDRAWN

Napier Polytechnic Library
The psychology of leisure travel: effect
GlenHd 9999 L4 Ray 8409594401

The Psychology of
Leisure Travel

THE PSYCHOLOGY OF LEISURE TRAVEL

Effective Marketing and Selling
of Travel Services

EDWARD J. MAYO, JR.
Director, Dick Pope Sr. Institute for Tourism Studies
LANCE P. JARVIS
Associate Dean

College of Business Administration
University of Central Florida

CBI   CBI Publishing Company, Inc.
51 Sleeper Street, Boston, Massachusetts 02210

Production Editor: Linda Dunn McCue
Interior Designer: Katrine Stevens
Cover Designer: Christy Rosso
Compositor: Trade Composition, Inc.

Copyright © 1981 CBI Publishing Company, Inc.
51 Sleeper Street, Boston, MA 02210
All rights reserved. This book may not be reproduced by any means without express written permission from the publisher.

Printed in the United States of America.

Printing (last digit): 9 8 7 6 5 4 3 2 1

Library of Congress Cataloging in Publication Data

Mayo, Edward J.
  The psychology of leisure travel.

  Bibliography: p.
  Includes index.
  1. Travel—Psychological aspects.
2. Travelers—Psychology. I. Jarvis,
Lance P., 1943–   . II. Title.
G151.M38   910′.01′9   81-10014
ISBN 0-8436-2204-0   AACR2

Distributed by:
**VAN NOSTRAND
REINHOLD (U.K.)**
MOLLY MILLARS LANE
WOKINGHAM, BERKS.
RG11 2PY, ENGLAND

NAPIER COLLEGE OF COMMERCE AND TECHNOLOGY

AC 84 095944 01 00 1137 /84

SIGHTHILL 910.019 MAY TT x

CON 0843622040 /24-75

To our parents
Marge and Ed Mayo
Erma and Bill Jarvis
Whose vision, encouragement,
support, and sacrifices made
many distant journeys possible.

TABLE OF CONTENTS

FOREWORD

The travel industry is a loosely organized composite of several distinct enterprises. Perhaps this is why, until now, there have been such wide gaps in our understanding of travel behavior and motivation. In this book, the insights necessary to close many of these gaps have been supplied for the first time. By exploring the very roots of travel behavior — perception, personality, attitudes, and other psychological factors — the authors clarify the questions and issues of greatest concern to our industry.

Why, for example, does a traveler decide to visit one country rather than another? As this book discusses in detail, the decision is in large part determined by the country's image. Image, in turn, is influenced by history — especially the textbook histories that we learned in school. An additional factor comes into play when we consider that many Americans have ancestral and emotional ties that link them to distant lands.

Of course, images are not static. Many countries are undergoing changes in appearance — changes that represent both real dangers and major opportunities for the travel industry. The outskirts of Paris are beginning to look like Detroit, and the same is true of Vienna and many other cities. The exotic nature of several African countries is changing as well. These changes are encouraged by the mistaken notion that what the modern traveler looks for in Africa is the same as what he looks for in Europe, the Far East, or Miami Beach.

Not only African countries but others, too, have lost much of their uniqueness by emphasizing standard tourist attractions instead of their own natural assets. I am reminded of a journey I once made all the way to India. During my stay in Shinagar in Kashmir, I was served barbecued hamburgers — misspelled, incidentally, as "humburgers." The organizers of my conference were shocked when I confided that what I wanted most was real Indian food. They explained that it had to be ordered at least a day in advance. Yet many people, like myself, travel to discover things that are different and new. This urge to experience and explore the unknown — previously underestimated in our industry — is acknowledged by the authors as a powerful motivating force behind much travel behavior.

This urge to explore the unknown is only one of many powerful desires and needs that are felt by consumers far more often than they are articulated. At times there are great differences between what people say they want from a vacation and what they really want. Sometimes an individual really doesn't know. The psychological insights and methods discussed in this book are perhaps the most effective means of tapping unspoken needs and desires. Travel agents and others who apply these methods will find themselves better equipped to understand what might best satisfy the consumer's travel needs.

Some people however, have difficulty taking any kind of vacation. They are so involved with work that sitting still for any period of time elicits feelings of guilt. Unconsciously, leisure time represents to them a foretaste of passive retirement and perhaps even death. These people must be encouraged to perceive travel as an active and productive experience, and the reader will discover several methods for accomplishing this within the pages of this book.

Most people revert to a childlike state when they travel. My own research indicates that the childlike or id state dominates the personality when one is away from the accustomed home, country, or language. People want to be pampered when they are away from home, and they want to have fun. Freudian and Transactional Analysis can aid us in understanding important personality factors that affect travel behavior and motivations. These topics are discussed here in depth, providing valuable insights that will enable travel service professions to develop and promote their products more effectively.

Although the major thrust of this book is a psychological one, the authors do not neglect the ramifications that political, sociological, and economic factors are bound to have on tourism trends and travel behavior. American tourists abroad, for example, are discovering that foreign-made goods have become too expensive to purchase and bring home. They are discovering that their own country is as much a "bargain" as Spain and Portugal once were. And that the American image has diminished to such an extent that they are often received with mistrust or hostility when abroad. The special travel behaviors of families and the pressures that various groups exert on individual travel decisions are subjects that deserve greater consideration than we have given them in the past. Fortunately, both subjects are treated at length in *The Psychology of Leisure Travel*, providing useful information for students and practitioners alike.

Now that travel has ceased to be the privilege of the upper classes, its pervasiveness demands a more comprehensive study of leisure behaviors in all their complexity. Statistical findings, by themselves, are no longer adequate. Broad generalizations no longer apply. The continued growth of our industry depends on a closer and more attentive scrutiny of *individual* travel needs. And Mayo and Jarvis prove themselves equal to this task, enriching the store of knowledge that will enable our industry to serve today's travelers — and tomorrow's — more effectively. For travel agencies, destination countries and their tourist offices, hotel and motel operators, airlines, and others in the travel field, *The Psychology of Leisure Travel* is an eminently enlightening and useful book.

Ernest Dichter

PREFACE

This book was written to better acquaint the travel industry with the consumer-traveler. This is not meant to suggest that the traveler is a complete stranger to the industry that serves him. But it does suggest that, by focusing on the individual rather than the "average" — and by understanding this traveler in psychological instead of merely demographic terms — new insights into travel behavior will be possible. These insights should enable the various segments of the travel industry to better serve their customers.

In the authors' experiences as consultants, researchers, and seminar leaders in the travel industry, a recurring theme voiced both by practitioners and students is the scarcity of knowledge about what really goes on in the consumer-traveler's head when he or she decides to travel. There is a need, they say, for a better understanding of the customers they serve.

The travel industry has made great strides over the years in operating more efficiently. Airlines, hotels, car rental companies, and others have learned how to manage capital assets more effectively. Travel agencies have learned that their businesses need to be managed as professionally as the multimillion-dollar carriers and lodging chains. And federal, state, and local tourism organizations have gradually learned that travel does not necessarily sell itself. Many practitioners readily acknowledge, however, that they are often uneasy when making decisions that require assumptions about how the consumer-traveler makes travel decisions. Many practitioners frankly admit that their knowledge of the psychological forces that affect travel behavior is very limited.

Some firms in the travel industry believe that they understand travel behavior as well as it needs to be understood. These organizations know that their "average" customer is 38.7 years old, has completed 1.3 years of college, has an income of $24,253 and has 2.1 children and two-thirds of a dog. Such customer profiles can be useful to a limited extent. But they fail almost completely to help us understand such important phenomena as:

· the failure of many travelers to use the services of travel agents
· the growing popularity of cruise vacations
· the rise and fall in popularity of various destination areas
· the appeal of certain lodging chains
· attitudes toward competing airlines and modes of transportation
· international travel, fly-drive programs, and packaged tours

Age, income, education, and other demographic information tell us whether an individual is a likely prospect for travel services in general — but rarely will such information help to explain why the traveler chooses one destination instead of another, why he prefers to fly instead of drive, why he prefers one airline over another, why he chooses to consult a travel agent, or why he resists paying for travel on an installment basis. Statistics alone cannot explain why two families living next door to one another and with nearly identical demographic characteristics exhibit diverse travel behavior. In the absence of a comprehensive understanding of how these types of decisions are made, there are few clues as to how an organization can better serve the consumer-traveler.

As we look toward the 1980s and beyond, there are several trends in the market for travel services that underscore the need for a more comprehensive understanding of travel behavior. These trends will have a profound impact on businesses that serve this $100 billion leisure travel market. There is little doubt that substantial changes can be expected in the intensity of competition, service offerings, and emphasis on the consumer-traveler.

First, from all indications the market will be considerably larger and different than it is today. More Americans will be traveling, and they will be doing so more often. A continued emphasis on the value of experience, coupled with deregulation of the airline industry and greater discretionary incomes, will substantially increase the number of traveling Americans. Many, of course, will be new travelers. In general, these travelers will be more discriminating. They will be better educated, more sophisticated, more experienced, and more demanding of those who serve them both prior to and during their travel experiences.

Second, more of this travel will span national boundaries as the horizons of both leisure and business travelers extend beyond traditional frontiers. The quantum increase in foreign travel to the U.S. should continue unabated. Increases in the real incomes of the citizens of other nations, together with their curiosity about America, all but ensure the continued trend toward increased foreign travel to the U.S. Likewise, more Americans will seize the opportunity to travel to other nations.

Third, prompted by opportunities afforded in this growth industry, competition within its various sectors will intensify. More well-financed organizations, including many that previously had no interest in serving the travel market, can be expected to enter it. The intensity of the competition will be particularly evident where new organizations attempt to move in on specialized market "niches" previously served by longstanding and well-known companies in the industry. The new entrants, often equipped with sophisticated research methods and a well-tuned arsenal of marketing techniques developed in other fields, will zero in on market segments that have been either inadequately served or neglected by the industry to date.

The new corporate entrants to the travel industry will question or ignore much of the conventional wisdom used by more experienced practitioners in the industry. Many of these mavericks will bring to the industry a knowledge of consumers and their needs gained from experiences in unrelated industries. The result will be increased competition and new, unconventional travel services. Standard practices — and even some traditional competitors — that have been mainstays in the industry for decades will quietly disappear. The result of this creative destruction among competitors will be a better-served consumer-traveler, and a corporate roster consisting largely of new and prominent competitors in the travel industry. Even the well-established survivors will be different. They will have to adapt and change themselves.

Lastly, consumerism and related issues that have become so prevalent in other industries are destined to assume an even larger role in operations of both large and small firms that serve the traveler.

All four of these trends have implications in common. Each represents both a threat and a challenging opportunity to organizations that presently serve the travel market. In addition, each trend underscores the necessity for companies to adapt in order to survive in a dynamic market where the only constant we can expect is continued change. Finally, and perhaps most important, only those competitors with a keen and fundamental understanding of travel behavior will succeed in adapting to each of these threats and opportunities.

This book focuses on the individual traveler's behavior from both a psychological and sociological perspective. In this sense, it differs markedly from the literature on tourism that (1) essentially describes rather than seeks to explain travel behavior, and (2) emphasizes the behavior of masses of travelers rather than the individual's. Clearly, it is the large numbers of people who travel that interest the travel industry. It is the decisions of individuals, however, that determine which destinations will be visited, how the traveler will get there, how much he will spend, and what types of accommodations and restaurants he will seek when he arrives. For this reason, we feel that an examination of the traveler as a decision-maker — from an individual, behavioral viewpoint — provides the needed insights to assist practitioners in dealing effectively with foreseeable trends in the industry, and to better serve the traveler.

To our knowledge, no other book has been written that views travel and tourism from a behavioral science perspective. Simply stated, we believe that human behavior is less unpredictable to the extent that the forces that influence it are understood. And, for the serious reader, there should be greater satisfaction and more profit to be gained from serving customers whose behavior is better understood.

This book is not intended to be an exhaustive inventory of everything that is known about travel behavior. No single book could incorporate all that is known. Instead, we present the reader with selected and well-accepted principles of psychology and sociology as they apply to travel behavior. These insights are supplemented by results from the growing volume of research that focuses specifically on the dynamics underlying travel behavior. We have drawn implications from this material that should be helpful to the practitioner in linking behavioral principles and research results to improved decisions about how to market and sell travel more profitably. The book is intended primarily for professionals in various sectors of the travel industry — travel agencies, airlines and other carriers, lodging chains, car rental companies, cruise lines, and restaurants, along with those federal, state, and local organizations that are concerned with promoting tourism. In each chapter, we present examples showing how insights into the traveler can be practically applied. In some cases, these examples focus on only one or two sectors of the travel industry. This does not, of course, preclude applications to other sectors.

The payoff to the practitioner who develops a keener understanding of the forces that influence travel behavior is not always immediate or direct. More often, this understanding is reflected over time in a heightened sensitivity to the needs of individual travelers, along with an enhanced ability to make decisions that profitably serve their needs and interests.

This book is also intended to assist students preparing to enter careers in travel and travel-related fields. The authors believe that it is essential for future practitioners in the travel industry to have a fundamental understanding of the psychological and sociological forces that affect the behavior of travelers. From a careful reading of this book, the student will acquire the fundamental knowledge necessary to understand and influence travel behavior.

All of us are students, of course, and we should recognize that tomorrow's traveler will differ in important ways from today's. In addition, tomorrow's travel market will include whole new segments of individuals who have previously had neither the means nor the interest to undertake travel. Accordingly, future travel behavior is likely to differ as well. However, the basic psychological and sociological processes that influence travel will most likely remain the same. For these reasons, students and practitioners are encouraged to put aside their mental images of today's "average" traveler while proceeding through the chapters of this book. Readers are encouraged to develop an intimate knowledge of the traveler's decision-making process and the forces that influence it, so that they will be ready to understand and profitably serve the needs of consumer-travelers in the future.

Human behavior rarely defies explanation. However, simple explanations of an inherently complex process are rarely satisfactory or insightful. This book is intended to be immensely practical — but it is not a "how-to" book that provides checklists and simple answers to the complex questions of why people travel and how they make decisions when they are away from home. It is our belief that human behavior does not lend itself to the checklist level of simplification. For these reasons, most of the book requires rather serious reading. We do not apologize for this necessity any more than the traveler must apologize for engaging in behavior that is not always easy for us to comprehend.

It is probably fair to conclude that the consumerism movement has resulted from the consumer's dissatisfaction with the performance of individuals and firms that serve him in the marketplace. All too often, organizations that are the targets of consumer wrath find it simply incomprehensible that longstanding products, services, and ways of doing business have suddenly come under attack. It is our hope that one outcome of reading this book will be a heightened sensitivity, concern for, and responsiveness to matters that sometimes cause dissatisfaction among consumer-travelers. To the extent that firms integrate the traveler's viewpoint into decisions that affect him, such dissatisfaction is unlikely to occur.

While this book shares with its readers much of what is known today concerning travel behavior, research in this field is still in its infancy. Hopefully, one byproduct of reading this book will be a greater commitment among both practitioners and academicians to support and conduct further research into the process of travel behavior. It is only through research-based insights that a more accurate and detailed portrait of the traveler will be possible.

Finally, we hope that each reader's journey through the pages of this book will be — like any rewarding journey — both enlightening and enjoyable.

Edward J. Mayo, Jr.
Lance P. Jarvis

ACKNOWLEDGMENTS

This book was written while the authors were on the faculties of the University of Notre Dame (E.J.M.) and Idaho State University (L.P.J.). Its completion would not have been possible without the moral encouragement and administrative support of four close friends and colleagues at these institutions. Associate Deans Hugh Furuhashi and Vincent Raymond of the College of Business Administration at Notre Dame understood the commitment necessary to develop a volume of this magnitude and provided much of the freedom that was essential to its completion. When their forbearance might have been tested, Dr. David Appel, Chairman of the Department of Marketing at Notre Dame, managed to find new ways to support the effort. More importantly, however, David was as eager as the authors were to see the book completed and helped sustain the enthusiasm that was needed to make it through to the final chapter. This was not a new experience for him.

Fifteen hundred miles to the west, James M. Kelly, Dean of the College of Business at Idaho State University, contributed immeasurably to the completion of the volume. From its inception, Jim enthusiastically offered to the authors his encouragement and support. His sensitivity to our needs and sustaining commitment removed most of the financial and logistical obstacles that would normally be encountered by two authors working half a continent apart over a two-year period. Jim's philosophy that a primary role for a college dean is to support and invest in his faculty's professional growth was seriously tested during this period. The book is a grateful testament to Jim's commitment to this increasingly rare administrative perspective.

A host of colleagues, students, and executives in the travel industry have made contributions of one kind or another to this book. Dr. Edward Kelly, Vice President of the Institute of Certified Travel Agents, reviewed an early draft of the manuscript and provided us with a number of critical suggestions that measurably strengthen the book. Ed also read the final draft of the manuscript and in his postscript provides a perspective that should help the serious reader to better understand and appreciate the psychological role of travel. Dr. John Kennedy of the University of Notre Dame shaped much of the thinking that went into the chapter dealing with personality and travel behavior. John Levy, a graduate student, provided constructive criticism of the chapter dealing with perception and travel behavior and also helped gather the hundreds of advertisements from which the illustrations appearing throughout the book were selected.

A number of original research projects conducted by the authors and reported in this book were underwritten by the organizations represented by Robert Hazard, formerly President of Best Western International; Ray Anderson and George Vondruska of the 3M National Advertising Company; and Brian Herron, Executive Vice President of the National Restaurant Association. These individuals not only provided financial support but, along with others associated with their organizations, made significant contributions to the interpretation of research findings. Dee Minick of the National Tour Brokers Association read an early draft of the manuscript. And numerous individuals with the Travel Industry Association of America, the American Society of Travel Agents, the American Hotel and Motel Association, the Old West Trails Foundation — as well as a number of state travel directors — provided opportunities to test and refine many of the materials in this book through seminar presentations and consulting and research projects.

We also wish to acknowledge and thank various travel industry organizations for allowing us to reproduce the travel advertisements that appear in this book. These advertisements help to illustrate important principles discussed in the text. Although we were limited to using primarily print advertisements, the reader will find them a valuable part of the book.

The manuscript for this book rolled through several different typewriters, but the one which did the bulk of the work belonged to Cheryl Barnum. She typed and retyped, collated, checked references, and generally managed the progress of the manuscript toward the publisher. For her devoted and meticulous care, we express our sincerest gratitude.

It is commonplace for writers to thank family members at the conclusion of a long list of acknowledgements, and after finishing this project we can understand why. The writing of a volume such as *The Psychology of Leisure Travel* puts a premium on endurance and persistence, and without family members who somehow understand this, it would be impossible to finish. Much thanks especially to Cindy and to Meg, Dobb, Jason, and Jennifer for their cooperation, tolerance, emotional support, and other intangibles — and for learning not to ask to often, "When will that book be finished?"

Finally, it is not uncommon for co-authors to emerge from the completion of a volume with emotional scars and a hope for eternal psychological and physical distance from one another. We are pleased to report to our friends and colleagues who alerted us to this danger that our decade-long close, personal, and professional bond has been strengthened during our co-authorship of this book. In fact, the preparation of *The Psychology of Leisure Travel* was a joyful experience that we hope is apparent to the reader. The distance of half a continent that separated us during the manuscript preparation period has, upon its completion, been reduced, perhaps symbolically, to the few feet between our offices in the College of Business Administration at the University of Central Florida.

1

THE STUDY
OF TRAVEL
AND LEISURE
BEHAVIOR

Much has been written in recent years about the leisure boom in the United States and other western industrialized nations. It is estimated that Americans spend better than $120 billion each year for their leisure. This money is spent for admission to sporting events, movies, stage plays, concerts, and other cultural attractions. It is spent on recreational vehicles, bowling balls, bicycles, cameras, cabin cruisers, fishing equipment, snowmobiles, mini-bikes and an endless number of other recreational items. It is spent on golf, tennis, hunting, fishing, boating, skiing, scuba diving, and scores of other leisure-time activities. And nearly half of the expenditure on leisure in the United States is for vacation travel, both within the U.S. and abroad.

Sixty-five percent of all Americans take at least one annual vacation trip, and many take any number of shorter vacations and weekend pleasure journeys. An estimated $61 billion is spent within the United States each year by travelers for hotel and motel rooms, airline tickets, gasoline, food, and other items. Americans who travel to foreign countries spend better than $9 billion outside of the United States. It is easy to see that travel and tourism is big business, and that its economic impact is great. In the state of Florida alone, out-of-state visitors spend more than $16 billion each year, thereby creating nearly 335,000 jobs for Floridians. In California, 93,000 people are employed in the hotel and motel industry alone, and they earn $664 million annually. In Vermont, one out of every seven nonagricultural workers is employed in the travel industry. In Pennsylvania, taxes on various travel services generate revenues exceeding $750 million a year.[1]

The leisure boom is not, of course, strictly an American phenomenon. Travel and tourism are of even greater economic importance to countries like Great Britain, Spain, Italy, Ireland, Mexico, Austria, Denmark, and Switzerland. In some areas, tourism is the single most important source of income and jobs. In balance of payments terms, tourism is an "export" and as such is an important source of income. Spain, for example, derives better than one-third of its foreign exchange from tourism — a dependence on a single industry, says one authority, that is unparalleled in western Europe. Tourism has become increasingly important to eastern European countries as well, because it provides these countries with an otherwise difficult way to earn "hard" currencies. Soviet statisticians have discovered that the average profit, if that be the right word, from one foreign tourist is equal to the profit earned by exporting two tons of grain.[2] Many emerging countries have embraced tourism because it sometimes can provide an easy way to earn foreign exchange. In addition, tourism is a "clean" industry — one that environmentally-oriented politicians and citizens can support.

Because of the importance of travel and tourism, governments often assume an important role in stimulating the tourist economy. In Portugal, for example, new hotels are exempt from property taxes for ten years. In Japan, travel agents are exempt from income taxes on monies earned from selling inclusive tours of Japan to foreigners. Many countries stimulate travel and tourism through airline subsidies, the development and expansion of airports with public money, and publicly financed travel promotion.

Total expenditures on travel advertising in the United States alone are estimated at around $500 million a year. A considerable portion of this sum derives from foreign countries and destination areas within them, as well as publicly-owned air and rail carriers. The province of Ontario, Canada, for example, spent $1.2 million on travel advertising in the U.S. in 1976. Other foreign advertisers who spend substantially on U.S. advertising include Bermuda, Quantas, Japan Airlines, Finnair, British Airways, Iberia Airlines, SAS, and Air Canada. The U.S. Travel Service, an agency of the U.S. Department of Commerce, has operated with a budget as high as $13 million a year, and one of its primary functions has been to stimulate foreign travel to the U.S. Within the United States, a number of states spend large amounts to stimulate travel. Michigan's state travel budget exceeds $3 million a year. The state of New York spent $9 million in 1978 on advertising alone to encourage people to visit New York.

In short, there is no question that tourism is a vital source of income and employment. Only oil, it is claimed, accounts for a greater percentage of international trade. Tourism is no less than the third most important industry in the large majority of states in the U.S. As a United Nations Conference on International Travel and Tourism concluded, travel and tourism are economic and social forces of major proportions in the world.

THE IMPORTANCE OF PSYCHOLOGICAL THEORY

The basic objectives of this book are to explain why people travel and to provide a foundation for understanding the various travel-related decisions that tourists and vacationers make, including destination decisions, mode of transportation, lodging, and use of travel agents. We will also examine the factors that influence such choices. The focus of this book, then, is on the individual traveler, his travel-related decisions, and how they are made. Economics helps us understand the importance of travel and tourism, and it indicates the size of the travel and tourism market. In other words, economic factors help to describe, in aggregate or total terms, the travel behavior of millions of people who periodically leave their homes in search of pleasures that, for one reason or another, are not always easily found in the living room or the backyard.

There seems to be a widespread assumption, however, that economic factors can also explain the behavior of, and the decisions made by, the individual traveler. Great efforts are put into collecting information about the travel behavior of masses of people — the number of visitors, say, to Florida or France each year, how much they spend, how long they stay, how many people they travel with, and so forth. Information like this is essential and important. But, as this book will clearly demonstrate, economic factors alone do a very poor job of explaining the behavior and the decisions of the **individual** traveler. To effectively and profitably serve the individual traveler, we need to understand the **psychological** forces that motivate him and that influence the various travel-related decisions he makes.

Economic factors do not tell us much more than which individuals are *able* to travel and which of these individuals might have an inclination to do so. There are, for example, an estimated 5.6 million people in the United States who have graduated from college and who earn incomes of $20,000 or more per year. Their above-average incomes should permit them, along with their families, to indulge periodically in pleasure travel. And their educations should have increased their awareness of the interesting and diverse world in which they live, stimulating their desire to see this world with their own eyes. We know, however, that a sizeable percentage of affluent, college-educated people in the United States choose to spend their leisure time in and around their own homes. Economic analysis does not explain why. Nor does it adequately explain the behavior of those who do travel.

It is useful, then, to distinguish between **qualifying** factors and **determining** factors. To be considered part of the market for travel, a consumer would have to have enough money. This, however, would only qualify her as a "prospect." It would not tell us whether she will choose to spend her money on travel, a college education, a new car, a new wardrobe, or a set of encyclopedias for her children. In short, traditional demographic factors like income, education, age, and occupation, only tell us that there is some likelihood that a given individual might choose to travel.

Explaining the decision to travel — and the variety of related decisions that accompany it — depends on an examination of relevant psychological and sociological factors. These, and not demographic factors, will actually determine whether an individual will travel, the specific destination to which he will travel, how he will get there, and what he will do when he arrives. It is through an understanding of the psychological forces that influence travel that we can better understand the traveler's specific attitudes, personality, and motivation. And, with these insights, we can serve the individual traveler more effectively and profitably.

OUTLINE OF THIS BOOK

Explaining travel behavior is not easy. There are just too many factors that influence an individual's behavior. In the psychologist's terms, one must understand how people **perceive** such things as destination areas, air travel, travel distances, and travel advertising; how they **learn** to consume and to travel; how they make decisions; and how **personality** affects those decisions. One must learn what **motivations** influence the individual's travel decisions and how these motivations interact. We must understand how **attitudes** are formed and how they influence the individual's behavior. And we must know how various **group influences** affect travel behavior.

Travel behavior is a special form of consumption behavior, and the factors noted here are recognized as major sources of influence on this type of behavior. Each of these factors — perception, learning, personality, motivation, attitudes, and group influences — is the subject of a chapter in this book.

The primary focus of the book is on the travel behavior of individuals. Thus, the focus is primarily a psychological one. There are other social sciences besides psychology, however, that can help to explain travel behavior. Throughout this book, therefore, we will occasionally utilize other perspectives: sociology (the study of group behavior), social psychology (the study of interpersonal behavior), anthropology (the study of societies and cultures), economics (the study of how people choose to spend money), and history.

This first chapter provides a foundation for understanding the psychological principles discussed in chapters two through seven of this book. It would be impossible, for example, to understand the travel behavior of individuals living in highly developed countries without at least briefly examining pleasure travel from a historical perspective. Therefore, we will begin with a historical overview of tourism.

Often, an individual's travel behavior is influenced more by the amount of time he has available for leisure activities than by the amount of money or the number of credit cards in his pocket. This is especially true of individuals living in economically advanced societies, where time pressures are greatest. Consequently, we must identify how these pressures affect travel and leisure behavior, and this is done in the second section of this chapter.

The third and final section of this chapter presents a framework or model for understanding individual travel behavior. This model will help readers understand from the outset the relationships among various key psychological concepts discussed throughout the book. In this way, readers can more easily integrate material as they proceed from one chapter to the next.

A BRIEF HISTORY OF TOURISM

The earliest human beings were not wanderers, but preferred to stay in one place. Only changes in climate, dwindling food supplies, or hostile invaders could drive people from safe retreats. This situation changed when people recognized that there might be something to be gained from a journey that took them far from their homes.

Travel in Ancient Times

Initially, commerce and trade motivated people to wander away from home for weeks or months — and sometimes years. The Phoenicians were among the first real travelers in any modern sense, moving from one place to another as traders. Early travel in the Orient was also largely based on trade.[3]

Of course, people in ancient times found other reasons to travel besides trade, commerce, and the search for more plentiful food supplies. Philosophers like Plato and Aristotle visited Egypt and Asia Minor. Herodotus, the Greek historian, toured the Black Sea region, Egypt, Phoenicia, and Greece in the fourth century B.C. Armies traveled to make war, while others traveled to visit famous temples and religious monuments.

In addition there were some, even in ancient times, who traveled simply for pleasure. In the fourth century B.C., thousands of people would flock each year to the ancient city of Ephesus, in what is now Turkey, to be entertained by acrobats, animal acts, jugglers, and magicians. Greek citizens journeyed to spas and festivals. And, beginning in 776 B.C., visitors from all over Europe and the Middle East traveled to Mount Olympus for the Olympic Games.

For the most part, however, travel for the sake of pleasure in ancient times was limited primarily to the well-to-do. Those lower down on the economic and social scales enjoyed few opportunities to engage in such frivolity. Though they may have had the time because of better than a hundred holidays a year, the absence of good communications, the paucity of disposable incomes, and real dangers to travelers posed serious obstacles to travel.

Travel in the Roman Empire

Ordinary citizens in large numbers came to indulge in pleasure travel during the time of the Roman Empire (27 B.C.–395 A.D.). In order to protect and administer the large empire, the Romans built an efficient network of roads that enabled the ordinary citizen to travel. As George Young points out, this pattern — an important advance in transportation technology brought about by military needs — should not be unfamiliar to the student living in the twentieth century.[4] Military uses of the airplane, for example, preceded its development for commercial purposes. The 1,500-mile Alaska Highway and the 42,000-mile Interstate Highway System were also built, in part, because of military considerations.

Traveling in the Roman Empire was safe and convenient to a degree unknown again until the beginning of the nineteenth century. A traveler could journey from one end of the Empire to the other, a distance of over 4,500 miles, over what were then first-class roads. By using relays of horses, it was possible to cover long distances in relatively short periods of time. If one were in a real hurry, as many as 100 miles a day could be covered.

The Romans also built hotels — or posting houses, as they were called — to accommodate the long-distance travelers using the Roman road network. This development also has its modern counterparts in the hotels invested in by stage-coach companies, railroads, and airlines to serve their passengers. Some of the Roman posting houses could only be used by officials with a *diploma tractatorium* — an official document carried by those on government business — a custom still surviving in today's airport VIP lounges.

The Roman roads were used heavily in the summer months. City dwellers escaped the heat of summer by traveling to coastal resorts. These seaside resorts — known as spas — offered medicinal baths, theatrical productions, festivals, and athletic competitions. Those who could afford it traveled abroad for their holidays — to Egypt, Greece, or Babylon.

Following the collapse of the Roman Empire in the fifth century, the conditions fostering extensive pleasure travel were absent for approximately the next thousand years. These centuries are often referred to as the Dark Ages, when travel became a dangerous undertaking. Commerce and trade became much less important, and people once again became immobile and tied to the land that sustained them. The great Roman roads deteriorated, and only the most adventurous would wander too far or long away from home. The only significant travel undertaken during the Dark Ages came during the Crusades — which were essentially military expenditions — and during pilgrimages to the important religious shrines of Europe.

The Reemergence of Pleasure Travel

Extensive pleasure travel reemerged in England during the reign of Queen Elizabeth I (1558–1603). Horse-drawn coaches and wagons made travel easier, and trade began to flourish once again. Educational travel also became popular. The young aristocracy — and, in time, the sons of the rising middle class — traveled to the Continent to complete their education. By 1670 this kind of educational odyssey, sometimes lasting as long as three years, had become known as the Grand Tour.

It is worth emphasizing here that the Grand Tour justified the fun and excitement of travel on the basis that it helped round out one's education. Presumably, the purpose of the Grand Tour was a practical one. As we shall see, this phenomenon — justifying an inherently enjoyable activity like travel in terms of important, practical purposes — helps to explain much travel behavior even today.

This need to justify pleasure travel was responsible for the growth in popularity of the spa. As early as the sixteenth century, the medical profession in England began prescribing visits to places where mineral waters flowed from natural springs. Mineral waters were thought to have extraordinary healing properties, and those places where springs could be found became extremely popular. Better-known spas included Bath, Turnbridge Wells, and Epsom in England, Spa in Belgium, Baden-Baden in Germany, Baines-les-Bains in France, and Lucca in Italy. In fact, hundreds of spas throughout England and Europe — and later in the United States — were patronized by those who would "take the waters" in search of better health.

Slowly, the spas evolved into vacation resorts which, more than anything else, helped to restore and maintain their visitors' psychological health. The spas offered a means of escape from the cities. As Young points out, "People of wealth and fashion gravitated towards them, even though they were in good health."[5] Accordingly, the spas became more consumer-oriented. They offered their guests better accommodations, along with the opportunity to indulge in various social events, games, dancing, gambling, and entertainment.

Sea bathing also became popular — again, in part, because people believed that sea water was curative. In time, people came to seaside resorts not in search of better health, but to have fun. The sea coast appreciably expanded the capacity of the budding tourist industry, since every small coastal community could easily be transformed into a seaside resort. When this happened tourism began to evolve, albeit slowly, into an industry that served not only the rich and well-to-do, but an increasingly large middle class as well.

Travel Since the Industrial Revolution

An important characteristic of modern tourism in the industrialized world is that it can be indulged in by nearly everyone. The Industrial Revolution of the late 1700s and 1800s is largely responsible for this. The Industrial Revolution refers to the social and economic changes that occurred when hand tools were gradually replaced by machine and power tools. With the help of machines, people were able to multiply their productivity. In time, the cobbler became an assembly-line worker who could help make hundreds of shoes a day. The seamstress became a pattern cutter who could help make hundreds of dresses a day. The farmer could plow ten acres a day instead of one.

Increases in the productive capacity of the average worker led to several important changes in the social and economic structure of industrializing societies. Not the least of these changes was the increased wealth that was generated — income that accrued to the middle-class industrialists instead of the landed aristocracy. Ultimately, and largely due to increasingly powerful trade unions, some of this new wealth also accrued to the workers. No longer did they toil long hours just to pay for the basic necessities of life. Instead, many workers now earned discretionary incomes that could be spent on some of life's luxuries — and, among other things, this ultimately included travel.

The Industrial Revolution also changed the nature of the tasks performed by the average worker, as well as the place where these tasks were performed. The Industrial Revolution called for large-scale production facilities. People flocked from the agricultural countryside to the city factories in search of better wages and a higher standard of living. One result of mechanized production was that the type of work performed became relentlessly monotonous for many. City and factory life — in comparison to the seasonality, variety, and leisurely pace of life in the countryside — was routinized, standardized, and frequently boring. Still, life for many was greatly improved. But there emerged an urgent need to escape periodically from the ever-present routines and pressures of city living. This created a new demand for travel and — together with the worker's newly found discretionary income — served as the foundation for the modern tourist industry, an industry that appeals to and serves the travel needs of large masses of people living in advanced industrialized nations.

The Industrial Revolution brought still another change that has had a significant impact on the development of the tourism industry: the emergence and growth of powerful trade unions. The trade union movement is largely responsible for a shorter work week, longer annual vacations, vacations with pay, and higher wages. Each of these factors, of course, stimulates increased expenditures of time and money on travel and tourism.

The Contribution of Thomas Cook

Even a brief historical overview of pleasure travel would be incomplete without mention of Thomas Cook. The invention of steam locomotion brought mobility to people who might not otherwise have been able to travel long distances from home. And it did this at unheard-of low prices. The initial impact of rail travel was to increase short day-trips. Excursion trains were more fully developed by Cook. His first publicly advertised excursion was from Leicester, England to a temperance demonstration in Loughborough on July 5, 1841. The round-trip fare was one shilling, and 570 people paid the price. From this relatively modest beginning, Cook went on to build an organization that has been a household word in travel ever since. In 1855, he started his first continental operation by marketing travel to the Paris Exhibition. This was the origin of the inclusive tour.

Cook offered an itinerary that might have taken the individual tourist weeks to organize and a good deal more to finance. Cook's success, however, can be attributed to other factors besides these. In the nineteenth century, there was no established tradition of extended travel among the new middle classes, and there were formidable practical obstacles to surmount. There were language problems, prejudices at home and abroad, confusing monetary exchange rates, and, finally, passports. The rich overcame these difficulties when traveling by using their money — by employing personal guides and patronizing hotels whose employees spoke the traveler's language. The new middle-class tourists could not afford these services, however, and so turned to Thomas Cook. Cook had the foresight to recognize these problems, and he built an organization which helped solve them. The influence of Cook in the field of travel cannot be overemphasized.

The revolution in travel has continued to the present day, influenced most in the twentieth century by technological developments in the transportation industry. The airplane, automobile, and tens of thousands of miles of good roads have created an impression of entire societies always on the move. These technological developments have lowered the cost of traveling so that, without too much planning or saving, millions can afford to travel to the other side of the globe in a matter of hours. People in even greater numbers have the means to climb into their automobiles and be hundreds of miles away, also within a matter of hours.

Conclusions

From ancient times to present, the opportunity to travel has become a financial reality for increasing proportions of the world's citizens. As individuals spend less of their incomes on life's necessities and more on leisure activities, travel becomes a stronger contender for these discretionary funds.

We have also observed that travel has simply become easier. Distance — the most formidable and expensive barrier to travel — has been overcome by more sophisticated means of transportation. These trends appear likely to continue in the future.

Historically, movements toward greater affluence and technological sophistication have likewise been accompanied by structural changes in society that have resulted in conditions favorable to increased leisure travel. Mechanization, urbanization, and the faster pace of life in industrialized nations have created the need for a periodic change of pace in our lives. Leisure travel is recognized by substantial and increasing numbers of individuals as one means of escape from the hectic and tense setting of everyday life.

Historically, people have justified travel by associating it with highly practical ends like education and health. This has been so in spite of the fact that much travel was actually undertaken for its own sake, because of the pleasurable experiences it could afford. Nevertheless, justifications to oneself and others were seen as necessary to rationalize pleasurable leisure travel.

Even today we find that what one says he is seeking in a travel experience often differs substantially from his primary motive for travel. This insight suggests that by simply observing travel behavior, or by accepting singular and superficial explanations for it, we miss the opportunity to understand the real psychological reasons for this behavior. In addition, the mere observation of travel behavior often provides not just a superficial, but an erroneous, basis for our understanding of destination, lodging, transportation, and other decisions.

Thomas Cook might best illustrate the benefits to travel marketers of gaining accurate insights into the psychology of travel. By taking the time to understand the real problems confronting early leisure travelers, Cook was able to offer services that substantially facilitated travel. Clearly, the success of the Cook organization resulted from his ability to understand travelers' needs and offer services that satisfied them. The lesson taught us by Thomas Cook is, of course, equally valid for travel marketing organizations today.

THE VALUE OF TIME AND TRAVEL BEHAVIOR

As indicated earlier, an individual's travel and leisure behavior is often influenced as much by the amount of time he has available to engage in recreational or leisure activities as by the amount of money or number of credit cards in his pocket. Individuals living in economically advanced societies are generally subject to strong time pressures, and these pressures often have a dramatic influence on travel and leisure behavior. This section will briefly examine how time functions as a source of pressure, how people cope with these pressures, and how their coping, in turn, influences their leisure and travel behavior.

The Increasing Scarcity of Time

The reason why time can have a greater impact on one's leisure behavior than the availability of money is that the supply of time available to any one person is fixed. A person has at his or her disposal just twenty-four hours a day — no more, no less. The supply of money at one's disposal, on the other hand, is not fixed. It can increase or decrease — and, for most people living in industrialized societies, it does increase throughout most of their adult years. This is an important point because, as we will see, increasing incomes help to create increasing time pressures.[6]

There are, of course, any number of ways in which people spend time. It will be helpful here to identify six categories of time utilization. These six categories include:

1. Work Time: time spent on productive work that earns monetary income

2. Maintenance Time: time spent on personal work, such as maintaining one's body and possessions
3. Consumption Time: time spent consuming various goods and services
4. Cultural Time: time spent on cultural activities such as playing the piano, reading, and painting
5. Social Time: time spent interacting with family, friends, and acquaintances
6. Idle Time: time spent doing nothing

An individual determines the optimal way to allocate his time to each of these six categories. For example, he may choose to spend the twenty-four hours of a typical day in the following way:

Hours	Category
8	Work Time
10	Maintenance Time
2	Consumption Time
1	Cultural Time
2	Social Time
1	Idle Time

Assume now that this individual is advised that his hourly wage will be raised by five dollars. Now he will be able to earn the same weekly wage by working fewer hours (assuming that he has the flexibility to make such a choice). Alternatively, he might be tempted to work more than eight hours a day, since the overtime will earn him more than it would have before. In either case, the raise may prompt him to think seriously about how he allocates his time.

The same question — of how to allocate time — could occur to this individual for any number of other reasons. He might meet a new friend, for instance, and be tempted to spend more time enjoying this person's company. Or he might be invited to play with the local symphony and be tempted to accept, although it would require him to devote ten or fifteen hours each week to this activity. He might discover a new and rewarding recreational activity, like skiing or camping, and be tempted to spend more of his hours on consumption time. In fact, most of us are forced to constantly reevaluate how we allocate our time because of new friends and acquaintances, new experiences, new career interests, changing values and attitudes, and any number of other factors.

We respond to these kinds of developments in our lives in two different ways. First, we attempt to rearrange the way in which we spend the hours of each day. If possible, we change the number of hours we spend working. We spend less time taking care of our homes and more time on a new recreational activity or with a new friend. We take time from being idle to play the piano or read a good book instead. There are numerous ways in which we can rearrange the hours in our days and how we spend them — but there are practical limits to how much rearranging of hours we can do. Most of us do not have the flexibility to change the number of hours we spend working on a typical day. The number of hours we spend on a maintenance activity like sleeping can be reduced just so far before Mother Nature objects. Such practical limits motivate us to find other ways to save time.

The second way in which we can make better use of our time is to find ways of using it more efficiently. Many people try to perform various tasks and activities in less time. Typically, they attempt to reduce the time spent on less pleasant chores or activities in order to provide more time for activities that are more highly valued. One person invests in a garden tractor so that he can cut his lawn in half the time and spend more time playing golf. Another person invests in a speed-reading course. Others take sleeping pills to reduce time spent in bed, while still others consume vitamin pills instead of taking the time to eat a nutritious breakfast. In fact, the list of labor-saving and time-saving products — automatic dishwashers, aluminum siding, frozen foods, microwave ovens — is seemingly endless.

So great are the pressures of time that the search for ways to save it does not stop with a reliance on so-called labor-saving products. People also modify their behavior with the aim of saving time. They learn, literally, to "eat on the run." Others become specialists in meal skipping, trying to survive on the nonnutritious foods available from the ever-present vending machine. We not only eat faster but cook faster as well — and take less interest, it seems, in the taste of our food. Child care is delegated to day-care centers. People avoid the small dinner party and attend only larger gatherings where they can socialize with a greater number of people. Some become adept at what is called "simultaneous consumption," consuming two or more things — breakfast and the morning newspaper, the evening news and conversation — at the same time. Increasingly, people rent instead of buy because the rented item — the apartment, the car, or the motor home — demands less time for maintenance. People shop around less, preferring instead to make their purchases at a single retail location. They rely more on brand names and various rules-of-thumb like "price equals quality," so that time will not be wasted in search of the best buy or studying competitive brochures and advertising.

This is just a small sampling of the ways in which people attempt to save time. The fact that such efforts are made is evidence that in an advanced economy time is a very precious resource. As people in an advanced economy surround themselves with more and more "things" — bigger homes, second homes, motor homes, second and third automobiles, larger wardrobes, larger families, swimming pools, snowmobiles, and any number of other items — and as they immerse themselves in careers that demand significant amounts of time, they find that they have less and less time to spend on the people and objects in their lives. The pace of life quickly becomes hectic as efforts are made to find time for everything and everyone. Idle time disappears. People substitute money for time by delegating the responsibility for child care, by putting older relatives into nursing homes, by hiring lawn care specialists and pool maintenance firms, and so forth.

Time Pressures in the Travel Environment

Leisure time, according to Aristotle and others, should be free of time pressures — but for many people, ironically, it is not. Time that is spent on what is often loosely referred to as leisure is frequently just as hectic as time spent earning a living and managing a home. People rush to their vacation destinations and to their weekend retreats. Some plan their leisure hours with too many things to do, hoping to accomplish as much as possible, but unaware that more can be gained from leisure when one is not concerned with accomplishing anything.

There is a certain uneasiness about leisure in an industrialized society like the United States. It is an uneasiness inherited from earlier generations unaccustomed to having both the time and the money to do something other than work. These earlier generations were strongly influenced by the Protestant Work Ethic, which discouraged the squandering of time on anything not considered useful or productive. As a result, a person's 'free' time was expected to be as productively spent as the time devoted to gainful employment. The legacy of this ethic, as we shall see, affects many people even today.

There is ample evidence that our leisure is spent at least in part with an eye on the clock, under pressure of the need to conserve time and to do things quickly and efficiently. We can point first to our desire to travel with as much speed as possible from one place to another. The airplane is the preferred mode of transportation among many pleasure travelers, because it minimizes the amount of time needed to reach a vacation destination. The automobile is perhaps even more symbolic. Even during the family auto vacation, when sightseeing is reportedly a major interest, we spend much of our time driving on interstate highways at speeds that interfere with any serious sightseeing efforts. The interstate highways themselves are often engineered in curves and lines around and sometimes through hills and mountains, so that breathtaking vistas are usually denied the speeding motorist. Road signs remind the motorist to maintain a minimum speed, and a limited number of exits discourage the travel party from wandering off the expressway in search of quaint villages and towns.

The Interstate highway has been called a tunnel of isolation–a description that seems to underscore its single-minded emphasis on "making time."

Some deal with the guilt that can come from taking time off and traveling by staying at home and working without pause. Many families rationalize their travel as an educational experience for the children. Some individuals deal with the problem by combining business and pleasure when traveling. An extra day or two is spent at some business destination taking in the sights, playing a round or two of golf, or spending a few lazy hours at the side of a swimming pool. So much the better when these few extra hours or days are spent with business associates, because productive work can be accomplished at the same time that some needed rest and relaxation are enjoyed. The business traveler can also manage to discharge his responsibility to provide time away from home for family members by occasionally taking them along on business journeys. He works and the family plays — and somehow everyone is thought to be better off as a result. The time-off problem is also solved when the business traveler attends business conventions and conferences at resort locations. In all of these instances, travelers minimize the guilt they may feel about taking time off while making efficient use of their time by combining business with pleasure.

Many pleasure travelers, accustomed to a hectic pace of life, also experience a time-related tension because of the time it takes to wind down and settle into the slower pace necessary to enjoy true leisure. To compensate for the loss of productivity that comes with time off, some people cram the hours and days immediately preceding a vacation journey with extra work — and with extra pressures. As a result, the first few days of a vacation journey are filled with excess tension. It takes most people some time to shift gears, so to speak, and psychologists now recommend that a change of pace be initiated before an actual vacation journey begins.

Even as they do on a day-to-day basis, some people practice simultaneous consumption when they travel as well, in order to make the most efficient use of their time. While they are transported from one place to another, air travelers are entertained with inflight motion pictures, occupied with stereo headsets, fed, and offered an assortment of beverages. No longer is it sufficient to sit back and relax, to take an occasional look out the window, or to talk with a fellow passenger across the aisle. Visitors to ski resorts are no longer satisfied with powdered snow and good skiing conditions. They demand, in addition, good restaurants, discotheques, saunas, swimming pools, entertainment, and the opportunity to meet interesting people.

Just as they do at home, vacationers rent things instead of owning them — lake cottages, travel trailers, camping equipment, motor homes, scuba gear, trail bikes, snowmobiles, and many other recreational items. In this way, the time that one must devote to the maintenance and repair of any given item is minimized. By renting rather than owning such equipment one pays someone else to repair it, paint it, maintain insurance on it, and so forth.

The scarcity of time affects leisure and travel behavior in countless other ways. Automobile travelers save time by eating at fast-food restaurants. An increasing number of people fly to their destinations and then rent an automobile. Visitors to western Europe tour eight different countries in twelve days. And, with so little time to leisurely explore each country, many try to make up for it by recording what they do see on film, so they can tour each country at greater leisure in their living rooms. We turn what used to be holy days into holidays and then reschedule the holidays, when necessary, in order to manufacture three-day weekends.

It is important to emphasize that individual decisions and behavior — including those related to travel — take place in a larger cultural and social setting that influences these outcomes. The scarcity of time and the accompanying psychological pressures created by it are felt by all members of modern industrial societies to one extent or another. People sometimes return more pressed and tense from journeys that were intended for rest and relaxation. As we progress through the chapters of this book, we should continually bear in mind that the scarcity of time influences our decisions and behavior even when we hope to escape it through leisure and travel.

A MODEL FOR THE STUDY OF TRAVEL BEHAVIOR

To understand individual travel behavior, it is helpful to view individual travelers as decision-makers. Whenever an individual leaves home, he must make many travel-related decisions. First of all, the decision to leave home itself must be made. Then, decisions must be made concerning where to go, what to do, how to get there, how much to spend, how long to stay, where to stay along the way, where to eat, and with whom to travel.

Routine and Extensive Decision-Making

The individual traveler can make these types of decisions by utilizing several different decision-making approaches, ranging from the highly routine to the very extensive (see Figure 1-1). Sometimes the traveler will use a routine decision-making approach. When this form of decision-making is used, decisions are made quickly and with very little mental effort. The auto traveler needing overnight accommodations, for example, may almost automatically look for a Holiday Inn. In this case, the traveler makes

Figure 1-1 The decision-making continuum.

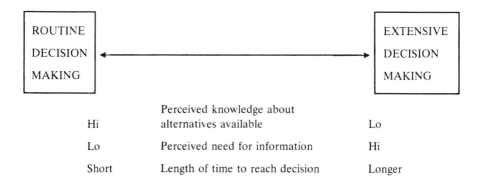

	Perceived knowledge about	
Hi	alternatives available	Lo
Lo	Perceived need for information	Hi
Short	Length of time to reach decision	Longer

a **routine** or habitual travel decision, so called because it is made so rapidly and with so little conscious thought that it appears to be based on habit. Similarly, the East Coast business woman who must travel to the West Coast might automatically and habitually choose to fly to her destination.

Although many travel decisions fall somewhere near the routine end of the continuum in Figure 1-1, others are reached by a more extensive process. When travelers use **extensive** decision-making, they spend considerable time and effort seeking information and evaluating the alternatives available. The decision processes used in any given situation will usually fall somewhere in between the totally routine and highly extensive ends of the continuum in Figure 1-1.

The approach used by an individual when making a particular type of travel decision does not necessarily remain the same. On one occasion, a traveler might routinely decide to stay at a Holiday Inn. On another occasion, however, the same traveler may spend considerable time deliberating over three or four lodging alternatives. There are times, too, when a decision made routinely in the past no longer yields the same level of satisfaction. Then the traveler may resort to a more extensive decision-making process in order to find a more satisfying alternative. For example, the family that tires of driving each winter from its home in Maryland to Florida may give extensive thought to flying or taking Amtrak.

We have seen, then, that the length of the decision process may vary at different times for a particular individual. It is also true that different individuals vary in the extensiveness of their decision processes, even when making the same kind of travel decision. One traveler, for example, will habitually stop at the nearest lodging establishment at about 4:30 p.m., wherever he happens to be. Another traveler, however, will consult various travel guides and consider a variety of accommodations before deciding where to spend the night.

Influencing Routine Decisions.   The type of decision-making process used by the traveler has important implications for the organization engaged in the marketing of travel services. By understanding these processes and knowing when they are most likely to be used, travel marketers can determine the amount, timing, and kind of information necessary to influence these decisions. For example, when an individual uses a routine decision process, he usually makes his choice based on an inventory of knowledge and attitudes that already exists in his mind. He is confident of an adequate store of information on which to base his choice and will not actively seek additional inputs when making it. Consequently, when the need for such a decision arises, this individual will be least susceptible to communications that are designed to influence his choice. Therefore, marketing efforts made *prior* to the time and need for a decision will be most likely to affect the outcome.

One decision that is probably made in a nearly instantaneous manner is the choice of a car rental company. Little thought or information-seeking activity is likely to precede a decision when the need arises for this service. Therefore, the company should develop image-oriented advertising or factual information that stimulates consumer awareness of their alternative long before the need for a decision is recognized by the traveler. Since the consumer is unlikely to seek out such information on his own, these communications must be highly visible.

Triggering Impulsive Decisions.   Another type of decision — made nearly instantaneously, but quite different from those we call routine — is commonly referred to as an **impulse decision.** In sharp contrast to routine decisions, which are usually repetitive, impulse travel decisions are not considered in advance. They are frequently triggered by billboards and other forms of outdoor advertising, although impulsive behavior can be provoked by almost any type of communication when it is strategically positioned. For example, a travel party enroute to a particular destination by car may see a billboard for a sightseeing attraction that is not on its itinerary, and decide to stop there. The decision to visit this attraction can be characterized as impulsive because it involves an unplanned choice that was actually stimulated by the billboard itself. Where a travel-related service has the potential to increase its volume of business through impulse decisions, advertising and personal selling can stimulate the need for a decision that was previously unforeseen and direct the choice itself. A travel agent is often in a unique position to stimulate such decisions by suggesting various travel options previously unconsidered by the client.

Influencing Extensive Decisions.   When an individual makes travel decisions using the extended decision approach, he is likely to be receptive to information that will assist him in making his choice. Under such conditions, the consumer feels his store of information is insufficient to support the decision that must be made. Under these circumstances, the marketing organization is in a better position to influence the outcome — particularly after the traveler recognizes the need for a decision, and before he feels he has enough information on which to base it. In fact, the consumer may be actively seeking such information.

During the extended decision process, an individual might turn to personal sources for assistance — travel agents, business associates, and friends. In addition, he will be receptive to advertising, brochures, and other impersonal sources of assistance relating to the choice at hand. Now that a decision must be made, he may recall information that was previously ignored, since it was not needed for any particular purpose.

There is much evidence to indicate that the choice of a vacation destination is, for many, the result of a fairly extended decision process. Previous information may have affected the particular alternatives that the individual is now willing to consider. However, it is primarily what he discovers in the information search process that begins *after* the question, "Where shall we go on vacation this year?" that will affect the outcome. Under such circumstances, the major thrust of advertising and personal selling efforts should coincide with the point in time at which people are in the sometimes lengthy and difficult process of making such decisions. Furthermore, all communications should be detailed and factual, since this consumer is looking for answers to specific questions that will assist him in making what he may consider an important choice.

Psychological and Social Factors

Understanding how individual travelers make decisions also requires an insight into the psychological factors that influence their choices. Figure 1-2 illustrates that the travel decision-maker, located in the center of the diagram, is affected by both internal and social influences. The internal psychological factors that influence travel behavior and that are discussed in detail throughout this book are (1) perception, (2) learning, (3) personality, (4) motives, and (5) attitudes. **Perception** is the process by which an individual selects, organizes, and interprets information to create a meaningful picture of the world. **Learning** refers to changes in an individual's behavior based on his experiences. **Personality** refers to the patterns of behavior displayed by an individual, and to the mental structures that relate experience and behavior in an orderly way. **Motives** are thought of as internal energizing forces that direct a person's behavior toward the achievement of personal goals. **Attitudes** consist of knowledge and positive or negative feelings about an object, an event, or another person.

Although these psychological factors operate as internal influences on

Figure 1-2   Major influences on individual travel behavior.

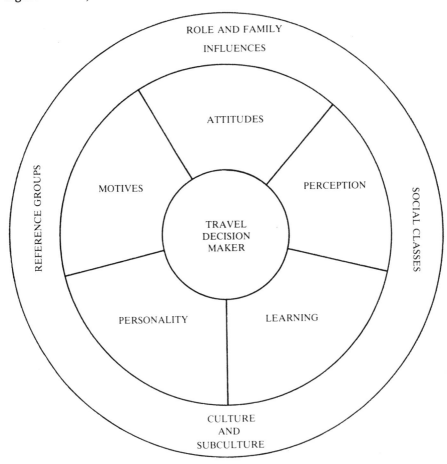

travel behavior, they do not operate in a vacuum. As we saw earlier, travel decisions are very much affected by forces outside the individual, and by other people as well. Thus, we need to analyze the effects of others upon an individual traveler's behavior. The forces that other people exert are called social influences. As Figure 1-2 illustrates, these social influences can be grouped into four major areas: (1) role and family influences, (2) reference groups, (3) social classes, and (4) culture and subcultures. These major social influences are discussed in Chapter 7.

REFERENCES

[1] The source of many of the statistics cited here is: Charles R. Goeldner and Karen P. Dicke, *Travel Trends in the United States and Canada* (Boulder, Colorado: Business Research Division, University of Colorado, 1978).

[2] George Young, *Tourism: Blessing or Blight?* (Baltimore: Penguin Books, Inc., 1973), p. 133.

[3] The material in this section is drawn from several sources, including the following: Robert W. McIntosh, *Tourism Principles, Practices, Philosophies*, second edition (Columbus, Ohio: Grid, Inc., 1977), pp. 3-19; Donald E. Lundberg, *The Tourist Business*, third edition (Boston: CBI Publishing Company, 1976), pp. 1-23; and Young, *Tourism: Blessing or Blight?*, pp. 9-29.

[4] Young, *Tourism: Blessing or Blight?* p. 10.

[5] Ibid., p. 14.

[6] The first part of this discussion is based in part on: Staffan Burenstam Linder, *The Harried Leisure Class* (New York: Columbia University Press, 1970).

QUESTIONS FOR DISCUSSION

1. Why are economic and demographic factors usually less than adequate in explaining travel behavior?
2. What effect do the Protestant Work Ethic and Puritanism have on leisure and travel behavior?
3. Explain the following statement: "This phenomenon — justifying an inherently enjoyable activity like leisure travel in terms of important practical purposes — helps to explain much travel behavior even today."
4. What effect did the Industrial Revolution have on travel and tourism?
5. What effect have trade unions had on travel and tourism?
6. What was the primary reason for the success of Thomas Cook? What lesson does Cook's success hold for today's travel marketers?
7. What are the two ways in which people try to cope with increasing time pressures? To what extent do you try to save time when you are a leisure traveler? Discuss.
8. Why are the hours and days immediately preceding a vacation journey filled with tension for many people? How can this tension be reduced? How might a travel service firm help reduce this tension for people?

2

THE PERCEPTION OF TRAVEL

The person who travels and who involves himself in leisure-time activities is a decision-maker, and his travel and leisure behavior results from any number of decisions. These decisions involve choice — the choice of one alternative course of action over others. When a person decides to spend a thousand dollars on a trip to Hawaii, he is choosing not to spend this same money on a trip instead to Bermuda, a backyard swimming pool, or a new set of encyclopedias for his children. At the same time, he is choosing how to spend his time. When he decides to spend a week in Hawaii, he is forsaking the opportunity to spend the same time somewhere else.

In choosing between Hawaii and Bermuda or some other destination, the decision-maker — usually not consciously — begins by subjectively evaluating each of the alternatives facing him. These subjective judgments reflect each alternative destination's predicted ability to satisfy the decision-maker's special needs. Let us say that the individual's primary needs are to escape from his present environment, to visit a destination where he can enjoy plenty of sunshine and relaxation, and to visit a destination where he is likely to meet other interesting people. The judgments that he makes about each alternative destination and its ability to satisfy his needs will be unique. That is, judgments like these are subjective and will vary from one individual to another. This, of course, is why some people go to Hawaii while others visit Bermuda — even though all may be looking to satisfy identical needs.

The subjective judgments that we make about the alternatives available to us depend on a number of factors. One of the most important of these is our **perception** of each alternative and its ability to satisfy our needs. An important beginning, then, in comprehending the psychology of travel and leisure behavior is an understanding of perception. Psychologists recognize the process of perception as a key variable in understanding all types of behavior.

This chapter discusses perception and the role that it plays in travel behavior. The first section discusses several basic psychological principles of perception, including a number of stimulus and personal factors that influence what we perceive and how we perceive it. The second section defines the actual process of perception as a filtering process and describes how this process affects a person's perception of travel phenomena. In the third section, we will see how people perceive distance, and how perceptions of distance influence travel behavior. The fourth section of this chapter discusses the perception of travel destinations, while the fifth section presents examples that illustrate how air carriers are perceived. In the sixth and final section, we will discuss several examples of travel advertising that utilize some of the basic psychological principles of perception discussed throughout the chapter.

A key point underlying the discussions in this chapter is that an organization that comprehends how travelers form perceptions of travel-related services is in a very strong position to influence them. This ability to modify perceptions can alter consumer patronage behavior in a favorable way.

PSYCHOLOGICAL PRINCIPLES OF PERCEPTION

Perception can be thought of as the process by which we make sense of the world. We perceive objects, events, and behavior. Once a mental impression is formed, it is organized — along with other mental impressions — into a pattern that is in some way meaningful to the individual. These impressions and the patterns they form influence behavior.

The process of perception is not a simple one, however, although it may occur instantaneously. No two people see the world in exactly the same way. We see different things. And what we see together, we nevertheless see and interpret differently. A planeload of vacationers bound for

Europe means something different to a tour operator, to the plane's crew, and to the relatives left standing and watching the plane taxi away. At the same time, the bystander who is waiting for the six o'clock commuter flight to Springfield may not even be consciously aware of the 300 tourists departing from the next gate. Why are some objects noticed and others not? Why is one object perceived differently by different people? Why are some things remembered and others forgotten? An understanding of the perceptual process can assist us in addressing these important questions, and thereby help us to better comprehend travel behavior.

To the travel marketer, perception is of particular interest because it involves the total impression that his services and promotional efforts create in the mind of the traveler. This total impression includes both what the traveler senses (the color of an airplane, the noises in a Roman street, the sign denoting the price of an evening's lodging) *and* the way in which he adds to, changes, or interprets these sensations.

Throughout much of human history, it was believed that what people perceived was the same as what there was to be perceived. In other words, people assumed that their perceptions were an accurate reflection of the world around them. We have come to recognize the fallacy of this assumption, largely as a result of research in the behavioral sciences. Today we recognize that "what we perceive is very often as much a product of what we want to perceive as of what is actually there."[1]

Factors That Influence Perception

Many factors contribute to how an object or product is perceived. These factors are not only extensive and complex, but all are not yet known. Those factors that are known to influence perception can be divided into two categories:

1. **Stimulus Factors.**   These are characteristics of the stimulus itself, such as size, color, sound, texture, shape, and surroundings.
2. **Personal Factors.**   These are the characteristics of the person himself and include his sensory processes (eyesight, hearing, etc.), intelligence level, personality, past experience, values, motivations, expectations, and mood.

Neither stimulus nor personal factors taken alone can explain a traveler's reaction to a particular travel advertisement, front desk clerk, or package tour offer. Both kinds of factors influence the traveler's total perception.

Stimulus Factors

Perception is affected partly by the nature of the physical stimulus itself. We see the world as made up of objects, objects with a unified wholeness that differentiates them from each other and from the background against which they appear. The analysis of perception in terms of unified wholes has been the primary concern of gestalt psychologists. **Gestalt** is a German word commonly translated as *pattern*, and gestalt psychologists emphasize the patterned organization of sensations. When we perceive an object, we are perceiving an organized whole — a gestalt. To understand the perception of objects, we therefore need to know how elements become organized into patterns. Gestalt psychologists have formulated a number of laws that help to explain these patterns. Four of these laws are:

1. The Law Of Similarity
2. The Law Of Proximity
3. The Law Of Symmetry
4. The Law Of Context

Similarity. Similarity is one of the major stimulus factors of organization. Other things being equal, similar things tend to be perceived as belonging together. Figure 2-1 shows how the principle of similarity works. Most individuals, when asked what they see in Figure 2-1, state that they see two sets of four white squares separated by one set of four black dots. Seldom do people see two horizontal lines, each consisting of squares and dots. In like fashion, many people perceive Puerto Rico, Bermuda, and Jamaica as very similar — despite the fact that in many important ways all three are quite unique. However, to many people, they are similar because they are all island resorts. In much the same way, it is quite likely that many people group Hawaiians and Orientals together because there is some similarity of appearance.

Proximity. Proximity is a second stimulus factor by which we organize what we perceive. Other things being equal, things near each other tend

Figure 2-1 The principle of similarity.

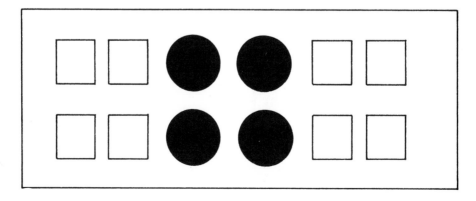

to be perceived as belonging together. This principle of *proximity* is illustrated in Figure 2-2. Instead of six vertical lines, we see three pairs of parallel lines. Similarly, many people perceive England, Scotland, and Wales as belonging together because they share the same island. They do, in fact, belong together politically as members of the United Kingdom. Yet in many important ways, each area is unique and strikingly different from the other two. The same can be said about Vermont and New Hampshire, about northern and southern Indiana, and about Spain and Portugal. What this serves to demonstrate is that most tourist destinations are studies in contrast — and yet many people tend to perceive in terms of a single object that represents them: Switzerland is the Alps, Italy is Rome, Hawaii is a beach, and San Francisco is a cable car.

Symmetry.   Symmetry is a third stimulus factor that prompts us to perceive objects that form a complete or symmetrical figure as part of a whole. Figure 2-3 is more easily seen as a hexagon than as one figure composed of dots and another figure composed of circles. In this case, similarity is competing with the principle of symmetry. Neither the circles nor the dots by themselves form a symmetrical pattern. Most people find this disturbing. We have a desire for symmetry and, if necessary, we will even supply missing elements in order to achieve **closure** — the perception of a meaningful and complete whole. This principle can be illustrated with United Airlines' advertising campaign slogan: "Fly the friendly skies . . . of United Airlines." After this slogan became very well known, the first line alone could have been sung in subsequent commercials, compelling the listener to complete it himself. This procedure — in which good form (closure) is purposefully not supplied — actually helps produce a longer-lasting impression by forcing the viewer to become involved in the commercial.

Figure 2-2   The principle of proximity.

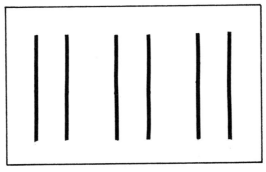

Figure 2-3   The principle of symmetry.

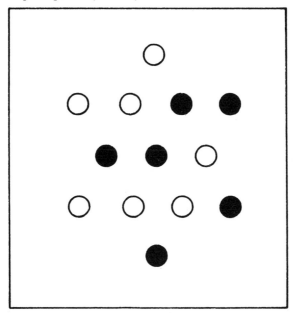

Figure 2-4   The principle of context.

Context.   Context refers to the environment or setting of an object, and it often determines how that object will be perceived. The reversible faces in Figure 2-4 illustrate the principle of context and how it works. If the background is perceived as black, the face emerges on the left-hand side of the figure. If the background is seen as white, the face is on the right-hand of the figure. A traveler, for example, may know nothing about Bora Bora, but when told that it is an island in the South Pacific, he will be able to begin forming some perception of it. The South Pacific, in this case, serves as the background or context.

Other stimulus factors.   People become accustomed to certain sizes, sounds, colors, movements, and other stimulus factors. Sizes, sounds, colors, and movements that contrast sharply with our expectations of them can have a very important influence on perception. Large **sizes** for example, normally produce more attention than small sizes. Thus, other things being equal, California attracts more attention than Rhode Island because it is 156 times as large. Loud **sounds** and bright **colors** normally attract more attention than quiet colors or sounds. The Mardi Gras, for example, attract more attention than a Memorial Day observance at Arlington National Cemetary. **Moving** objects often attract more attention than stationary objects. Niagara Falls, for instance, would normally attract more attention than a placid mountain lake. A combination of these contrasting effects would help to explain why New York City would be perceived quite differently by someone from Butte, Montana than it would by someone from Chicago. Similarly, the Mardi Gras is undoubtedly something quite different for a resident of Las Vegas than it is for someone from Midland, Michgan.

Personal Factors

As indicated earlier, the perception of certain objects in the environment is a simple matter. A chair, for example, presents little, if any, perceptual ambiguity. Many other objects, however, present a great deal more. This would seem to be especially so in the travel and leisure areas.[2] The Mardi Gras, New York City, and the South Pacific are many things to many people. Skiing, camping, and mountain climbing probably represent something a little bit different for each of its participants. No two people perceive a jet airplane, an ocean liner, or an automobile in quite the same way.

Because the travel and leisure area is a complex perceptual environment, personal factors play a very important role in the perception of its objects, activities, and events. The personal factors which appear to influence the perception of travel phenomena include interests, needs and motives, expectations, personality, and social position.

Interests.   Perception is selective. What we choose to perceive is related to what we care about. Our interests, in other words, aid us in filtering out that which is of no importance or relevance to us. Research suggests that people interested in travel would more readily perceive travel advertisements than other types of advertising.[3] A person planning to visit Japan would more readily notice news about Japan than news about some other foreign country. A frequent air traveler probably pays more attention to news of changes in airline fares than someone who does very little traveling by air.

In addition, since an individual's needs and interests are constantly changing, stimuli that previously went unnoticed may now be attended to. The Japan-bound traveler probably pays more attention to news about Japan now than he did before the trip. Advertisements for Hawaii may be noticed with greater frequency by Idahoans during the long winter than they are during more pleasant weather.

Needs.   Both our physiological and our psychological needs have a strong impact upon how we perceive various stimuli. The man dying of thirst sees an oasis where one does not exist, and the starving man sees food where there is none.

Of special significance to those interested in travel is a psychological need called the **Ulysses factor.** Some anthropologists and psychologists believe that man has a deep need to explore, and that some force other than mere adventure explains this need. Most exploration is of no apparent practical value. Although some other animals have a curious nature, most of their exploring is done for the purpose of finding new food sources. Human beings, however — almost from the time of birth — are constantly exploring and extending the boundaries of their environments. It is imperative for most any person to *know* what is beyond his next horizon. The Ulysses factor is a physical as well as an intellectual need. To read, to listen to others, is not enough. We must go ourselves, see for ourselves, find out for ourselves.[4]

This need to know probably has much to do with why people travel and with how they perceive various destinations. Man traveled to the moon for several reasons — but perhaps the most important one was simply that he has never been there before. In the same way, people travel to Europe because they have never seen it. For many — perhaps for all — that is reason enough.

The need to know, then, colors our perceptions of all the places to which we have never been. Whether it be Yellowstone Park, Europe, or the moon, the destination is perceived as a mystery, as an unknown. Though we may hold some image of it in our minds, we realize that our perception is incomplete and inadequate.

Our psychological need for **status** also affects our perceptions in the travel environment. In an earlier time, only the privileged were able to travel with regularity to distant places, and this entitled them to membership in the leisure class. Travel gave them status. It was a symbol that told the rest of the world that these were people who had it made.

Now, however, nearly everyone in the economically advanced portions of the world has the money and the time to travel. So it is no longer whether one travels or not but where he travels to, how he gets there, how long he stays, and what he does while he is there that matters. These are the things that give status.

Our social position and our need for status color our perceptions of destinations, modes of travel, and various leisure-time activities. The travel environment is full of status symbols. The first class cabin on a jetliner distinguishes its occupants from those sitting in the coach section. A week in St. Croix symbolizes more than a week at Virginia Beach. Even if there were no significant physical differences between first class and coach or between St. Croix and Virginia Beach, people would perceive important differences. They would attach status to one seat and not to another, to one destination and not to another. The need for status is a very important one in travel behavior and is discussed more fully in subsequent chapters.

Perception is also affected by strong but **momentary motives** and needs. Periodically, we all become psychologically drained. The rat-race catches up with us, and we experience a strong need to escape. Often, this need to escape calls for a change of environment. And when the need becomes strong enough, it can lead us to some significant perceptual distortions. All of a sudden Europe does not appear very far away. The cost does not seem too high. A family visit to Disney World suddenly seems more appealing. Travel decisions are made more impulsively.

Expectations.   Our perceptions of travel phenomena are also affected by our prior experiences and our expectations. To an extent, a person perceives what he expects to see. Sprinters in a track race expect to hear a starter's gun, and any stimulus — a cough or a movement, for example — is perceived as a gunshot, causing one of the sprinters to "jump the gun."

A first-time visitor to Hawaii expects to see Diamond Head, boulevards lined with palm trees, bronze-skinned Hawaiians on surf boards, bikinis, and mammouth waves washing onto the beaches of Waikiki. These expectations could derive from "Hawaii Five-O," United Airlines television commercials, or the experiences of friends who have previously visited the fiftieth state. Such expectations have a critical effect on what the visitor actually perceives because they determine what he pays attention to. Accordingly, he sees Diamond Head, the palm trees, the surf boards, and the bikinis. But because of his expectations, he may hardly notice the out-of-place McDonald's stand, the urban blight of Honolulu, and the relatively quiet surf at Waikiki. In this way, our expectations play a major role in the selection of what we perceive.

Personality.   An individual's personality is manifested in a consistent pattern of responses to the world, and it influences the manner in which the individual's world is organized and perceived.[5] Personality is most frequently described in terms of particular personality traits. As just one example, some people are more authoritarian than others, and consumer behavior research suggests that the authoritarian person is more likely to consider fewer alternatives prior to making a decision.[6] If this holds true in the case of travel, it means that the authoritarian tourist considers fewer potential modes of transportation, fewer potential destinations to visit, and so forth. In other words, his personality influences his perception by narrowing his focus to only a limited number of alternatives.

In 1971, the Canadian Government Travel Bureau conducted a study of the personality profiles of Canadian vacation travelers. Some of the findings of this study help to further demonstrate how personality influences the perception of travel phenomena.[7] Air travelers were found to be extremely active and confident people who displayed strong leadership tendencies. People who traveled by train, on the other hand, were found to be less confident; they were described as passive personalities with a high need for security. These personality traits obviously helped to explain, at least in part, why some people traveled by air while others traveled by train. Air travel was perceived as riskier and train travel as safer. Thus, those with more confidence traveled by air, while those with a higher need for security traveled by train. At the same time, those who preferred to travel by automobile did so in part because they were courageous, venturesome, and inquisitive personalities who were willing to venture away from familiar surroundings. Other findings from this study are discussed in more detail in a subsequent chapter.

Social Class.   Much of the individual's environment is made up of symbols, and this is especially true of the travel environment. Modes of travel, various destinations, different leisure-time activities, and even travel itself — all are symbols. Various social factors help to determine what each of these symbols means to different people.

Social class, for example, has a powerful effect on the perception of travel phenomena. Society is stratified on the basis of wealth, skill, and power. One's income, education, and occupation determine the social class to which he may belong. An individual shares similar values and attitudes with other members of the same social class. And in a general fashion, members of the same social class tend to behave in similar ways.

Some of the important contrasts between two social class groups — the middle class and the lower class — are listed in Figure 2-5. It is easy to see how the contrasting attitudes and values of these two classes could affect perception. Because of its wider horizons, the middle class would seem to be more interested in travel. To this class, travel would be perceived as a means of exploring its larger world.

Lower-status people, on the other hand, would perceive the world in more limited terms. A trip to Europe or some other far-off destination may be perceived as unnecessary, frivolous, and therefore of no interest. The

---

FIGURE 2-5   Social Class Patterns.

Middle Class	*Lower Class*
1. Pointed to the future.	1. Pointed to the present and past.
2. Viewpoint embraces a long expanse of time.	2. Lives and thinks in a short expanse of time.
3. More urban identification.	3. More rural identification.
4. Stresses rationality	4. Essentially nonrational.
5. Well-structured sense of the universe.	5. Vague and unclear structuring.
6. Horizons vastly extended or not limited.	6. Horizons sharply defined and limited.
7. Greater sense of choice making.	7. Limited sense of choice making.
8. Self-confident, willing to take risks.	8. Very much concerned with security and insecurity.
9. Immaterial and abstract in thinking (idea-minded).	9. Concrete and perceptive in thinking (thing-minded).
10. Feels tied to national happenings.	10. World revolves around family.

Source: Pierre Martineau, "Social Classes and Spending Behavior," *Journal of Marketing*, Vol. 23 (October, 1958), pp. 121–30.

ideal vacation for a lower-status individual may be a trip to some domestic destination or, perhaps even better, three weeks each summer at a family cottage at a nearby lake. The lower-status person sees his home as his castle, and he loads it down with hardware — heavy appliances, swimming pools, and expensive furniture — that serves as a symbol of security. The middle-class person, on the other hand, tends to be less interested in material objects. He does not have the same need for symbols of physical security, and is more willing to spend his money on intangibles — like travel. Thus, the middle-class person places a greater value on travel and is therefore more likely to perceive travel phenomena. Although the lower-status person may place less value on travel, his perceptions can be modified to the extent that he aspires to membership in the middle class. In such a case, travel may represent one way of demonstrating his qualifications for membership in the higher social class.

Other Personal Factors.   Other personal factors that can influence the perception of travel phenomena include the standard demographic factors — age, income, occupation, sex, nationality, and ethnic origin — along with attitudes, beliefs, moods, and memory. All across the United States, for example, there are tightly knit ethnic communities — of Italians, Portugese, and Greeks, to name a few — whose members perceive travel as a link to family and friends in the old country.[8]

Age also plays an important role in the perception of travel. Older middle-class people perceive travel differently than they once did when their children lived at home. Financial security has been attained. Career goals have either been attained or become less important. Travel is then viewed in a new light.

THE PROCESS OF PERCEPTION

We now turn to the actual process of perception. As we noted earlier, this process is a highly selective one. It has to be, because the environment in which we live — our homes, our places of work, and the cities around us — are cluttered by millions of objects. Millions of events take place around us every day. We are surrounded by hundreds of thousands of people. And it is impossible to notice, be aware of, and remember every thing. Our mental capacity is limited to noticing and registering just a very small fraction of all that exists or happens around us.

Our personal environments are so complex and cluttered that we must economize our perceptual efforts. Because our attention span and immediate memory are limited, and because we approach a perceptual situation with specific attitudes, we must be highly selective in what we are exposed to, notice, comprehend, and remember. In fact, perception is often characterized as a *process of successive filtering of stimuli*. Information from the environment must first be noticed, it must then be interpreted and integrated with other perceptions, and then it must be retained for some period of time if it is to subsequently influence behavior.

Selective Attention

Since we cannot perceive everything, we become selective in what we allow ourselves to notice. Selective attention is a form of **perceptual defense:** the blocking out of things that are non-essential, irrelevant, or otherwise personally or culturally unacceptable to us. For example, it may be that most air travelers no longer notice air travel insurance machines because, in part, they no longer think of air travel as dangerous. The travel writer visits a foreign country and is conscious of tourist attractions, hotel accommodations, and restaurants, but perhaps very little else.

A traveler's interests will often aid her in filtering out stimuli that are irrelevant or threatening. The traveler who suddenly decides to rent an automobile at her destination might pay more attention to advertisements for this service in an inflight magazine than the traveler sitting next to her who has been "on the road" for a week and looks forward to spending time with his family. Similarly, the person thinking about a vacation that offers rest and relaxation at a destination no more than a day's drive from

Peoria is not as likely to focus his attention on an advertisement for Singapore as the traveler who has set her sights on a vacation in the Orient.

Another way in which the individual deals with the overload of stimulus information he is exposed to is by using pencil, paper, cameras, and tape recorders. Each of these aids is designed to lengthen the noticing process. They allow us to go back over the verbal or visual picture to which little attention could be directed at the time and, if desired, to extract the last ounce of meaning or enjoyment from an object or event. This helps to explain the popularity of cameras among tourists. The 21-day tour of twelve European countries provides little opportunity for the careful and leisurely examination of landscape, architecture, culture, people, and history. The camera allows these visual impressions to be stored and reexamined at a later date.

Of course, some stimuli force us, involuntarily, to pay attention: loud sounds, bright colors, movement, contrast, and novelty. All other things being equal, we are likelier to notice a Calder-designed Braniff jet than the traditional silver-colored 727. The unusual headline, ''Ski the Big Potato,'' probably attracts considerable attention to advertisements promoting skiing in Idaho.

We should remember, too, that while people tend to limit their attention to the essential and relevant in their everyday lives, vacation travel often represents a departure from this tendency. The vacation provides us with the freedom to open our senses to previously unnoticed stimuli. Many people prefer to visit new places and meet new people. This suggests an awareness that there is much to be enjoyed and learned by lowering our perceptual barriers. For most, however, this perceptual freedom is limited to just two or three weeks out of every year. As a perception-expanding experience, vacation travel becomes all the more valuable for its contribution to the quality of our lives.

Comprehension

The fact that an individual notices or pays attention to a stimulus is no assurance that it will be understood in the manner intended or consistent with objective reality. Again, perception is best described as a subjective filtering process. The meaning we attribute to a stimulus often derives from our own needs, attitudes, and interests, as well as our need to economize our perceptual efforts while dealing with the complex world around us.

One means by which we comprehend stimuli is by categorizing people, behavior, events, and objects. Long ago Walter Lippman called this **stereotyping.** The occupants of the first class cabin on a jetliner are quickly stereotyped as corporate presidents, affluent socialites, or independently wealthy jetsetters. Stereotyping means that people, objects, events, and behavior are perceived according to preconceived categories of meaning. Thus, based on only a limited amount of information or cues, an individual places the stimulus into a mental category.

The process of stereotyping economizes the amount of perceptual work that is done, since only a small amount of information is needed in order to make a categorical judgment. The price of stereotyping is that information is not used to its utmost, and people "see" the stereotypes they have created. In addition, the limited information used to form the perceptual judgment may be inappropriate for the purpose of categorization. Germans, for example, are often stereotyped as strong-willed aggressive, stubborn, beer-drinking people. This stereotype may be a disservice not only to a German, but also to the individual who will miss seeing something in Germans or Germany because of his preconceptions.

In the case of the travel marketer, stereotyping may enhance or detract from an individual's perception of his product or service. After seeing a brightly colored airplane, for example, the traveler may conclude that the airline is an exciting, adventurous, contemporary one. On the other hand, the traveler who is greeted at a motel desk by an unsmiling, indifferent desk clerk may conclude that all hotels or motels belonging to the same lodging chain are cold, unfriendly, and unprofessional. In both instances, then, based on only limited cues from his environment, the traveler has arrived at a categorical conclusion that may very well be inaccurate.

In general, people tend to avoid contradictory or dissonant information. They seek information that agrees with their beliefs, and they try to ignore information that does not. What happens, though, when an individual is confronted with a stimulus that conflicts with his attitudes, values, or prior information? Under these circumstances, the meaning of the stimulus may be changed in a way that deviates from objective reality. That is, the stimulus may be interpreted in such a way that some of its attributes are amplified, while others may be diminished or ignored. This distortion occurs to make the stimulus more consistent with the individual's own preferences and beliefs. This mechanism, called **perceptual distortion,** enables the individual to cope with the vast amount of information that is inconsistent with what he knows, believes, or prefers. The individual is psychologically more comfortable interpreting the stimulus in this manner.

Perceptual distortion is particularly likely to occur when a consumer perceives advertising messages, and it may take one of at least three forms:[9]

1. distortion and misinterpretation of appeals to make them consistent with attitudes;
2. rejection of the message and the source of the message as being biased; and
3. absorbing factual information, but ignoring persuasive appeals.

A traveler opposed to staying in hotels or motels that are part of a standardized, look-alike lodging chain may read the advertisement in Figure 2-6 and completely distort the message. He may overlook any reference to individual property differences and simply notice some attractive hotel and motel properties. Possibly he will reject the message concerning lodging chain size as incorrect, because his own prior knowledge tells him that Holiday Inn really has more properties. Finally, he may retain such factual information as cleanliness, quality, comfort, and value standards — and ignore the appeal to stay at a Best Western.

Thus, exposure to a stimulus — a person, object, event, or advertisement — by no means ensures that the stimulus will be interpreted in a manner consistent with objective reality. Those with contradictory beliefs can completely distort the message. Of course, travelers who favor the use of standardized lodging chains are far less likely to distort the advertisement in Figure 2-6.

Generally, the more ambiguous or complex the stimulus, the greater the opportunity for the individual to see what he wants to see. The corporate executive may see the attractive stewardess as a pleasant part of the interior decor of an airplane. His female counterpart, however, may see an attractive and capable young woman whose physical assets receive more attention than her mental abilities because of the nature of her job.

Selective Retention

Finally, information that is perceived by an individual may or may not be retained by her over a period of time. Generally, it is believed that individuals store in memory that which is relevant to their needs, values, and predispositions. Information that has no such relevance is often rapidly forgotten. In addition, there is some evidence to support the proposition that retention is likelier to occur, and with greatest accuracy, when the information to which we are exposed is consistent with our attitudes, biases, and life styles.[10]

There is reason to believe that the traveler who dislikes national lodging chains will forget specific information contained in the advertisement on page 37. Furthermore, it is likely that he will not even recall seeing it. Retention of specific advertising claims drops rapidly after exposure — probably reflecting the indifference of most consumers to the vast quantity of advertising to which they are exposed.

Only those perceptions that are retained can influence subsequent behavior. If on his first visit to a major U.S. city a farmer from the Midwest is mugged, the experience will stand out for years in his mind, forming the basis for his overall perception of that city. He may forget, however, many enjoyable experiences he had while visiting the metropolis.

Thus, we see that our predispositions give rise to selective exposure,

FIGURE 2-6

World's Largest Lodging Chain

Why? Best Western has over 2000 attractive, well-furnished and dependably clean motels, hotels and resorts conveniently located in more than 1300 cities.

Each one looks refreshingly different, yet all offer the same personal and efficient service. Every Best Western is regularly inspected to assure that it meets Best Western's high standards of cleanliness, quality, comfort and value.

Wherever you travel, get your money's worth at Best Western. And stop at any Best Western for a free copy of our 1978 Road Atlas & Travel Guide.

Best Western serves 70% of the major U.S. airports. You may be on your way to one.

(800) 528-1234

Call toll-free for reservations or see your travel agent. In Arizona (800) 352-1222 • Phoenix 279-7600

Best Western

Copyright © Best Western/B-W advertising agency, inc, Phoenix, AZ. Reprinted by Permission.

comprehension, and selective retention. These phenomena, in turn, have the tendency to *reinforce* our existing predispositions. It is for this reason that many promotional communications play on and are intended to reinforce existing beliefs. To bring about even minor perceptual and attitudinal changes is a much more difficult — although not impossible — task.

In the sections that follow, we will see from detailed examples how these principles of perception operate to influence travel behavior. We will discuss how people perceive distances, how they distort them, and how perceived distances influence travel behavior. We will examine the perception of travel destinations, and how these perceptions influence the destination choices made by travelers. Perceptions of air carriers and how they influence airline choices will also be discussed. And in a final set of examples, we will see how certain travel advertisements utilize the gestalt principles discussed earlier to attract and hold a reader's attention, to create a favorable image of the travel service, and to communicate important information about it.

The examples discussed in the following sections should help to demonstrate the importance of knowing how travelers perceive a particular travel product or service. Knowing how a product or service is perceived by consumers will help to explain its relative popularity in the travel market. Furthermore, this knowledge is a starting point for efforts designed to create a more accurate and improved image of travel products and services in the marketplace.

THE PERCEPTION OF DISTANCE

Travel takes place through time and space. Travel, therefore, can be measured both in terms of time (minutes, hours, and days) and in terms of distance. Many people, in fact, perceive distance in terms of time: a trip to the drug store takes ten minutes; a flight to Pittsburgh takes two hours; London is seven hours away by plane.

The perception of time and distance influences travel behavior and attitudes. For example, when a family embarks in its automobile for a trip, from Chicago to St. Louis, each person may know or be told that the trip will take approximately six hours. The perception of six hours, however, will differ for each member of the family. For the father, who may be used to driving long distances, six hours may not seem like a very long time. For the mother, six hours might be perceived as "a whole day in the car with the children." To the children, meanwhile, it might seem that they are embarking on a trip that will never end.[11]

Distance as a Deterrent to Travel

The perception of distance affects travel behavior and attitudes in two ways. It acts, first of all, as a deterrent to travel. With respect to pleasure travel, however, distance can also stimulate travel.

Geographers refer to the concept of the **friction of distance.** What this means is that there are certain costs associated with travel. There are monetary costs, time costs, convenience costs, physical costs, and often emotional costs incurred when a person travels from one place to another. These costs, by themselves, serve to discourage travel. And, unless there are certain benefits to be obtained from traveling that will more than compensate for all of these costs, travel will not take place. These costs act as friction. They inhibit travel.

As distance increases, the costs of traveling increase — and the less likely it becomes that travel will take place. This principle can be illustrated by taking two cities of approximately the same size — Atlanta and Buffalo, for example. The number of people attracted to Disney World from Atlanta is much greater than the number of people attracted to Disney World from Buffalo. The obvious reason for this is that Buffalo is much farther away from Orlando, Florida than is Atlanta. The cost of traveling to Disney World — the friction of distance — is much higher for the residents of Buffalo. The same principle helps to explain why visitors to the United States from Canada and Mexico far outnumber visitors from all other foreign countries.

Distance as a Stimulant to Travel

There is, at the same time, a phenomenon that competes with the friction of distance and stimulates the kind of travel with which this book is concerned: pleasure travel, or tourism. Research suggests that the far-off destination is especially attractive to the pleasure traveler simply because it is far off.[12] There may be little difference between the amount of enjoyment a vacationer would experience by visiting either Hawaii or Tahiti. The vacationer might do essentially the same things and enjoy them equally at either destination. But because Tahiti is the more distant destination, it has an extraordinary attraction about it. Thus, while the friction of distance would have our hypothetical tourist stop at Hawaii, there is a competing force that attracts the tourist to the more distant destination — simply because it is more distant. The greater distance in this case helps to create a perception of the far-off destination that makes it more attractive. The same phenomenon would explain why a New Yorker might find Aruba more appealing than Nassau, and Las Vegas more alluring than Atlantic City. Thus, when finances do not prohibit the traveler from doing so, she might easily be persuaded to travel to the more distant destination.

Perceptual Distortion of Distance

People seem to have a distorted perception of the geographic world in which they live and around which they travel. Figure 2-7 is a composite

FIGURE 2-7 Comparison of actual and perceived geographic locations.

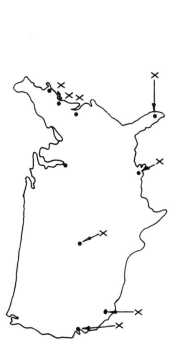

● indicates correct geographical location of city

✗ indicates perceived geographical location of city

Scale of Miles

ATLANTIC OCEAN

map showing the relative geographic positions of eight U.S. and three European cities as perceived by a group of graduate students in the Midwest. The point of reference is Chicago. The map reveals a number of perceptual inaccuracies.

First, the three European destinations were perceived to be much farther south than they actually are. Rome, for example, was perceived to be roughly at the same latitude as Miami — about 1,100 miles south of its true position. Second, the two U.S. cities most distant from Chicago — Los Angeles and San Francisco — were also subjectively perceived to be much farther south of their true geographic positions. Thus, it appears that for some reason — perhaps because of perceptions of dramatic life style, cultural and climatic differences — cities that are relatively far away from some base point tend to be perceived as farther south than they actually are. This was true for Los Angeles and San Francisco as well as the three European cities. The reader can examine Figure 2-7 for other perceptual inaccuracies.

These types of perceptual geographic distortions can influence how a tourist seeks to fulfill his travel needs (his choice of destination, for example). They can also have an impact on his satisfaction with any particular destination.

PERCEPTIONS OF TRAVEL DESTINATIONS

When an object or event is perceived, it is normally part of a family of similar objects or events. Bermuda is just one of many different island resorts, and it is also part of a broader category of objects we call tourist destinations. Likewise, an Eastern Airlines '747' is just one of many different types of airplanes, as well as part of a broader category of objects we call transportation vehicles. Eastern Airlines itself is also just one of several major air carriers in the United States.

When choosing a destination, a vacationing traveler must decide from among any number of possible destination alternatives. The choices a traveler must make force her to compare alternatives. These comparisons are made on the basis of the perceptions the individual has of each alternative in terms of any number of **decision criteria.**

We must know what these decision criteria are and how the individual perceives the alternatives facing her if we are to understand how she makes her travel decisions. Several examples follow that show how vacationers perceive various destination areas, how they go about organizing these perceptions, and how they select one destination area over another.

Perceptions of the United States

The United States Travel Service has conducted research in a number of foreign countries to determine the image of the United States as a travel destination and thereby explain the relative attractiveness of the U.S. to foreign travelers. The U.S.T.S. image studies in eleven foreign countries are summarized in Figure 2-8.

Figure 2-8 underscores a number of important points made earlier in this chapter. No two people see a destination in exactly the same way. Our perceptions are selective, and they vary not only from person to person but from one country to another as well. Foreign perceptions of the U.S. depend, among other things, upon prior experience and values. And the foreigner's perceptions of the U.S. are often influenced, as Ernest Dichter points out, in no small way by "movies, the old westerns, which they see on television continually, through stories about mugging, raping, and racial difficulties which have been featured much more prominently in foreign publications and on TV than the positive aspects of the U.S."[13] The result, says Dichter, are some rather distorted perceptions of the U.S.

Figure 2-8 clearly indicates that most foreign travelers have a stereotyped view of the United States. Most do not perceive that there are many places of significant historical interest to visit in the U.S. Most do not view the U.S. as a place to visit if the objective is to participate in winter sports activities. Most do not expect an exciting night life or an abundance of good restaurants in the U.S. And many do not associate vistas of sheer natural beauty with the U.S.

Dichter identifies several psychological factors — fear, emotions, prejudice — that also play a role in distorting foreigners' perceptions of the United States. To some foreigners, according to Dichter, America is tomorrow's newspaper, and it's full of bad news. They fear that the U.S. today is a picture of what their own countries and cultures will look like tomorrow — cities that look too much like New York; crowded highways; a hectic pace of life; women who are liberated and autonomous; too much urbanization; and high crime rates. In short, a visit to the U.S. can be threatening because it may force the outsider to confront an image of what his own life might be like some day. A visit to the U.S., Dichter says, might also threaten the foreigner with feelings of inferiority about his own country. In this case, the traveler will focus his attention on the negative aspects of the U.S. in order to support his decision to travel somewhere else. Some foreigners are also apprehensive about the overall size of the U.S., and some fear that they might not really be welcomed as visitors to this country.[14]

As indicated earlier, our perception of objects like vacation destinations may often be distorted. There are just too many factors that interfere

FIGURE 2-8   Images of the United States as a travel destination.

Travel Expectation	Mexico	Japan	United Kingdom	West Germany	France	Australia	Venezuela	Italy	Netherlands	Sweden	Belgium
To experience a different culture and way of life		+			+	−	+	+			+
To enjoy an exciting night life, good restaurants, dancing, and entertainment	+	+									
To visit places of significant historical interest	−	−	−	−	−	−	−	−		−	−
To see beautiful scenery		−				−					
To meet interesting new people		+	+		+		+	+	+		
To learn new things helpful in one's business or social life	+	+	+	+	+	+	+	+	+	+	
To get a bargain-priced vacation	+		−	−	−			−	−		−
To purchase interesting gifts and souvenirs		−					−	+			
To participate in warm-weather sports or lay in the sunshine							+	+	−		
To participate in winter sports and activities	+	−	−	−	−	−		−	−		−
To experience a relaxing atmosphere					−			−			−
To participate in outdoor activities like hiking and camping	+	+					+				−

Note: A "plus" (+) indicates that the travel expectation is particularly important in motivating travel to the U.S. A "minus" (−) indicates that the travel expectation is a particularly important deterrent to travel to the U.S.

Source: United States Travel Service, *International Travel Market Reviews of Selected Major Tourism Generating Countries* (Washington: U.S. Department of Commerce, 1977).

with the development of clear, comprehensive, objective perceptions. The foreigner, for example, is exposed to only a relatively small amount of information about the United States — and, unfortunately, this information is often selected for him by the news media. The typical foreigner's awareness of tourist attractions in the U.S. is generally limited to four or five major points, such as New York City, the Grand Canyon, San Francisco, and two or three other points of interest like Niagara Falls or Disney World.

One also sees what he wants to see, and what he wants to see is often dictated by attitudes, prejudices, and needs, along with various cultural and stimulus factors. The United States is, in addition, a large and complex "stimulus" — and this, in turn, creates perceptual ambiguity. It should be no surprise, given all of these influences on perception, that to many foreigners the U.S. is represented by the Grand Canyon, Disney World, crime in the streets, urbanization, industrialization, and a hectic pace of life. Considering these distortions, it is somewhat surprising that most foreign travelers do, in fact, have a very strong urge to visit the U.S.

Of course, the generalizing and the stereotyping by foreign travelers misses much of the real America — the small towns, the friendliness, the mountains and the valleys, the museums, the universities, the national parks. The challenge to those interested in stimulating even more foreign travel to the U.S. is to improve its image in an honest and thorough way.

Regional Destinations in the United States

It is helpful to realize that perceptions of competing objects — in this case, travel destinations — are organized in our minds much as they are in geometric space. It is possible through the use of some sophisticated statistical procedures and computer technology to approximate how these perceptual organizations actually exist in our minds.[15] They can be thought of as a picture of what exists in our minds when we organize perceptions of similar objects. They are often referred to as **perceptual maps.**

Figure 2-10 presents such a perceptual map.[16] It is based on information provided by 700 summertime auto vacationers who were interviewed at twenty-four geographically dispersed locations throughout the United States. The information these travelers provided dealt with the extent to which they felt eight regional destination areas in the U.S. were similar or dissimilar, their attitudes toward each of these eight destination areas, and the importance of various attributes of each of these areas. Figure 2-9 identifies the states comprising each of these eight "Discover America" regions.

The perceptual map shown in Figure 2-10 represents the average respondent's perceptual organization of the eight regional destination areas. In other words, this map shows us how this person's perceptions of the

---

FIGURE 2-9   Composition of "Discover America" regions.

New England
  Connecticut
  Maine
  Massachusetts
  New Hampshire
  Rhode Island
  Vermont
Eastern Gateway
  New Jersey
  New York
George Washington Country
  Delaware
  Washington, D.C.
  Maryland
  Pennsylvania
  Virginia
  West Virginia
The South
  Alabama
  Arkansas
  Florida
  Georgia
  Kentucky
  Louisiana
  Mississippi
  North Carolina
  South Carolina
  Tennessee

Great Lakes Country
  Illinois
  Indiana
  Iowa
  Michigan
  Minnesota
  Ohio
  Wisconsin
The Old West
  Colorado
  Montana
  Nebraska
  North Dakota
  South Dakota
  Utah
  Wyoming
The Frontier West
  Arizona
  Kansas
  Missouri
  New Mexico
  Oklahoma
  Texas
The Far West
  Alaska
  California
  Idaho
  Nevada
  Oregon
  Washington

---

eight destination areas are organized in his mind. Among other things, the map indicates the degree to which the eight regional areas are perceived as being either similar or dissimilar. The closer that two destination areas are on the map, the more similar they are perceived to be by the typical summertime auto vacationer. The Far West region, for example, is perceived to be quite similar to the Old West region as a vacation destination area. Each of these regions, however, is perceived as being quite unlike either New England or the Eastern Gateway region.

In order to understand how the perceptions of vacation destination areas affect destination decisions, it is necessary to know what factors are used by a traveler to evaluate the alternatives. Earlier, we referred to these factors as decision criteria. Two of the key decision criteria that summertime

FIGURE 2-10   Perceptual map of eight "Discover America" regions.

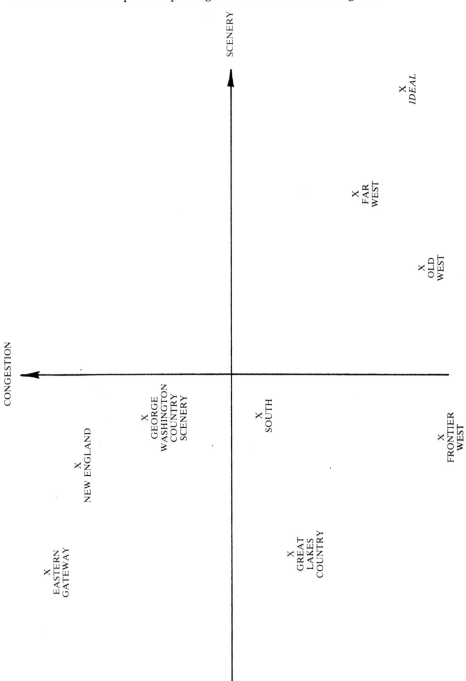

auto vacationers use to evaluate alternative regional destination areas are (1) degree of congestion and (2) scenery. These two factors are used to label the axes of the perceptual map in Figure 2-10 because they help the traveler to organize his perceptions of the regional destination areas.

Figure 2-10 indicates the overall image of each of the eight U.S. regional destination areas in terms of congestion and scenery. Also included on the map is a hypothetical "ideal" destina ion area which serves as a point of reference. The position of this hypothetical ideal indicates that the typical auto vacationer would, all other things being equal, prefer to visit a destination area with an abundance of scenic beauty and one that is not congested with either people or industry.

In order to appreciate the value of understanding how perceptions of alternative destination areas are organized, the reader is invited to examine the position on the perceptual map of the Eastern Gateway region. This area — which consists of the states of New York and New Jersey — is generally perceived as a highly congested one with little to offer in the way of scenic beauty. It would seem that this image of the region is closely tied to the image many travelers have of New York City. Yet, anyone familiar with upstate New York and the New Jersey shoreline will readily acknowledge that the Eastern Gateway is much more than the concrete, congestion, and hectic pace of metropolitan New York. The region has had an image problem. Vacationers have had a distorted perception of the area. Because of the prominence of New York City in the media, it is easy to understand why this would be so.

Realizing that it did indeed have an image problem — and acknowledging, too, the economic importance of tourism — the state of New York recognized the need to create a more realistic and favorable image for itself. Beginning in 1977, an imaginative television advertising campaign featuring the "I Love New York" theme promoted not only Broadway shows, but upstate New York's mountain and lake regions as well (see Figure 2-11). A colorful, 96-page travel guide describing 400 attractions in some 250 locations throughout the state was also produced. Vacation packages were developed to appeal to automobile travelers as well as those traveling by motorcoach, train, and plane. Travelers were told about dude ranch vacations, white water canoe trips, high country hiking and backpacking, and other activities that many people associate with locations elsewhere in the United States.

The results of New York's efforts to create a more complete image of the tourist attractions available in the state speak for themselves. Upstate motel occupancy has topped 80 percent for the first time in several years. Travel spending for summer vacations in the state has increased several times faster than in the nation as a whole. State tax revenues from travel service businesses have increased substantially. It is not likely that all of this would have happened had not New York realized that it indeed had an image problem and taken steps to create a more comprehensive image of the state as a travel destination. Once perceptions of the state began to improve — once pleasure travelers saw that New York was more than Times Square, Central Park, the Statue of Liberty, and the United Nations — people found more reasons to vacation in New York.

FIGURE 2-11

Wells, Rich, Greene, Inc./767 Fifth Avenue/New York, N.Y. 10022/Plaza 8-4300

"I LOVE NEW YORK"
(Phone Version)

New York State Department of Commerce   30-seconds

I live in New Hampshire, but I love New York.

I live in North Carolina, but I love New York.

ANNCR: Call Toll-Free for our free 100 page vacation guide.

It's filled with affordable vacation packages and ideas.

Find out why outdoor lovers

from the Carolinas to Canada love New York.

I live in Brooklyn, but I love New York.

SINGERS: I LOVE NEW YORK, WHAT A GREAT VACATION.

American Indian Reservations

As suggested earlier, some stimuli present a great deal of perceptual ambiguity. To many foreigners, the image of the United States is ambiguous because it is large and complex. It consists of seashore, mountain ranges, and plains. It is — depending on location and time of year — arid, tropical, and frigid. It is urbanized and highly industrialized; at the same time, it is one of the largest agricultural producers in the world. Because of its size, complexity, and diversity, the United States would be difficult, if not impossible, to describe in just a few words.

A similar perceptual problem exists with respect to a large number of American Indian reservations that are interested in tourism as a means of economic development. Rich as they are in history and cultural heritage, these reservations would seemingly stand to experience significant economic growth by encouraging pleasure travelers to visit. Despite their efforts, however, along with the assistance of the Bureau of Indian Affairs and the Travel Industry Association of America progress has come slowly — and one of the primary reasons is that the American Indian reservation is generally a perceptually ambiguous travel destination.

Research indicates that travelers do not have a clear idea of what might be seen or experienced if they were to visit a reservation during their vacation journeys. In a large-scale study of the attitudes of automobile vacationers, a sizeable number of people referred to the "depressing social environment" that one would be likely to encounter at a reservation.[17] These vacationers may think that, since many reservations are economically depressed, they must be socially depressed areas as well. It should be noted that during the year or two prior to the study, the plight of the American Indian had been featured in newspapers and on television because of demonstrations at Wounded Knee and several other reservations. At the time of the study, at least, it was clear that the pleasure traveler feared that what he was likely to see during a visit to a reservation would not be very pleasant.

Once again, awareness of what one is likely to see and experience during a visit to any particular travel destination area goes a long way toward attracting greater numbers of tourists. Those auto vacationers who feel that they have at least some knowledge and, therefore, some unambiguous expectations of the American Indian reservations report that they are more likely to visit a reservation during their vacation travels. Their expectations do not have to include majestic landscapes, rewarding interactions with "real" Indians, or participation in authentic tribal ceremonies. Rather, they merely need to be realistic expectations. This suggests that one of the worst enemies of successful tourism is perceptual ambiguity. The traveler must be able to form some realistic expectation of what he may experience during a visit to a particular destination. He is less likely to visit such a destination if it is not clear what type of experience he may have. All of this underscores the importance of advertising and other forms of communication that help prospective travelers to formulate expectations about travel destinations.

Rocky Mountain States

The preceding examples demonstrate that the image of a destination area may have as much to do with its ability to stimulate tourism as its more tangible recreation and tourism resources. Many factors, of course, contribute to the overall perception that potential visitors have of an area.

It has been found that perceptions of four Rocky Mountain states as vacation destinations depend, among other things, on the overall impression of each state's resident population, its landscape, and its climatic conditions.[18] In a survey conducted among people in several cities outside of the Rocky Mountain region, participants were asked to indicate which couple in Figure 2-12 looked most like the people who lived in each of four Rocky Mountain states (Colorado, Montana, Utah, and Wyoming). The participants were also asked to describe their perceptions of the residents of each of the four states in terms of population distribution (urban vs. rural), average annual income, political tendencies (liberal vs. conservative), receptiveness to visitors, and progressiveness (see Figure 2-13).

Figure 2-13 summarizes how the respondents perceived the residents, landscape, and climate of each of the four states. The information presented in Figure 2-13 is enlightening because of the fact that two out of every three participants stated that among the four states Colorado would be their most preferred vacation destination. Colorado was perceived as mountainous, with abundant snow in winter and moderate temperatures in summer. Residents of Colorado were perceived quite differently than those of Montana, Utah, and Wyoming. Colorado's residents were perceived to have incomes slightly above the national average, middle-of-the-road political tendencies, progressive attitudes, and high receptiveness to visitors from other states. Their dress and behavior were perceived as contemporary.

The state found to be least attractive as a vacation destination area was Utah, and an examination of its image suggests why. Utah was perceived primarily as a desert, where the summers are very hot and where the winters bring only a moderate amount of snow. It was undoubtedly more than just coincidental that in terms of opportunities for skiing, Utah was rated poorly — despite the fact that it does offer what some consider to be outstanding skiing opportunities: steep terrain, heavy annual snowfalls, and light powdery snow that delights skiers. Utah's general image,

FIGURE 2-12 Drawings of couples representing how residents of Colorado, Montana, Utah, and Wyoming might look and dress.

FIGURE 2-13	Perceptions of four Rocky Mountain states.			
	Colorado	*Montana*	*Utah*	*Wyoming*
Landscape	Mountains	Grassland/ Rangeland	Desert	Grassland/ Rangeland
Climate				
Winter	Much snow	Much snow	Moderate snow	Much snow
Summer	Moderate	Cool	Very hot	Hot
Resident Population				
Income	Above average	Below average	Below average	Below average
Politics	Middle-of-the-road	Conservative	Conservative	Middle-of-the-road
Attitudes	Progressive	Backward	Backward	Backward
Receptivity	Highly Receptive	Receptive	Receptive	Receptive
Dress	Contemporary	Cowboys Farmers Ranchers	Western pioneer Religious	Cowboys

however — an arid state where winter brings only a moderate amount of snow — would not easily be associated with good skiing conditions.

Utah's desert image serves as the background against which people, in the absence of sufficient information, formulate specific attitudes about the state. To improve these attitudes it would be necessary, in gestalt terms, to change the context that helps shape Utah's image. Figure 2-14A is an advertisement that Utah has used to create greater awareness of the attractions that it feels would interest vacationers. Aimed as it is at summertime automobile vacationers, the ad might have been considerably more effective had it also clearly positioned Utah as part of the Rocky Mountain region. This, in fact, is accomplished in another advertisement, shown in Figure 2-14B, directed at retail travel agents.

Perceptions of Australia

Australia was an early promoter of tourism in North America. In 1930, it opened an office in San Francisco to service tourist inquiries and to encourage potential visitors to take the long voyage to Australia and "spend winter in Australia's summer." However, with the introduction of regularly scheduled air services and the growth of discretionary income, the

FIGURE 2-14A

Copyright © Utah Travel Council, Department of Community and Economic Development, Salt Lake City, UT. Reprinted by permission.

FIGURE 2-14B

Give your clients a new season...

UTAH'S AUTUMN

Slopes of Mt. Timpanogos

Cache Valley Threshing Bee

Peach Days—Brigham City

Harvest of fresh Utah Trout

Oktoberfest—Snowbird Resort

Salt Lake Mormon Temple

Bottleneck Peak, San Rafael Swell

Provo Canyon

Autumn in Utah is like no other season your clients have experienced before. From the golden cottonwoods lining the streams of the south, to the flaming oak and aspen slopes of the north, it's a totally unique season with a splendor all its own.

It's also uncrowded and loaded with activities for all types of vacationers.

There's backpacking, horsepacking and river-running for the active set; aerial tours, excursion trains, festivals, art and craft exhibits, and leisurely sightseeing for the more easy going. There's also a variety of all-inclusive tours, featuring comfortable trips through our five national parks, visits to our Indian lands, historical and cultural tours, city sightseeing—a variety of activities and attractions ideal for your clients.

This year, don't just suggest a new vacation. Suggest a new season. Utah's Autumn.

I'd like to receive your fall color tours and events brochure.

Name _____

Address _____

City _____

State _____ Zip _____

The Utah Travel Council
Dept. HL-10
Council Hall
Salt Lake City, Utah 84414

Copyright © Utah Travel Council, Department of Community and Economic Development, Salt Lake City, UT. Reprinted by permission.

North American market became an important source of tourism for many countries. By the 1950s, Australia enjoyed only a very small share of this market. This was because of the high cost of travel to what was perceived as a distant destination with ill-defined attractions.[19]

The problems of distance and cost were met in part by the introduction of jet services to the Pacific. Jets, with their faster speed and lower cost, overcame some of the rigors of the journey while also increasing the size of the market that could afford to travel to far-off destinations like Australia. This, however, did not solve the main problem of motivating people to want to travel there. The Australian Tourist Commission analyzed the problem and concluded that an effort had to be made to alter the geographic definition of the South Pacific to include Australia. By 1964, Australia had persuaded New Zealand, Fiji, Tahiti, and New Caledona to join in promoting the entire South Pacific region. And, by 1970, it was apparent that the joint promotion had been successful for Australia. The number of Americans who traveled to Australia increased from little more than 5,000 in 1960 to more than 41,000 in 1971, an average annual increase of 64 percent. For every year during the same time period, overseas travel by U.S. citizens increased 23 percent. It is clear, therefore, that Australia's strategy of positioning itself as part of the South Pacific region was an effective one. Each year, more Americans who visited the South Pacific also visited Australia.

Australia's strategy employed the gestalt principles of proximity and context, an approach that has been used frequently by many other destination areas. Aer Lingus, for example, promotes vacation travel to Ireland by packaging it with travel to Britain, its "next-door neighbor." "Ireland's so close to Britain," Aer Lingus says in its advertising, "it's almost sinful to visit us without adding on Britain." Portugal, in an effort to stimulate more tourism following political unrest in 1975, recognized the popularity of Spain as a tourist destination — and, instead of competing directly, used Spain's popularity as a way of promoting travel within its own borders. In advertising directed at travel agents in the United States, Portugal stated: "If your clients are interested in going to Spain, include Portugal in their plans and they can enjoy both for the same bargain price."

PERCEPTIONS OF AIR CARRIERS

Another type of decision that illustrates how perceptions influence travel behavior is the traveler's selection of an air carrier. The choice of carrier is more difficult to understand than the destination choice because differences between carriers are more subtle and difficult to isolate. Though Bermuda and Hawaii are similar in many respects, their differences are obvious enough to promote unique perceptions of each island resort. But what about the differences between United Airlines and American Airlines? What about the differences between Pan Am and TWA? What about the differences between a carrier that serves a particular air travel market with 747 aircraft and one that serves the same market with the 727? Three case studies will serve to illustrate the role of perception in the choice of air carriers.

Transatlantic Air Travel

The differences among various air carriers are difficult to identify because each one offers essentially the same basic product: air transportation to a particular destination. Suppose you are making plans for traveling from New York to Paris. Which of the two flights described below would you choose?

> **Flight A:** A 707 flown by British Airways will depart within two hours of the time you would like to leave and is often late in arriving in Paris. The plane will make two intermediate stops, and it is anticipated that it will be 50 percent full. Flight attendants are warm and friendly, and you will have a choice of two movies for entertainment.
>
> **Flight B:** A 747 flown by TWA will depart within four hours of the time you would like to leave and is almost never late in arriving in Paris. The flight is non-stop, and it is anticipated that the plane will be 90 percent full. Flight attendants are cold and curt, and only magazines are provided for entertainment.

This hypothetical decision was presented to a number of experienced transatlantic air travelers in a study designed primarily to determine how air travelers evaluated the 707 vs. the 747 in transatlantic travel.[20] Using a new set of analytical techniques from mathematical psychology, the researchers in this study were able to isolate the factors that would best explain how air travelers perceive Flight A and Flight B, and why one flight might be chosen over the other.

The air travelers in this study were found to have a particularly strong preference for TWA over British Airways. This strong preference for TWA, however, had relatively little to do with the fact that TWA was offering 747 service.

The benefits an air traveler expects or desires on a transatlantic flight to Paris were found to be most strongly related to four factors: (1) departure time, (2) punctuality of arrival, (3) number of intermediate stops, and (4) attitudes of flight attendants. The factors that do not *significantly* influence air travelers' perceptions of the two flights, in addition to the type of aircraft,* were discovered to be passenger load and entertainment.

---

*It should be noted, however, that over time air travelers have apparently come to place greater value on the comfort provided by wide-body jet aircraft. This is especially so for flights of over two hours.

The findings of this study suggest at least two important implications. First, the value of time to an air traveler is very important — more important, in fact, than the type of aircraft in which he flies and the type of entertainment with which he is provided.[21] This was found to be true both for vacationers and for business travelers, although slightly more so for the business traveler. The air traveler is interested in departing at the most convenient time and arriving at his destination when he is scheduled to. He also prefers the nonstop flight, presumably because it will not normally encounter any enroute delays. Thus, the traveler chooses nonstop Flight B — even though its departure time is not quite as good as Flight A's.

The findings of this study also place in perspective the importance of the attitudes of flight attendants. Besides the time conveniences offered by competing airlines, there is little else that distinguishes one air carrier from another. Each offers transportation to the same destination, often at exactly the same price. Thus, one of the few ways in which a carrier can differentiate itself from its competitors is service. Air travelers especially value warm, courteous, and friendly service. Consequently, most airlines attempt to provide the best service possible. As most air travelers know, however, some carriers do better at this task than others.

The Chicago-Los Angeles Air Travel Market

The quality of service is no less important to many domestic air travelers. This fact was supported by the findings of a study of air traveler perceptions in the Chicago-Los Angeles air travel market.[22] Because this is a long-haul market with a substantial volume of air travel, it was considered a very lucrative one for any of the four major carriers serving the travelers in Chicago and Los Angeles at the time of the study (1971). Thus, it was — and still is — a very competitive market.

The carriers needed to attract as large a share of this market as possible. To do so, they had to differentiate themselves from their competitors. But these domestic carriers, like their transatlantic counterparts, offered the same basic product: air transportation to the same destination. In addition, each carrier normally offered this product at the same basic fare; any fare reductions were typically associated with sacrifices in convenience.

In this case, perceptual mapping helped to identify service as one of the key factors in establishing a positive airline image. Figure 2-15 presents a two-dimensional perceptual map showing service measured along the vertical axis. In terms of this factor, Continental was perceived by air travelers in the Chicago market to offer the highest quality service.* Because

*The perceptions described here are those of the average air traveler in the Chicago-Los Angeles air travel market. The perceptions of certain groups (business vs. non-business, male vs. female, and first class vs. coach) sometimes differed significantly from the overall general image of an airline.

at the time of this study (1971) the Chicago-Los Angeles market was one of Continental's most lucrative, it spent a lot of money promoting itself in these two cities. In addition, it was the only one of the four carriers to emphasize curbside check-in services. It was also the only one to have on board each of its Chicago-Los Angeles flights a male passenger service representative whose function was to supervise the flight attendants, to give special attention to passenger problems, and to generally conduct inflight public relations for Continental. In short, Continental was perceived to provide more than its competitors of the warm, genuine, helpful, friendly, and personal services that air travelers desire.[23]

In terms of the quality of personal services, two of Continental's competitors — American and TWA — were given moderate ratings. United, however, was felt to offer less than its three competitors in terms of personal service. The reason for this was not entirely clear. It is quite possible that United's personal service in the Chicago-Los Angeles market actually was poor in comparison to the services of its competitors. The perception might also be attributed to United's size. Because it is the largest air carrier in the U.S., people might have inferred that United was incapable of offering genuinely warm and courteous personal attention to its passengers. In fact, this perception could very well be the target of the "friendly skies" theme that United has used in its national image-building campaign for years.

The horizontal axis in Figure 2-15 suggests that the second factor explaining the perceptual organization of the four airlines is the perceived size of the carriers. In this case, size conveys a positive meaning. United, American, and TWA are three of the four largest air carriers in the U.S. At the time of the study, each of these airlines carried three to five times the number of passengers carried by Continental. In addition, each of the three major carriers was spending $15 to $20 million per year on advertising, a substantial portion of which was spent on national campaigns. Meanwhile, Continental — although allocating a substantial portion of its advertising budget to the Chicago and Los Angeles markets — was spending less than $100,000 on national advertising. It seems reasonable to conclude, therefore, that Continental's perceived image was not that of a large domestic air carrier. Its three competitors, however, were perceived in exactly these terms. Size was regarded positively by these travelers who concluded that larger air carriers can offer more flights per day because of their larger fleets of aircraft — whether or not this is so in fact. More flights mean greater departure convenience for travelers, and many concluded that larger carriers are better able to offer more of this convenience.[24]

The results of the Chicago-Los Angeles air travel study suggest that schedule convenience is an overriding consideration for the air traveler. Once the need for time conveniences is satisfied, the air traveler then turns to a consideration of the quality of personal services provided by the airline.

FIGURE 2-15 Perceptual map of four Chicago-Los Angeles air carriers.

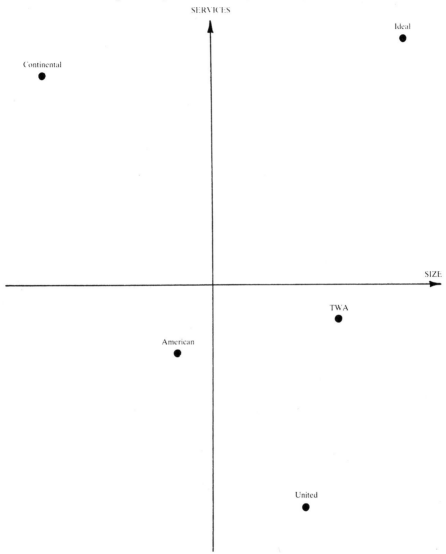

In the Chicago-Los Angeles market, Continental Airlines was perceived as offering outstanding personal service and attention. But because it was not considered a large air carrier, travelers may have perceived that it was unable to offer the scheduling conveniences of its larger competitors. On the other hand, United Airlines was perceived to offer considerable scheduling convenience because of its size. Yet, it was perceived as unable to provide personal service and attention of high quality — again, perhaps because of its size.

Perceptions are not static, however. They change over time — and, in some cases, they can change in a very short period of time. An airline's image can begin to change quickly when it institutes significant service changes and announces them with plenty of promotional fanfare. The Chicago-Los Angeles air travel study reflected perceptions as they existed in 1971; it would be reasonable to suspect that these images have changed in some important ways during subsequent years.

Intrastate Air Travel in Texas

People see the same object differently at different points in time. This is because people themselves change, and because objects — or communications about objects — change as well. This was illustrated when Southwest Airlines, a small intrastate air carrier in Texas, began carrying passengers between Dallas, Houston, and San Antonio in 1971. Competing with Braniff International, which carried 80 percent of the intrastate air passengers in Texas, Southwest considered how it could capture a profitable portion of the air passenger business in Texas by first examining how its competition was perceived by air travelers.[25]

As Figure 2-16 indicates, the image of the major competitor, Braniff, was found to have shifted over a period of three or four years. The perceptual position labeled Braniff-1 indicates how Braniff was perceived three or four years before the appearance of Southwest. This was referred to as the Mary Wells Braniff, in recognition of the image built for the airline by advertising executive Mary Wells. Braniff at this time was described as a fun and highly visible airline. Over time, however, the Braniff image became dull. The bold-colored planes that were the inspiration of Mary Wells began to appear dated. The image began to lose some of its freshness and appeal. As a result, Braniff came to be perceived as a conservative rather than a fun airline. It became more subtle and less obvious.* This new image is depicted in Figure 2-16 as Braniff-2. Finally, as indicated by the perceptual position labeled Braniff-3, the image of Southwest's major competitor moved farther into the conservative-subtle sector of the perceptual map.

At this time, Southwest decided to position itself where Braniff had once been — at Braniff-1 on the perceptual map. They created an obvious-fun image. Their hostesses were clad in tangerine hot pants, clinging orange sweaters, and white go-go boots, and they were trained by a woman

---

*It is noteworthy that to the management of Southwest, "an airline is a woman," and it literally tried to build an image evocative of the personality of Ali McGraw and the looks of Raquel Welch. This gives a clue to the meaning of the words "subtle" and "obvious" used in Figure 2-16.

FIGURE 2-16   Perceptual map for Braniff International.

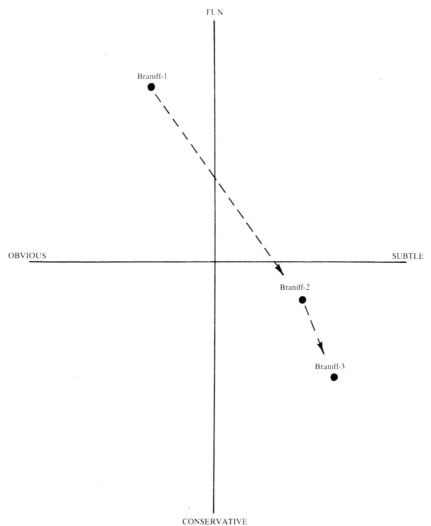

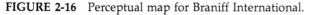

who had trained the Bunny hostesses on Hugh Hefner's planes. Each passenger was greeted with, "Welcome to the Love flight," (Southwest was headquartered at Love Field in Dallas). Southwest sold drinks for $1 — less than the $1.50 charged by Braniff. A passenger who, for any reason, voiced a complaint was given a free drink. A passenger who showed up at least five minutes before a flight and found it full was the first to board the next flight, flew for free, and received all drinks free of charge. In this way, Southwest tried to create a fun image, and purposely gave its passengers more personal care and attention than its competition did — or, in fact, could.* At the same time, Southwest was able to offer scheduling conveniences and time savings that Braniff sometimes found impossible to match. Because Texas weather is normally ideal for flying, 99 percent of Southwest's flights arrived within five minutes of schedule. Many of Braniff's flights, on the other hand, originated out-of-state and were sometimes behind schedule. In addition, Southwest sold tickets at the flight gate, while Braniff did not.

In short, Southwest recognized how air travelers perceived its major competitor and built its image on the qualities that most appealed to air travelers. It recognized the consumer's desire for personal service, time-saving conveniences, and fun, and it made sure that it delivered these benefits to its passengers. The results of Southwest's image-building strategy speak for themselves. In 1972, its first full year of operations, Southwest captured nearly 40 percent of the Dallas-Houston air travel market, while Braniff's share of this market fell from about 75 to 50 percent.

TRAVEL ADVERTISING

Consumer advertising plays an indispensable role in the marketing of travel products and services. Most of the principles of perception discussed in this chapter are employed in travel advertisements to create favorable perceptions of the services that they promote. Three examples are discussed below to illustrate how some of these principles can be used effectively in travel advertising.

Allegheny Airlines

Over the years, the scope and size of many regional air carriers have increased substantially. Frontier Airlines serves Atlanta, Air Florida has scheduled flights to Amsterdam and Brussels, Texas International flies to the Bahamas, and Western makes transcontinental flights to Miami. This trend will only increase with airline deregulation, as the formerly regional carriers begin serving destinations that fall outside of the limited geo-

---

*Braniff, because it was an interstate air carrier regulated by the Civil Aeronautics Board, could not legally do some of the things that Southwest could as an intrastate carrier not regulated by the CAB.

graphic areas they formerly served. Yet, travelers' perceptions of regional air carriers are often inconsistent with this new reality.

Unfortunately for these airlines, the regional character of their names reinforces perceptions of their limited size and route structure. Allegheny Airlines addressed this problem by renaming itself US Air, a name that more accurately reflects the geographic extent of the markets it now serves. Prior to the name change, Allegheny had addressed the perceptual inaccuracy created by its name through advertisements like the one reproduced in Figure 2-17. The headline in this advertisement — "Did you know Allegheny is 2 million passengers bigger than Pan Am?" — compared Allegheny to an international carrier that many Americans might have thought was among the largest in the world. Although most travelers would probably have underestimated the size and scope of Allegheny's operations, they also might have overestimated Pan Am's due to its international character. These two stereotypes make the objective comparison in this advertisement — passengers carried — a particularly effective one.

Figure 2-17 also illustrates the value of comparison in conveying information to an individual. The fact that Allegheny carried nearly 11 million passengers in one year would have little meaning to most readers, who have no reference point with which to compare this figure. Allegheny's passenger count does, however, have both meaning and impact when compared with that of another airline whose size is better established in the mind of the traveler.

It is unlikely that either Allegheny's or Pan Am's passenger counts will be retained due to their lack of relevance to most individuals. The message, however — that Allegheny is bigger than a large international airline — is both easier to remember and more meaningful as a bit of information to file away for future use.

If the reader notices anything in a print advertisement at all (selective attention), it is usually the headline and/or illustration. For this reason, it is particularly important that an advertisement convey its essential message in these two elements of the advertisement alone. Most readers will not read the body copy.* The advertisement for Allegheny makes particularly good use of headline and illustration, effectively communicating its message in these two elements. The headline and the illustration reinforce each other, further adding to the advertisement's ability to convey its message in little more than a glance. The reader's attention is directed to the prominence of Allegheny's plane in the foreground of the illustration, with its nose ahead of the Pan Am aircraft.

---

* In a recent issue of *Sunset* magazine, for example, the typical travel advertisement, according to a Starch Readership Report, was seen by two out of every three readers. Only an estimated 15 percent of this audience, however, read half or more of the written material in the typical travel ad.

FIGURE 2-17

Did you know Allegheny is 2 million passengers bigger than Pan Am?

Passenger Totals	
ALLEGHENY	**10,905,000**
Pan Am	8,257,000

Source: CAB, latest available 12-month data. Does not include 1,431,000 passengers flown by the 12 Allegheny Commuters.

When you're a big airline you count passengers by the millions.

When you're a good airline you never forget that every passenger is a person.

At Allegheny we mean to be as good as we are big. (And you're starting to know how big we are.)

Come fly Allegheny. Relax in the comforts of our single-class jet cabins.

We've got the cities you want. The business-day schedules you want. The discount fares you need, so you and your family can travel without breaking the bank.

And one thing more. We've got people who care about other people, which everybody wants.

Next time you fly, let us show you how good we really are. Just see your travel agent or call Allegheny. Welcome aboard!

ALLEGHENY®

It takes a big airline.

Rhode Island

As this chapter has emphasized, the traveler's perceptions of destinations does not always correspond with objective reality. He does not always perceive all that there is to perceive when he thinks about a given destination area. When considering a vacation to New England, for example, travelers may think in terms of only a few states (Massachusetts, Vermont, and New Hampshire), several specific destinations (Martha's Vineyard, Cape Cod, and Mount Washington), and a few attractions (historic landmarks, fresh seafood, and scenic countryside). The traveler's mental picture of New England may be neither accurate nor complete. Nonetheless, it is this personal mental picture, rather than the objective reality, that will serve as the basis for his destination-choice decisions.

The advertisement "If You Haven't Seen Rhode Island, You Haven't Seen New England" addresses this kind of perceptual omission (see Figure 2-18). When thinking about New England, the state of Rhode Island and its own specific destinations and attractions are very likely not considered by many travelers. In fact, many travelers may not even consider Rhode Island part of the New England region.

The goal of the advertisement reproduced in Figure 2-18 is to convey to the reader that Rhode Island *does* belong within his mental picture of New England, and that Rhode Island does offer many worthwhile attractions. In other words, the advertisement hopes to bring the state of Rhode Island into the pattern of possible destinations for the New England-bound traveler. Note, again, that the headline conveys the essential message by itself. It says to the traveler: "Your mental picture of New England is not complete unless it includes Rhode Island."

The Wickenburg Inn

Advertising for an individual resort usually has a difficult task. First, it must compete for the reader's attention with much larger space advertisements that feature air carriers, destination areas, and lodging chains. Second, for reasons of cost, resort advertisements often appear in black and white. Nonetheless, they must somehow draw the reader into the copy and convey their message quickly. A particularly effective job in both regards is accomplished by the advertisement for the Wickenburg Inn, reproduced in Figure 2-19.

The headline that proposes saddling up for a tennis clinic makes effective use of inconsistency — relating two activities not normally thought of as belonging together. The illustration reinforces this inconsistency by

FIGURE 2-18

IF YOU HAVEN'T SEEN RHODE ISLAND, YOU HAVEN'T SEEN NEW ENGLAND.

You can see the best New England has to offer. Right here in Rhode Island. Get a free Rhode Island Vacation Kit tailored to your special interests by mailing this coupon to: Rhode Island Tourist Promotion Division, One Weybosset Hill, Providence, R.I. 02903.

I'm interested in: ☐ Tours of historic mansions and sites
☐ Bicentennial events
☐ Camping   ☐ R. I. Seafood and clambakes   ☐ Boating
☐ Sports fishing   ☐ Golf courses   ☐ Museums
☐ Art shows, concerts, theater   ☐ Scenic bus and boat tours   ☐ House and garden tours   ☐ Windjammer cruises
☐ Craft fairs   ☐ Antiques   ☐ What the kids can do.
☐ Tall Ships '76 – Newport, June 26-July 1

Toll Free Information Number: 800-556-2484
Phone Monday thru Friday, 8:30 AM - 4:30 PM

Name _____

Address _____

City _____ State _____ Zip _____

BHG

Copyright © Tourist Promotion Division, Rhode Island, Providence, RI. Reprinted by permission.

FIGURE 2-19

1978 AAA◆◆◆◆and Mobil ★★★★ Resort

Saddle up for a super tennis clinic!

The Wickenburg Inn offers a superb combination of sunshine, the romantic Old West and relaxing resort luxury.

Weekly clinics* are conducted by our teaching professionals in a Tennis Center featuring 11 acrylic courts and the latest teaching devices. Classes are designed for maximum individual improvement.

Between court sessions, you can enjoy swimming, arts and crafts, nature activities and trail rides over 4700 acres of magnificent Arizona high desert.

The Wickenburg Inn, designed for 125 guests, is sixty miles northwest of Phoenix. Its friendly, informal atmosphere and undisturbed natural setting are perfect for an adventure in better tennis.

See your Travel Agent.
Or call toll free 800-323-1776
(In Illinois dial 800-942-8888)

THE WICKENBURG INN
Tennis and Guest Ranch
P.O. Box P, Dept. HA, Wickenburg, Az 85358 • (602) 684-7811

8 day/7 night tennis clinic from $571 per person double occupancy, includes instruction, all meals and activities.

Copyright © The Wickenburg Inn, Phoenix, AZ. Reprinted by permission.

placing a basket of tennis balls adjacent to a saddle. In this case, inconsistency serves as an attention-getting device, luring the reader into the copy where the riddle of inconsistency is solved. Even if the reader disregards the body copy, three highly visible elements — the headline, the illustration, and the signature ("The Wickenburg Inn — Tennis and Guest Ranch") — will still communicate the essential message in a glance.

This advertisement appeared in the November issue of an inflight magazine. Therefore, people were exposed to the advertisement at a time when tennis and riding are normally unavailable to many Americans.

Timing the advertisement in this way enables it to penetrate the perceptual defenses of those tennis and horseback riding enthusiasts who cannot enjoy these activities close to home during the winter months.

SUMMARY

An important starting point for understanding travel behavior is an understanding of perception. This chapter has identified a number of basic psychological principles of perception and shown how they influence the perception of various travel phenomena. Perception is a filtering process. A person selects what he will perceive based on what is important and relevant to him. He then forms an interpretation of a stimulus based on his perception of its characteristics. This interpretation may also be influenced by the individual's expectations, personality, experiences, needs, motives, and mood.

Perception is a complex process because the world is a complex environment. No wonder, then, that two people can respond to the same stimulus in entirely different ways. This explains why people with identical sets of needs and motives will choose different ways to satisfy them. In a travel setting, this helps to explain why people travel to different destinations, why some prefer to fly while others drive, why people have preferences for different air carriers, and why they patronize different types of lodging accommodations.

The influence that perceptions have on various travel decisions underscores the prospective traveler's need for information that helps him to develop accurate images of travel products and services. Travel is an intangible and highly symbolic product. For these reasons, the perception of travel phenomena is much more complex than it is for many other types of products and services.

A key point of this chapter is that an organization that comprehends how travelers form perceptions of travel-related services is in a very strong position to influence them. And since the perceptual process is an integral part of the traveler's decision-making, the ability to modify perceptions can alter consumer patronage behavior in a favorable way.

REFERENCES

[1] James H. Meyers and William H. Reynolds, *Consumer Behavior and Marketing Management* (Boston: Houghton-Mifflin Company, 1967), p. 3.

[2] This is suggested by: Clifford T. Morgan and Richard A. King, *Introduction to Psychology* (New York: McGraw-Hill Book Company, 1966), p. 37.

[3] David Krech, Richard S. Crutchfield, and Egerton L. Ballachy, *Individual in Society* (New York: McGraw-Hill Book Company, 1962), pp. 22–24.

[4] The Ulysses factor is the subject of an entire volume: J.R.L. Anderson, *The Ulysses Factor* (New York: Harcourt Brace Jovanovich, Inc., 1970).

[5] Harold H. Kassarjian and Thomas S. Robertson, eds., *Perspectives in Consumer Behavior* (Glenview, Illinois: Scott, Foresman and Company, 1968), p. 196.

[6] John A. Howard and Jagdish N. Sheth, "A Theory of Buyer Behavior," in Kassarjian and Robertson, *Perspectives in Consumer Behavior*, pp. 467–87 at p. 486.

[7] Canadian Government Travel Bureau, *1969 Vacation Trends and Recreation Patterns* (Ottawa, Canada: Canadian Government Travel Bureau, 1971).

[8] Donald E. Lundberg, *The Tourist Business* (Chicago: Institutions/Volume Feeding Management Magazine, 1971), p. 126.

[9] J.F. Engel, D.T. Kollat, and R.D. Blackwell, *Consumer Behavior* (New York: Holt Rinehart & Winston, Inc., 1968), pp. 218–20.

[10] Rom J. Markin, Jr., *Consumer Behavior* (New York: Macmillan Company, 1974), p. 321.

[11] For an interesting discussion of what is called durational expectancy, see: Alvin Toffler, *Future Shock* (New York: Random House, Inc., 1970), pp. 42–44.

[12] This principle was the subject of a research study reported in: Edward J. Mayo, "The Attractiveness of the Far-Off Destination: A Study of Subjective Distance," a paper presented at the Sixth Annual Conference of the Travel Research Association, San Diego (September 11, 1975).

[13] Ernest Dichter, "Finding Out What Motivates Today's Traveler to the U.S.," a speech presented before the Travel Research Association, Quebec, Canada (August 15, 1972).

[14] Ibid. This topic was also discussed by Robert Carlson of International Research Associates, Inc. at a meeting of the New York chapter of the Travel Research Association, January 16, 1973.

[15] One of the techniques that has been widely used for these purposes is called multidimensional scaling. For a discussion of this and related techniques, see: Paul E. Green and Frank J. Carmone, *Multidimensional Scaling and Related Techniques in Marketing Analysis* (Boston: Allyn and Bacon, Inc., 1970).

[16] The perceptual mapping discussed here is based on: Edward J. Mayo, *Regional Travel Characteristics of the United States* (Bedford Park, Illinois: 3M National Advertising Company, 1973).

[17] Edward J. Mayo, *Tourism and the American Indian Reservation* (Notre Dame, Indiana: University of Notre Dame, Center for Business Research, 1973), pp. 32–34. Also see: Richard W. Stoffle et al., "Reservation-Based Tourism: Implications of Tourist Attitudes for Native American Economic Development," *Human Organization* (forthcoming).

[18] John D. Hunt, "Image as a Factor in Tourism Development," *Journal of Travel Research*, Vol. 13 (Winter, 1975), pp. 1–7.

[19] Australia's efforts to increase tourism are described in: "Promoting Australia in North America," a management case distributed by the Intercollegiate Case Clearing House, Boston, Massachusetts.

[20] See: Paul E. Green and Yoram Wind, "New Way to Measure Consumers' Judgments," *Harvard Business Review*, Vol. 53 (July–August, 1975), pp. 107–117.

[21] The importance of time and scheduling conveniences has been documented in a number of other independent research studies. See: Kit G. Narodick, "What Motivates the Consumer's Choice of an Airline?" *Journal of Retailing*, Vol. 48 (Spring,

1972), pp. 30–38, 96; Kit G. Narodick, "Determinants of Airline Market-Share," *Journal of Advertising Research,* Vol. 12 (October, 1972), pp. 31–36; and *1975 Survey Results* (Dallas: Airline Passengers Association). The relative importance of airline-choice factors among business and vacation travelers was also examined in a recent study in Calgary, Canada. This study indicated that vacation travelers often considered fares and safety factors more important than flight schedules. The importance of fares to vacation travelers has undoubtedly grown since deregulation of the airline industry. See: J.R. Brent Ritchie, Everett E. Johnston, and Vernon J. Jones, "Competition, Fares and Fences — Perspective of the Air Traveler," *Journal of Travel Research,* Vol. 18 (Winter, 1980), pp. 17–25.

[22] Edward J. Mayo, "Airline Choice: The Role of Perceived Images," a paper presented at the Seventh Annual Conference of the Travel Research Association, Boca Raton, Florida (June 23, 1976).

[23] The reader may also be interested in T. O'Brien, N. de Gennaro, and G. Summers, "Customer Perception of Product Attributes in the Airline Industry," *Journal of Travel Research,* Vol. 15 (Winter, 1977), pp. 9–13.

[24] These points are discussed in some detail in: Kit G. Narodick, "Researching the Airline Passenger: The Boeing 747 Experience," a paper presented at the Fourth Annual Conference of the Travel Research Association, Sun Valley, Idaho (August 13, 1973). Also see: O'Brien, de Gennaro, and Summers, "Customer Perception of Product Attributes. . . ."

[25] The material here is drawn from: "Southwest Airlines (A)," a management case distributed by the Intercollegiate Case Clearing House, Boston, Massachusetts; and Walter Joyce, "Love Boxes in Braniff in Texas," *Marketing/Communications* (January, 1972), pp. 20–24.

QUESTIONS FOR DISCUSSION

1. Describe, in a sentence or two, your overall impression of Disney World. (It doesn't matter whether you have ever visited there.) Then ask someone else to give you his impression of Disney World. Compare the two sets of impressions. Can you explain why they might differ?
2. "Most leisure travel serves no practical value." Do you agree with this statement? If not, then why is leisure travel so popular?
3. What is meant by the "Ulysses factor?" How does it influence our perceptions of distant destinations?
4. Give an example of how a person's need for status would influence his perceptions in the travel market.
5. When the need to travel or get away becomes very strong, how does this influence our perceptions in the travel environment?
6. Instead of spending a vacation traveling to some far-off destination, a person of a lower social class might prefer to spend a few weeks at a lake cottage not far from home. Explain why.
7. The far-off travel destination can have a special attraction about it simply because it is far-off. What are some of the reasons why this might be so?
8. Many people in foreign countries have a negative image of the United States

as a place to visit. Why? Might any of your answers also help to explain the travel attitudes of Americans toward various areas of the U.S.?

9. Why is perceptual ambiguity a liability for those promoting travel to a specific destination area? Isn't the lure of the unknown enough to make people want to visit a particular destination area?

10. Why is it so important for a travel advertisement to have a powerful headline and/or illustration?

11. Perception is often referred to as a filtering process. How does this filtering process work? What are some of the factors that influence the way in which the filter works?

12. Identify a travel destination which you personally found to be quite different from your preconception of it. Why was your earlier image of the destination so inaccurate?

13. Perceptions of travel phenomena are much more complex than for many other types of products. Why?

3
LEARNING AND TRAVEL BEHAVIOR

Psychologists are of the opinion that all human behavior involves some form of **learning.** Over time, an individual's behavior changes, and these changes can often be attributed to the learning process. John Doe decides to start making travel arrangements through a travel agency that recently opened a new branch office near his home. He learned or became aware of its existence. He became interested in the agency because of an advertisement he read in the local newspaper (more learning). The travel agency that he has patronized for about three years no longer seems to give him the kind of personalized attention he likes. A close friend tells him that he has done business with the new agency at a different location and that he likes their efficiency and the personalized service they provide (another form of learning). John Doe starts doing business with the new travel agency, forms several impressions of it (more learning), and decides that he will continue to give his business to the new agency.

Travelers are consumers and problem solvers. How one solves various travel problems — where to go, when to go, how to get there, how long to stay, and where to stay — changes over time for various economic, psychological, social, and cultural reasons. Our incomes fluctuate, as do the prices for different travel products and services. Our motivations and perceptions change. We grow older, and our group affiliations change. And, as we move from one age category to another, we find that our behavior must often change as well. The young adult is free to travel alone, but must pay her own way. The aging individual discovers that he can no longer climb mountains or tolerate the noise and confusion of crowded tourist attractions. We change, physically and psychologically, and the environments in which we live change in ways that force us to alter our behavior. We are forced to adapt. We adapt in ways that enable us to continue to attain our desired goals. Learning plays a central role in this process, because adaptation is learned. We learn new goals and new ways to achieve them; we learn about our changing environment and about ourselves; we learn new means to adjust to life and the world in which we live.

The process of learning — adapting to changes in ourselves and our environment — can have a very significant impact on our travel behavior. As we shall see in this chapter, learning is a psychological process that can have a profound effect on our perceptions, personalities, motivations, and attitudes — in other words, on many of the key psychological factors that influence travel behavior.

Consumers learn motives and attitudes, they learn how to consume, and they learn how to deal with the doubts that sometimes follow the decisions they make in the marketplace. The first section of this chapter discusses what the consumer-traveler learns that allows him to solve specific travel problems and how best to satisfy specific travel needs. What the travel service firm can do to show potential customers how its product can help to satisfy particular travel needs is discussed in the second section of this chapter. The family is considered the single most important leisure group in western societies, and the third section of this chapter discusses the topic of family travel decision-making.

WHAT IS LEARNED?

Some travel problems require an individual to systematically evaluate alternative courses of action. The careful, deliberate, and logical travel decision is one in which an individual applies what he has learned from past experiences. A person accustomed to spending two weeks each summer touring a new state in his motorhome may have logically decided against doing so during the summer of 1979. Aware of the gasoline shortage that summer, he may have foreseen that a long motorhome journey could very well leave him stranded far from home for some period of time. After weighing the risk, he decides either to stay at home or to fly to some vacation destination. The decision not to vacation in his motorhome is based on newly learned information — information that he uses to draw logical conclusions. Thus, some travel behavior can only be fully comprehended by appreciating that it is based on what the individual traveler knows.

Other kinds of travel behavior result from habits, and these too are learned. An individual learns habits when he discovers that certain actions are rewarding. The psychologist refers to this process in terms of **stimulus-and-response.** According to this principle, an individual will learn to respond in a certain way to a given stimulus if the possibility of being rewarded in some manner is present. Pavlov's well-known experiments showed that a dog could be taught to salivate in response to the ringing of a bell if the sound was followed immediately by the reward of food. For some time afterward, the bell *alone* produced salivation — until the dog learned that food would not necessarily accompany the ringing of the bell.

There is little question that a great deal of human behavior is guided by this type of learning. An individual learns, for example, that a mid-day hunger pain (a stimulus) can disappear (the reward) by stopping at McDonald's (the response). In other words, the stimulus and the response are linked by a reward. When a stimulus-and-response link like this one is repeated several times, it becomes more and more likely that the next mid-day hunger pain will prompt the individual to think about McDonald's. Before long, the mid-day visit to McDonald's becomes a habit. Almost without conscious thought, the individual turns to McDonald's when he feels hunger. And after a time, the visit to McDonald's may be triggered not by a hunger pain but by the clock on the wall.*

An automobile traveler may learn through trial and error that Holiday Inn offers reliable overnight accommodations. The need to rest (the stimulus) prompts her to seek out Holiday Inn accommodations (the response), and she obtains a good night's rest (the reward). As long as the response is rewarded, the traveler will be likely to continue seeking out Holiday Inn accommodations. If she is a business traveler, the individual may learn that making travel arrangements through a travel agent saves her considerable time. The time saved is the reward and, as long as she continues to travel (the stimulus) and to receive this reward, she is likely to continue using the services of a travel agent (the response).

For many people, pleasure travel itself may be a habit. The stimulus may be the tension brought on by working for long, unbroken periods of time. The individual learns that travel rewards her with a reduction of tension. And as long as this stimulus-response behavior produces a satisfying reward, she will continue to travel. In this way, travel may become

---

*The habit may be broken periodically, of course, when the individual tires of a consistent diet of McDonald's food and, for the sake of variety, visits other eating places.

a habit. In fact, the urge to travel may be triggered as much by a glance at a calendar as by the tension that arises from living and working in a fast-paced urban and industrial society.

Learning is a pervasive activity. In the normal individual, it begins at birth and continues until death. It is involved continuously with the application of new information to problem solving situations and even plays an important role in the development of our feelings and emotions, our self-concepts, and our total personalities.[1] Learning involves the development of personal rules and strategies that help one to act out the role of purchaser and consumer of various products and services. In other words, we learn how to shop for and purchase goods and services, and we learn how to consume them. A travel decision maker learns to solve problems by learning the kinds of products and services that best serve his specific needs. Motives and attitudes exert a considerable influence on this problem solving process, and both can be learned.

The Learning of Motives

We can define a motive as a need, a goal, or a want. In more technical terms, a motive is a biological or psychological tension that prompts us to behave in a way that reduces it. Travel motivations are discussed at length in Chapter 5, which builds a case for considering the basic urge to travel as an **innate** need. Nearly everyone is born, it seems, with a need to explore — for the baby to see what lies beyond his nursery; for the child to explore the neighborhood in which he lives; for the adult to see his country, foreign lands, and even other planets. For some people, the basic urge to travel is dampened over time because of experiences, often very early in life, from which they learned to fear the unknown. It seems clear, however, that most people are born with the need to discover what lies beyond their immediate surroundings.

Aside from the basic urge to explore, most other motives that can influence our travel behavior are learned rather than innate. In fact, many psychologists agree that "most of the motivational characteristics of the adult human are learned or acquired."[2] So, while many of our drives and needs are biological in nature (innate), most are learned from family members, friends, acquaintances, and others who help transmit cultural norms.[3] Many authorities contend that a person learns needs and motives such as the following: status, power, aggressiveness, anxiety, fear, affiliaton, achievement, strength, independence, self-confidence, and self-respect. An individual's need for status, for example, is not something with which she is born. She learns that social or professional status provides her with prestige, bolsters her self-image, and makes her more attractive to people who are important to her.

The learned need for status can have a tremendous impact on travel behavior — on choices of destination, mode of transportation, and accommodation, to name a few. The motive of fear also influences travel behavior, inhibiting some people from traveling in airplanes and others from traveling to lands too foreign or cities too large.

Because needs and motives such as these are learned, travel behavior can and does change as they are learned, unlearned, and learned again in some new way. The need for status may be absorbed relatively early in life, but the way in which status is achieved changes from one stage of life to another. Obviously, what gives status to a ten-year-old is not the same thing that gives status to a 20-year-old person or to a person sixty-five years of age. For one, a trip to Disney World gives status. For another, status means a week in Ft. Lauderdale during the late winter months. For still others, status is a Caribbean cruise. Those who market theme parks, destination areas, cruises, and other travel products can help people to satisfy specific urges like the need for status. This is by no means an easy task, but it is one way to successfully market a specific travel service.

A specific need or motive can also represent the need to achieve a larger, higher, or more general goal. We can think, in other words, of a hierarchy of needs and motives, all of which may be learned.[4] An example of such a hierarchy is illustrated in Figure 3-1. At the top of the means-end chain in Figure 3-1 is the learned motive of anxiety, a motive of considerable importance in urban and industrialized societies. One way of coping with anxiety is by affiliating with selected groups of people. Membership in formal organizations (such as the Elks) or informal groups (such as a particular social class) can provide an individual with confidence, esteem, respect, and status—all of which can reduce anxiety. Travel is often viewed as a way of qualifying for membership in certain groups. Figure 3-1 suggests that one way of coping with anxiety, a learned motive, is by affiliating with an appropriate group. And one means of achieving affiliation, another learned motive, is by traveling. What Figure 3-1 suggests is that while travel may be an innate drive and an end in itself, it also serves as a means of satisfying other needs.

The particular destinations visited by the individual traveler might be selected on the basis of prestige, cost, luxury, and other factors — a third set of learned motives. This third set of motives is particularly important to the travel marketer because they are among the criteria which the individual traveler uses to evaluate alternative travel products and services. The fact that they are learned suggests that travel decisions can also be influenced by encouraging the individual traveler to learn new motives.

The Learning of Attitudes

The role of attitudes in influencing travel behavior is discussed in detail in Chapter 6. This section, about the *learning* of attitudes, should be pref-

FIGURE 3-1

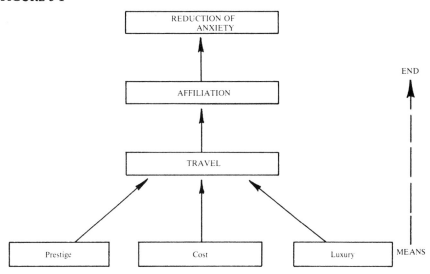

aced by emphasizing that most of the major topics in this book — perception, learning, personality, and motivation — contribute to the development of attitudes; and, under most circumstances, our behavior is influenced by our attitudes. If we have a positive attitude toward travel, we are probably inclined to travel. And if we have a positive attitude toward foreign travel, we will travel to foreign countries if we are able to do so.

The attitudes a person holds result from learning processes. Such attitudes are based in large part on our beliefs and opinions. These we learn from family, friends, acquaintances, and teachers. We learn them from reference groups to which we belong, from the society in which we live, and from the news media. These and other sources of influence provide us with the information that serves as the basis for our opinions and beliefs which, in turn, serve as the foundation of our attitudes. Family, friends, and acquaintances also provide us with models of how we should feel about various objects — and these feelings also help us form attitudes.

Attitudes are also learned by virtue of the roles we play. Each individual assumes a variety of roles at every stage of life. A small child, for example, might play the roles of daughter, sister, first-grade student, playmate, niece, and granddaughter. As a mature adult, she might play the roles of mother, wife, lover, business professional, citizen, church member, neighbor, and daughter-in-law. Each role is learned, and part of the learning requires that one take on the attitudes appropriate to a given role. One normally has some latitude in choosing a specific set of attitudes, but to reject an appropriate set of attitudes is to reject the role. A mother, for example, can choose to be lovingly permissive in her attitude toward her children or lovingly authoritative — but, on the whole, her attitude is expected to be one of loving concern. From both parents, the children will learn certain attitudes toward travel, and they will be taught how to travel as well.

The value of education is a good example of an attitude that people — parents and teachers especially — transmit to the young. This may take the form of pressure to earn good grades in school, to read books, to prepare for college, and to think seriously about entering one of the professions. Apparently, the attitude that education is all-important is learned well, because it continues to be transmitted from one generation to the next. It is an attitude that often has a great influence on travel behavior. As we will see in Chapter 4, travel that might not otherwise be undertaken is more easily justified when it is seen to serve a worthy educational purpose.

The learning of attitudes is also greatly influenced by perception, which was discussed at length in Chapter 2. Through perception, we learn how to generalize and label things. We learn to place New York, New Orleans, and San Francisco into the same category, and Colonial Williamsburg, Gettysburg, and Pennsylvania Dutch Country into another category. We learn that different categories of vacation destinations have the potential to satisfy different travel motives. If we are disappointed by a visit to Sturbridge Village in Massachusetts, our attitudes toward other Early American attractions are likely to be questioned or modified.

Broad cultural and societal reforms also lead us to form new attitudes and change old ones in ways that can have a marked effect on travel behavior. In recent years, for example, people have learned that it is not only acceptable but often healthy to view the family in a new light. No longer does society dictate that parents sacrifice so much for the well-being of their children. A generation ago, family solidarity was an important value. Today, however, family members have learned that there may be nothing shameful about doing things separately. Parents are more aware that they need time away from their children and from each other; their children, too, need time to be alone. Changing attitudes of this kind are learned and can have a dramatic influence on travel behavior. More couples, for example, are taking vacations without their children and also taking vacations alone.[5]

Attitudes toward women's roles in society have also changed a great deal in recent years. According to one authoritative source, women now constitute up to 28 percent of all business travelers. United Airlines estimates that 16 percent of its customers on business trips are women, and that their numbers are growing three times as fast as those of men.[6]

As women in larger numbers join the labor force — and especially the management ranks — they are required to travel more. This, in turn, requires them to learn a new set of roles, along with the attitudes that accompany them. No longer is the woman the demure companion of her executive husband who registers her in hotels, picks up the check in restaurants, and protects her from the difficulties of being away from home. Instead, the woman today is more likely to travel alone — and, like any traveler, she must cope with various travel-related problems. She brings with her a unique set of problems, however, because she is a woman. Unlike her male counterpart, for example, she must concern herself more with physical security. Conducting business meetings in a hotel room dominated by a bed can sometimes be awkward for a woman traveling alone, and so can the purchasing of a drink or a meal in a hotel lounge or restaurant. These and other concerns have a tremendous impact on the attitudes that the female traveler develops toward the hotels, restaurants, and other travel firms that serve her.

Attitudes are also learned as a result of our experiences and from purchasing and using travel services. For example, what we learn from other people, from advertising, and from other sources of information forms the basis for our preliminary attitudes toward a particular travel agency. Our direct experience with this travel agency, however, will confirm or modify our earlier attitudes, or prompt us to form entirely new ones. Direct experiences, therefore, have a primary role in determining what attitudes are formed. Of course, the attitudes we develop as a result of our experiences with travel products are influenced by the expectations we have of them. These expectations, in turn, develop from the process of learning how to consume.

Learning How to Consume

Learning how to travel implies, among other things, that an individual must learn how to discriminate between competitive travel products and services; that is, he must learn how to be a good shopper in the travel marketplace. As a consumer-traveler, he must learn how to evaluate competitive travel products and services and how to deal with the risk and uncertainty that is a part of any purchase decision. We should also keep in mind that even the most experienced traveler continues to learn and change his travel behavior. This is so because of changes in the prices of travel products and services, because of advertising that conveys new information, and because of changes in the availability of specific travel services. The experienced traveler also continues to learn because, over a period of time, his income may increase and allow him to afford what he could not in the past. We are also forced to learn anew what we have learned but forgotten in the past.

Learning from experience is a psychological result of the decisions we make in the marketplace. Learning takes place when we discover what differentiates one brand of travel service from another. We learn through experience how to evaluate competing hotel chains, airlines, car rental firms, and resort areas. We also learn from the experiences that our friends have and share with us.

A discussion of how we learn to consume and how this learning influences our behavior as travelers must emphasize the impact that risk and uncertainty have on the decisions we make in the marketplace. Risk and uncertainty accompany just about any decision an individual makes. But, as we shall see, risk and uncertainty are especially likely to accompany the purchase of travel services. Any decision a consumer makes has the potential to produce consequences that were not anticipated—sometimes very unpleasant ones. A consumer, then, may perceive risk when he makes decisions because the outcome may be quite different than he anticipates.[7] He may perceive some risk that when he rents a car it will break down. There is a risk when he travels south in the wintertime because of the possibility that Florida will experience a week of unseasonably cold weather. Even when the traveler has a confirmed reservation with a hotel or an air carrier, there is a risk that he will be "walked" or "bumped." Risk is also involved when he spends time at a prestigious resort, because of the possibility that his peers will consider the resort out of fashion.

Consumers learn how to cope with these and other kinds of risks. To understand how travelers reduce risk, it is first necessary to understand two major types of perceived risk: **functional** risk and **psychosocial** risk. Functional risk exists when there is a possibility that the product or service purchased will not work as expected. The rental car that breaks down, the airplane that experiences mechanical failure and must land somewhere other than its intended destination, and the malfunctioning air conditioning in a hotel room — each of these is an example of functional risk.

Psychosocial risk involves the question of whether a product or service will enhance an individual's sense of well-being, enrich his self-concept, or improve the way that other people think about him. Clothing, automobiles, and many travel services are highly visible and symbolic products, high in psychosocial risk. There is a risk, for example, that a skiing trip to the Poconos will communicate something negative about an individual or that during a trip to Hawaii one might meet people who do little to enhance one's self-image.

Perceived risk also exists because of the possibility that a person may waste money and time when he purchases a product that does not satisfy *either* functional or psychosocial goals. Perceived risk can become quite uncomfortable when the purchase is an expensive one — a late-model automobile, a new home, or an expensive vacation trip.

The amount of functional, psychosocial, and financial risk associated with a given product can have an important bearing on how the consumer deals with it and how a firm can best help the consumer to reduce the perceived risk. A person can perceive risk in a buying situation for reasons that include the following:

· **Uncertain buying goals**   Although an individual may have decided to take a vacation, she may be undecided about what kind of trip to take. Should she spend a relaxing week in Hawaii or an exciting, adventurous week in South America?

· **Uncertain purchase rewards**   Assuming the buying goal is clearly identified, the individual may be uncertain as to which purchase will best satisfy the buying goal. If the major purpose of a vacation trip is to relax, which would be more rewarding: a week in Florida, or a week in Arizona?

· **Lack of purchasing experience**   The individual may have little past experience with the purchase decision and therefore perceive risk. This might be the case with someone contemplating his first trip to a foreign destination.

· **Positive and negative consequences**   The individual may perceive that all of the alternatives have both positive and negative consequences. Traveling by air is the quickest way to reach a destination, but it prevents sightseeing along the way.

· **Peer influence**   The purchase decision might differ from the decisions that would be made by most members of an important peer group. An individual's peers may spend heavily on travel to foreign destinations and may look askance at a group member who purchases an expensive motorhome.

· **Financial considerations**   The individual perceives risk when he anticipates that there could be important changes in his financial situation. This might be the case for someone who recognizes the possibility of losing his job in a depressed economy.

It is common for people to perceive a certain amount of risk in any given buying situation. It is also common for them to attempt to reduce this perceived risk in some way. They can be aided in this task by travel service firms that recognize the varied causes of perceived risk and know how to help people reduce them. In fact, the professional travel agent occupies a unique role in that she specializes in helping travelers cope with and reduce perceived risk. We will discuss how she does this later in this chapter.

There are three ways in which people attempt to reduce perceived risk:

1. expecting less from the product or service
2. regularly purchasing the same product, service, or brand
3. acquiring information

Expecting Less from the Product or Service.   One way to reduce perceived risk is to lower our expectations of a product or service. We could expect to get less than EPA estimated gas mileage from a new automobile, or we could expect that the weather in Florida during a vacation there will be less than ideal at least part of the time.

According to some authorities, however, expecting less from a product or service is not among the more popular strategies for reducing perceived risk.[8] It would seem that this would be especially so in the case of travel and tourism services. Vacationers tend to idealize their travels.[9] They fantasize about the destinations to which they will travel and never really imagine that it might rain in Hawaii, that they might have to wait in several hour-long lines at Disney World, that they might only be grudgingly accepted by the natives in some foreign lands, or that foreign drinking water might make them ill. It is conceivable, in fact, that people would be less interested in travel if they were not allowed to idealize about their future vacation journeys. "Anticipation is the greater pleasure," Thomas Aquinas once said, and this may be particularly true of pleasure travel. Travel agents and others face the dual problem of encouraging their clients' fantasies while preparing them for the realities of travel so that they do not return disappointed and disillusioned. This, obviously, is no easy task.

Regularly Purchasing the Same Product, Service, or Brand.   A more popular strategy that consumers use to reduce perceived risk is the repetitive purchase of one product or service. The business traveler who patronizes only Sheraton hotels, who always flies with American, and who rents his cars from Hertz alone may do so in order to reduce perceived risks. He patronizes only Sheraton hotels because, through experience, he has learned to expect at least a reasonably good night's rest at any Sheraton, and he sees no reason to patronize other hotels and run the risk of spending a restless night. For a similar reason — to reduce perceived risk — he loyally gives his patronage to American and Hertz.

Brand loyalty does not necessarily mean that an individual is completely satisfied with the product. His brand-loyal behavior may merely indicate that he finds the product acceptable. As such, he may see no reason to spend the time and energy or endure the risk of finding a better alternative.

In Chapter 1, it was suggested that brand loyalty is one way of saving time. In addition, brand loyalty can also reduce perceived risk. Especially in the travel market, where the product is in many ways an intangible one, consumers are very likely to rely on brand loyalty as a risk-reducing strategy. Unlike tangible products such as automobiles, appliances, and clothing, it is sometimes very difficult for a consumer to evaluate an intangible service. Intangible services are difficult to describe, to demonstrate to the buying public, and to illustrate in promotional material.[10] Most travel products are actually services, and the quality of these services often depends on individual employees within the service firm — the reservation agent and flight crew of an airline, for example, or the front desk, restaurant, and housekeeping personnel of a hotel. In fact, the quality of a service can vary dramatically from one customer to another, and from one day to the next. An automobile is subject to relatively stringent quality control standards. This is not the case with personal services, which tend to be viewed with greater uncertainty as a result. Thus, the travel consumer relies more heavily on brand loyalty, because the perceived risk involved in most travel-related purchases is relatively high.

This line of reasoning underscores the importance, for those who market and sell travel services, of encouraging brand loyalty. One way to accomplish this is to develop training and educational programs that prepare employees to deliver maximum personal service and attention to customers. This is a standard procedure for some firms in the travel industry, and a wise one because it is one of the few ways that the quality of a firm's services can be effectively controlled. By providing a high quality of service, a travel firm can hold on to present customers. By providing a higher quality of service than its competitors, a firm can attract new customers as well.

Acquiring Information.   The third and most popular consumer strategy for reducing the risk associated with a buying situation is the seeking of information. As a general rule, the more reliable information a consumer possesses, the less risk she will perceive in a buying situation. Suppose, for example, that a traveler acquires information about Holiday Inns through her own experience, through the experiences of others, and through Holiday Inns' advertising. This information convinces her that Holiday Inns offer a highly standardized product and that, indeed, there are rarely any surprises at a Holiday Inn. The accommodations this lodging chain provides and the opportunity for restful sleep are highly predictable and, therefore, present little risk to the consumer. Clearly, one of the major reasons for Holiday Inns' success over the years has been exactly this — that it reduces perceived risk for the traveler. This does not necessarily mean that people are totally satisfied with Holiday Inns, but it does clearly demonstrate the importance of helping the traveler reduce the risk she may perceive when it comes to selecting overnight accommodations.

For years, communication researchers and advertisers viewed the process of communication primarily as a one-way street. It was assumed that advertisers directed persuasive messages at consumers who passively received them. The more modern viewpoint of the communication process is that consumers actively participate in it. Consumers, according to this viewpoint, will actively seek, acquire, transmit, and process information when they have a high need for it. Consumers perceive risk in most buying situations, and they learn that information will help them reduce this risk.

They decide on the sources, type, and amount of information they will use in making a purchase decision. This does not imply that consumers are not passive at times. It is when consumers have a need for information that they will become most actively involved in the process of acquiring and evaluating it. This also suggests that consumers are more likely to utilize an advertiser's message when it meets their information needs.[11] A person contemplating a trip to Europe, for example, is more likely to pay attention to advertising by transatlantic air carriers and foreign tourist boards. She is also more likely to seek the advice and opinions of people she knows who have visited Europe themselves.

A consumer who recognizes that he has a need for information will even pay for the information. People pay for information at the racetrack, when they buy *Consumer Reports,* and when they subscribe to the *Official Airline Guide.* The traveler pays for information with his time when he visits a travel agency or reads brochures.

Consumers seek out information that they consider will be most relevant to the type of perceived risk they are trying to reduce. If a person perceives high functional risk — risk that the product will not work as well as he thinks it should — he will seek out performance information. One source of this type of information is the firm's advertising or promotional literature.[12] A person contemplating a Caribbean cruise might consult a travel agent or brochure for factual, performance-related information concerning the size of staterooms and departure dates. A traveler contemplating a vacation trip to a specific resort area should be able to rely on published information provided by the resort concerning average temperatures, distance from transportation facilities, number of tennis courts, and so forth.

In addition, the traveler may also consult friends or travel agents to corroborate what he has learned from the brochures concerning a particular resort. In fact, this type of information — from "impartial" personal sources — is believed to be more influential in the consumer's final decision than seller-provided materials because it is considered less biased and therefore more complete and authoritative.

If a person perceives little functional risk but a great deal of psychosocial risk, he is much more likely to rely on interpersonal sources of information rather than the information provided by a manufacturer or producer. Psychosocial risk usually elicits a need for a specific type of information, and although image-oriented consumer advertising and brochures can assist in reducing psychosocial risk, they are probably incapable of providing the types of information that would reduce it entirely. Moreover, for this type of information, the producer or manufacturer is not looked on as a very reliable or trustworthy source.

The consumer who perceives an intolerable level of psychological and social risk will normally seek information to reduce it from friends, acquaintances, and other interpersonal sources. According to a number of authorities, advertising and promotional brochures or literature will not be relied on extensively to reduce this type of perceived risk.

It is important to point out that the professional travel agent can play a very important role when psychosocial risk is perceived to be high. To the extent that the travel agent is viewed as one's personal travel counselor, she can have an important impact on the travel decision process. To the extent that she is viewed merely as an order taker, however, the influence on travel decisions will be minimal. All of this underscores the importance for the travel agent to be very familiar both with the travel products she sells and with her clients. It also emphasizes the importance for travel service firms to work closely with travel agencies when these organizations account for a sizeable amount of the sales in the firm's sector of the travel industry.

Learning to Deal with Postpurchase Doubt

The previous section discussed the uncertainty that can *precede* a consumer decision and what the consumer is likely to do to reduce this uncertainty. Uncertainty can also exist *after* a purchase decision has been made. A considerable amount of research has been conducted that investigates post-purchase uncertainty — what consumer behavior theorists call **postpur-chase dissonance.** It has been found, for example, that postpurchase uncertainty is common among purchasers of homes, automobiles, major appliances, and many other expensive items.[13]

There are two broad reasons why a consumer might doubt or regret the decision to purchase a product. The uncertainty may, in part, be a carry-over from the prepurchase difficulty of deciding from among several possible choices. Suppose, for example, that a couple chose to spend a winter skiing holiday at Playboy's Lake Geneva resort in Wisconsin, rather than spending the holiday at a ski resort in Colorado. Presumably, they selected the Lake Geneva resort because they judged that it would best serve their needs. This does not, however, resolve the doubts that may exist after making the choice — doubts occasioned by some of the unattractive aspects of Lake Geneva or the attractive features of the Colorado resort that they rejected. These doubts may arise immediately after making the decision and before leaving for the trip, upon returning home from the trip, or both.

Postpurchase doubts may also arise if the couple has a disappointing experience at Lake Geneva or encounters unanticipated trouble. If the snow conditions are poor, for example, or if the entertainment seems less than first-rate, postpurchase doubts may be experienced. The same feelings might also arise if, upon returning home, their friends comment, "Why did you go *there?*" instead of "You must have had a great time!"

Postpurchase dissonance can arise when there is no reassurance that the decision the consumer made was a good one. The lack of reassurance can cause psychological discomfort in the consumer, who wonders: "Should I have made a different decision?" The resulting psychological tension motivates the consumer to reduce it. Consumers learn that there are ways in which this can be done. Understanding them is important to those who market and sell travel services, because the customer who feels she has had a satisfying experience with a particular service is likelier to purchase it again and report favorably about it to others. Accordingly, the travel firm's interest in its customers should not simply terminate when they use their services.

One of the primary methods that consumers utilize to reduce postpurchase doubt is exposure to new information.[14] If a decision is regretted, an individual will seek information that he perceives as likely to support it. At the same time, he will avoid information that favors the unchosen alternatives. Both of these activities are examples of **selective exposure,** a perceptual process that was discussed in Chapter 2. In effect, the consumer controls the type of information he is exposed to in a way that will help confirm in his own mind that he made a good decision. Research has shown, for example, that new car owners read more advertisements for the car they purchased than for other cars.[15]

A person can also reduce postpurchase dissonance by forgetting the favorable characteristics of an unchosen alternative, by remembering its unfavorable aspects, or both. This perceptual technique was referred to in Chapter 2 as **selective recall,** and it can be quite effective in reducing postdecision doubts. The individual returning from a three-week automobile trip to the West Coast, for instance, might purposely forget about the time he would have saved by flying and focus on the hundreds of dollars he saved instead.

One other way in which dissonance can be reduced occurs when a person rationalizes her decision by concluding that the alternative she chose led more or less to the same end result as would have occurred had she made some other choice. Although she may have spent a long time deciding to spend a winter holiday in Arizona instead of southern Florida, she might conclude afterwards that it really didn't matter after all. She would have spent, she now thinks, a restful week at either destination, returned with as good a tan from either destination, and met just as many interesting people in either place.

How Travel Firms Can Help Reduce Postpurchase Doubts.   By helping their customers to reduce postpurchase doubts, those who market and sell travel services provide a valuable service and increase the chances that these customers will continue to give them their business.

Perhaps the most effective means of accomplishing this goal is through direct communication with the traveler. One means that is popular with many travel agencies is the "welcome home" card, which thanks the client for his business and solicits comments and suggestions. While this indirect gesture may serve the travel agency's needs, there is good reason to believe that it is less than effective. Better than the "welcome home" greeting would be a phone call, because it provides an occasion for direct and personal dialogue between the travel agent and her client. A personal dialogue gives important feedback to the agent and provides an occasion for the customer to talk about the positive aspects of his experience. In the process of doing so, considerable postpurchase anxieties may be reduced — and this, of course, increases the likelihood that the client will be a repeat customer. The form-letter-like "welcome home" greeting card gives little, if any, dissonance-reducing opportunities.

There are other ways in which travelers can be encouraged to conclude that they have indeed made wise travel decisions. The airline ticket jacket, for example, is often kept by passengers long after a trip has ended. The jacket could be used to communicate information suggesting that the traveler made a good carrier choice. Normally, however, the space available for communicating this type of message is sold to car rental firms or hotel chains for advertising their products and services. Inflight magazines could also be used to reduce customers' postpurchase doubts, but they, too, do not seem to be used for this purpose.

Postpurchase dissonance can arise before as well as after a particular travel service has been consumed. A traveler can experience serious doubts about the wisdom of his choice after making a reservation, or after making a financial commitment in the form of a deposit that guarantees a reservation. Suppose, for instance, that a person deposits money with a travel agent six months in advance for a two-week stay at the Mauna Kea Beach Hotel in Hawaii. During the six-month waiting period, the individual will probably be exposed to a great deal of information that causes him to have second thoughts about the wisdom of his decision. He may, for example, see advertising that promotes different hotels in Hawaii or even different kinds of vacations, such as Caribbean cruises. He may be exposed to airline advertising that promotes bargain fares to other vacation destinations that all of a sudden seem just as attractive as two weeks in Hawaii. Friends and acquaintances may unwittingly suggest what they consider ideal vacations that are very different from the Hawaiian trip planned. The travel agency, the hotel, the airline, and other firms involved in this vacationer's trip to Hawaii should recognize that there is a possibility that he will change his mind — that he may develop enough doubt about his decision to cancel his reservation and decide to travel elsewhere. Worse still for these firms, the individual may decide to cancel his travel plans altogether and spend his money on something other than travel.

A traveler who makes reservations well in advance of his vacation will normally receive some type of written notice — from a resort, for example — confirming his reservation. Typically, this is all that this written notice does; in a computer-like fashion, it tells the traveler that a room has been reserved for so many days at a specified rate. What is missed by such a businesslike notice is the opportunity to confirm that the traveler has made a wise decision. It would cost little to include with the written confirmation a modest promotional pamphlet specifically designed to reassure the customer that he has made a very good choice. It could include pictures that the customer has not previously seen, and perhaps include testimonials by former guests. It might also be helpful to send the customer additional promotional materials, or even a personalized letter — especially if the time between placing the reservation and the date of arrival at the resort spans several months. The purpose, of course, is to reinforce the customer's decision, minimizing any chance that he may cancel the reservation.

Those who market and sell travel services profit by satisfying their customers' needs and helping them to solve problems. These needs and problems do not cease to exist when a sale or a reservation is made. Customers need to be reassured about the travel decisions they make. By satisfying this need, the travel service firm performs a valuable service for which it is rewarded when the customer follows through with his travel plans, when he returns to the same resorts, and when he patronizes the same travel service firms in the future. It is insufficient for the organization — be it a travel agency, a cruise line, a resort, a hotel, an airline, or a car rental firm — merely to say, "Thank you for your business." This focuses more on the need of the firm than on the needs of the customer. The message that should be communicated is one that reassures the customer that he is wise for having purchased the firm's product. In an article titled "Closing the Sale," *Travel Agent* magazine suggested that agents close their sales with words to this effect: "You know, I should thank you, but instead I'm going to congratulate you and shake your hand on making an excellent choice and a great purchase. Also, thank you. We really appreciate your business. Be sure to stop by or give me a call when you get back. I'll be excited to hear about all the fun you had. If you get a chance, here's my card, drop me a note. And when you're ready to go again, please stop back. You're great to work with."[16]

HOW WE LEARN

At the outset of this chapter we noted that psychologists are of the opinion that all human behavior involves some form of learning. An extension of this idea is that learning is also responsible for many of the changes in an individual's behavior over time. Changes in the behavior of the travel-consumer, our major interest, result from learning from two broad sources: experience and information. In other words, learning takes place as a result of the experiences we have and the information to which we are exposed. We turn now to a discussion of the learning process itself, because it can further our understanding of how travelers and the decisions they make can be influenced.

Experience as a Source of Learning

In many respects, the very essence of learning is related to what the psychologist calls **generalization.** A travel-consumer normally desires to minimize the time and effort necessary to make travel decisions, and one way of doing this is by generalizing. Generalizing takes place when a person responds to a given situation in the same way that he has responded to different but similar situations in the past. For example, after a pleasant vacation at a Club Med resort in Cancun, an individual might conclude that a vacation at any Club Med resort would offer a similar experience; therefore, he might choose for his next vacation a trip to the Club Med resort at Playa Blanca. Another individual, after flying a number of times with United Airlines, might conclude that all United flights must be enjoyable and choose to fly United whenever possible. Moreover, he might also conclude on the basis of his experience with United that Western International Hotels, United's "partner in travel," would provide pleasant accommodations.

Generalization also works in the other direction. After an unpleasant journey on board a United Airlines plane, an individual might conclude that all United flights are undesirable. Another person might conclude that all travel agents are nothing more than ticket writers who are incapable of helping their customers avoid second-rate hotels and long waits between connecting flights — all because of one disappointing travel experience that was planned by a travel agent.

Marketing managers have long been aware of the principle of generalization. Some firms try to capitalize on the consumer's tendency to generalize by using "family brands," such as Betty Crocker or Heinz's "57 varieties." It is hoped that the consumer's experience with one of the products in the "family" will be good, and that he will generalize this experience to other products in the line. Numerous examples of this marketing approach exist in the travel industry, including Club Med and Six Flags, Ask Mr. Foster (travel agents), and Travelodge. These organizations group their individual resorts, theme parks, offices, or lodging facilities under a family name.

Some travel firms, however, do little to associate their various products or services with each other, or else take actions to discourage such associations. A traveler visiting Sea Pines Plantation in South Carolina, for instance, may not be aware that the Sea Pines Company also operates the Amelia Island resort in Florida. Similarly, it does not seem likely that many people realized that TWA formerly owned and operated Hilton International Hotels, or that Holiday Inns owned Trailways Buslines for a long time. (In the latter case, Holiday Inns presumably did not wish to associate the frequently negative image of bus travel in the United States with its hotel and motel business.)

Actual buying experiences are learning experiences, and they influence how one makes subsequent buying decisions. This process is a continuous one for most of us. From experience, for example, one might learn that at times the choice of a connecting airline at a large airport should be based as much on the terminal location of competing airlines as on published departure times; or that greater importance should be given to parking convenience when selecting a hotel or motel.

Information as a Source of Learning

Learning occurs when an individual is exposed to and processes information. The kind of information that concerns us here comes from two major sources: (1) the commercial environment, which includes advertising, promotion, and personal selling; and (2) the individual's social environment, which consists of family, friends, acquaintances, and others.

The Commercial Environment.   A travel company promotes its services to prospective buyers primarily by communicating information about itself in pictures and words. Such information is thought to influence the potential buyer in several ways. First, the creative communication of promotional information can *intensify* whatever motives the buyer already has. A minute or two spent looking through the pages of a TWA "Skiing the Rockies" brochure might be sufficient to intensify a person's motives and prompt her to make an impulse (unplanned) decision in favor of the suggested vacation. A well-trained sales person can also create sufficient intensity of motive to prompt immediate action on the part of the buyer. There are a number of techniques for closing a sale with a travel consumer — techniques whose purpose, in effect, is to intensify a buyer's motives. These include the following:

> "Did I tell you that it was necessary to be ticketed thirty days in advance for that special fare?"
> "We didn't reserve a flight far enough in advance for Mr. Jones and that flight was all filled up. And he wasn't going for another six weeks!"

"Oh boy, do you know how popular that cruise is!"
"I think your wife will really like this. Why don't you surprise her?"
"You owe it to yourself to go on this trip."
"I hope I can get out of here for a couple of weeks this winter, too. I'm just not ready for all that snow again."

Commercial messages can also influence the consumer's travel decisions by persuading him to change the way he makes them. A travel agent does this, for example, when she overcomes a client's objections to the total price of a vacation package by saying, "It's true that this package costs $400 more than you were planning to spend. But, you know, the superior package only amounts to an extra $30 or so a month over the next year if you put the whole thing on your credit card."

Commercial messages can be particularly powerful for travelers who have no prior experience on which to rely. Such messages can help an inexperienced traveler learn how to make important travel decisions. A first-time traveler to a foreign destination, for example, can learn a great amount from travel advertising and from retail travel agents.

A travel firm can also communicate information that changes or adds to the list of alternatives from which a prospective buyer will choose. When Portugal began advertising iself as "The Portuguese Alternative," it was trying to gain inclusion in the set of destination areas to which European-bound travelers might give serious consideration (see Figure 3-2).

Finally, commercial messages directed at travel consumers can unintentionally remind them of negative qualities in a specific travel service or product. For example, an airline that stresses efficient maintenance procedures in its advertising may be reminding people that air travel can be dangerous. When Holiday Inns said "The Best Surprise Is No Surprise," it was communicating the fact that it offered predictably reliable accomodations for travelers; at the same time, however, it may have unwittingly suggested that its accommodations were boringly standardized. When Best Western refers to itself as the "World's Largest Lodging Chain," people may be reminded that "biggest" does not always mean "best." A travel agent who says "You've picked one of the most popular resorts," may be simultaneously suggesting that the client should be prepared for large crowds.

The Social Environment.   The social environment of the traveler — family, friends, acquaintances, and others — is a major source of information from which one learns. The effects of information from the social environment are somewhat different than those from the commercial environment. Friends and acquaintances are likely to interpret and give meaning to information before sharing it with others. Before telling a friend about a trip aboard Amtrak, a person will evaluate his experience on the basis of

FIGURE 3-2

In Portugal you can still afford and get the best of everything. For example, just compare Portuguese prices with those in London, Paris and Rome.

In Lisbon, the average price of a luxury hotel for two is $35. In London the price is $83. In Paris $101. In Rome $81.*

A full-course meal at a luxury restaurant costs on the average, $15 in Lisbon, $21 in London, $30 in Paris and $25 in Rome.*

These same values apply to almost anything you'd want to do or buy, because Portugal is still a shopper's paradise for Americans.

That's why more Americans than ever before are enjoying the Portuguese

Alternative with its tradition-rich museums, storybook palaces, beautiful beaches and exciting nightlife.

So this fall go to Portugal, where your dollar goes further. And go on one of the many TAP tours available. Each combines Portugal's unique values with the lowest air fare to continental Europe. See your Travel Agent.

TAP Tour Department
P.O. Box 941, Woodside, N.Y. 11377
In New York call (212) 421-8500.
For toll-free number in your area call: 800-555-1212.

Please send me information on
The Portuguese Alternative and TAP Tour Brochures
on Portugal, Spain & Northern Africa.

Name_____

Address_____

City_____

State_____ Zip____

*Source: 1978 Michelin Red Guides to Portugal / Great Britain / Paris / Italy, taking average of prices of Luxury Hotels and Restaurants of each city.
Prices are supplied to Michelin by Hotels and Restaurants etc., and are their responsibility.
U.S. dollar prices arrived at by using exchange rates in effect June 1978.
Prices may fluctuate slightly.

THE AIRLINE OF PORTUGAL
Tour with TAP
We're as big as an airline should be.

Copyright © TAP Airline of Portugal, New York, NY. Reprinted by permission.

how well Amtrak served his own needs. He will then give a subjective report to his friend. His friend, in turn, will probably attach greater credibility and importance to this first-hand account than to information that comes from the commercial environment. Friends and acquaintances, in other words, are seen as more trustworthy and more likely to give unbiased opinions than commercial sources of information.

Information that comes from a traveler's social environment can have a particularly strong impact on his motives. For example, the relative importance of travel for educational purposes, foreign travel, outdoor sports, and cultural activities will be strongly influenced by one's peers and the various reference groups to which one belongs. In much the same way, the social environment can determine the types of travel alternatives seriously considered by an individual traveler. This would be particularly true when the individual lacks personal experience. Those who sell travel can profit from knowing what kinds of social influence a prospective customer has been exposed to. Answers to a rather innocent question like, "Have you heard anything about Lake Tahoe?" can provide substantial insights into the types of social influence a prospective traveler has had up to that point.

Information may be actively sought by the traveler from his social environment not only because it is perceived to be more trustworthy than information from the commercial environment, but also because of the ease of two-way communication in social situations. The social environment allows the individual to ask questions, and to obtain evaluative information that permits him to reduce risk and uncertainty. Word-of-mouth information enables the individual to form judgments about *what it means*, if anything, to spend a winter vacation at Sun Valley instead of Aspen, to stay at Stanford Court rather than the Fairmont in San Francisco, or to vacation in St. Martin instead of Puerto Rico.

The Search for Information

People differ in the extent to which they actively seek out information that will help them to make important travel decisions, and it is useful to know how they differ in this regard. The intensity with which a traveler deliberately seeks out information will depend on how experienced as a traveler the person is, how much risk and uncertainty he perceives in the decision, and how important he feels it is to make an optimal or perfect choice. It is probably accurate to say that the need and search for information is greatest among individuals who a) are inexperienced as travelers, b) perceive a high degree of risk in the travel decision, and c) feel that it is imperative to make the very best possible decision.

Let us take a closer look at how this last factor — the importance of making an optimal travel decision — affects information search behavior. Whether a winter holiday would be better spent in Florida or in Arizona may be of little importance to one individual and of critical importance to another. In other words, some people would find any one of a number of alternatives satisfactory, while other people would worry over which alternative was actually best. In technical terms, the first group is called **satisficers** while the second is called **optimizers**.[17]

The travel market consists of both satisficers and optimizers. In fact, the same individual may be both. For certain travel decisions — such as which airline to fly or which hotel to stay at — the individual may accept any satisfactory alternative. For other travel decisions — such as the choice of a vacation destination or mode of transportation — the individual may be very concerned with making the very best possible choice. Because they will be comfortable with any one of several alternatives, satisficers are less active in their search for information. Optimizers, who want to make the best possible decision, need more information and will be more active in searching for it.[18]

With respect to vacation travel, a satisficer may simply have the need for diversion from his normal routine. An optimizer's needs, on the other hand, are likely to be more complex. While he may express the desire to simply get away from it all for awhile, he may also feel the need to get maximum value and satisfaction from the time and money he spends on travel.

Studies of people in a camping environment illustrate some of the basic personality differences between satisficers and optimizers. Camping activities can be classified according to several different types, one of which is referred to as **symbolic labor**.[19] Activities that fit into this category are productive in the sense that they are characterized by the quest for "trophies" — tangible symbols which signify that the time and effort expended by the individual were not in vain. The person who goes fishing or hunting and returns empty-handed will be sorely disappointed if he is the type of personality who needs proof that he did not waste his time. The child who returns from a romp through the woods with a bag full of rocks and pine cones has proof that he accomplished something during his journey. The person who returns from a winter vacation in Florida with an attractive tan can show that his time was well spent. Optimizers have a strong need for tangible evidence that they made the very best use of their time and energy. For satisficers, on the other hand, a solitary walk through the woods with nothing tangible to show for it or an afternoon of fishing without even a nibble causes no great alarm.

These examples suggest yet another important difference between satisficers and optimizers. A satisficer might choose to spend a winter holiday in Arizona instead of Florida without laboring over the decision, and without suffering any doubts or regrets afterwards. An optimizer, on the other hand, will probably expend a great deal of time and energy evaluating the two alternative destinations. In the process, he will gather considerably more information in the interest of making the very best choice. The optimizer is likely to worry over many of the details of his vacation — the numbers and types of people he will meet, the size of his room, the quality of the food, the popularity of the entertainers, the condition of the golf courses, and the costs involved.

The distinction between the satisficer and the optimizer would be of only passing interest to us unless there were some way to identify one from the other. There are a few obvious signs. Since the optimizer requires more information, he is likely to ply the seller with questions about minute details, and to do so over repeated visits. Obviously the optimizer is the more time-consuming customer, who is harder to sell and please as well.

Studies of the process by which families make vacation travel decisions indicate a *tendency* for wives to behave as satisficers and husbands as optimizers. In one survey of 670 married couples vacationing by automobile, both males and females were asked to indicate the degree to which they either agreed or disagreed with the statement: "It is not important where I go on vacation — just that I can get away."[20] Female respondents expressed agreement with this statement much more often than did male respondents, suggesting that for the typical married couple, the wife normally behaves as a satisficer. As such, she chooses to take a less active part in the choice of vacation destinations — at least with respect to those destinations visited on *family* automobile vacations. As we will see, the husband often plays the more active role in making family travel decisions, a fact that holds important implications for those who market and sell travel.

FAMILY TRAVEL DECISION-MAKING

To better understand the vacation choices of families, it is first necessary to recognize that any travel decision is not an isolated mental exercise but a step in a series of activities. As Figure 3-3 indicates, travel decision-making can be broken down into five steps.

The first of these steps involves the recognition of need. It is during

FIGURE 3-3 Five-step decision-making process.

this first step that a person (or a family) will say, "I need to get away from here for awhile," or, "I have two weeks vacation time coming. Should we go somewhere?" The organization that sells or markets travel services can play an important role in activating the consumer's feeling that a particular need exists. Figure 3-4, for example, represents an effort by Palm Springs to remind the potential traveler that cold weather is a fine time to escape to a warmer climate. The intention of the ad, of course, is to stimulate the traveler to feel the need for a winter vacation.

If the decision is made to travel, certain questions must then be addressed: Where should we go? Where should we stay? How should we get there? What should we do there? How much should we spend? How long should we stay? Information will be needed to help answer some or all of these questions, which brings us to the second step of the decision-making process: the search for information.

During the information search stage, as the consumer seeks alternative ways to satisfy her need, travel organizations can be of real assistance by making information available that aids the decision-making process. The State of Georgia's advertisement in Figure 3-5 shows the traveler that a wide variety of travel needs can be satisfied within the state, and it encourages the consumer to write for more information that will help her to evaluate Georgia as a vacation destination.

Once enough information has been gathered, it is evaluated. At this stage, the consumer is frequently faced with several attractive decision alternatives. The promotional objective at this point is to indicate the advantages of one alternative over others in hopes that a decision will be made to purchase this alternative. Figure 3-6, an advertisement for the Barbary Coast, proclaims to the Las Vegas-bound traveler the advantages of their hotel and casino over others nearby.

In the third step of the decision-making process, a series of final decisions is made. In the fourth step, various travel products and services are consumed, and in the fifth step, judgments are made about whether they adequately served the traveler's needs. As suggested earlier, these postpurchase feelings are of great importance because they provide feedback on which to base future decisions of the same type.

Our primary interest at this point is in the first three decision-making steps — problem or need recognition, search for information, and final decision — along with the roles played by the typical husband and wife in taking them.

Family Decision-Making Styles

Family decision-making can take any one of four different forms, depending on whether or not a person exerts dominant influence on the decision

FIGURE 3-4

Copyright © Palm Springs Convention and Visitors Bureau, Palm Springs, CA. Reprinted by permission.

FIGURE 3-5

If you love the outdoors, Georgia's a natural for your vacation this year. And our vacation guide was made with people like you in mind.

It doesn't stop with the highlights; it includes the ruggedly remote, as well. In fact, there are full descriptions of 333 different attractions, recreation areas and historical sites. We give you directions and pinpoint each on a handy reference map. You'll be able to find your way to everything from whitewater rapids to quiet lakes, with advance knowledge of practical information like visiting hours or whether you'll need to have reservations.

Are there RV hook-ups at the mountain campsite? What about boat rentals at the fishing lake? A quick glance at the book gives you immediate answers. 48 charts cover state parks, national forests, camping, tennis, golfing, fishing and university facilities. (The one on state parks has 32 different categories.)

"This Way to Fun" is divided into seven Georgia regions, previewed by 82 full-color photographs. If you like breathtaking views and the roar of waterfalls, read about our Northeast Mountains on pages 12-21. The intriguing Okefenokee Swamp is just one of 89 places you'll want to see in the Colonial Coast region — pages 32-45.

Send for your free guide today. Once you read it, you won't stop thinking about Georgia until you get here. It's only natural.

Georgia

Copyright © State of Georgia. Reprinted by permission.

FIGURE 3-6

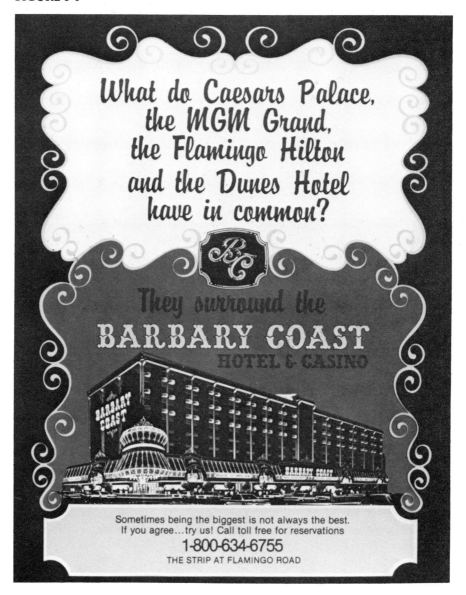

Copyright © Barbary Coast Hotel, Las Vegas, NV. Reprinted by permission.

and whether the actual decision is made individually or jointly.[21] The resulting family decision styles can be summarized as follows:

1. **Husband dominant decisions.**   In these situations, the husband exerts primary influence over the purchase decision and actually makes the final choice. In such cases, the wife will usually have little influence on recognition of the problem or need for the product, on gathering information to assist in the choice, or on making the actual purchase decision. This type of family decision-making style characterizes the purchase of such products as life insurance, lawnmowers, and automotive services.

2. **Wife dominant decisions.**   Here it is the wife who exerts primary influence over the purchase decision and actually makes the final choice. The husband has little, if any, role in the recognition of problems, gathering of information, or final decision process. Examples of products for which this decision-making style is typical include cleaning products, kitchenware, children's clothes, food, and certain household furnishings.

3. **Joint influence — individual decision.**   In many purchase situations, the eventual decision is made by one spouse although considerable influence over the outcome may be exerted by the other. Alcoholic beverages, for example, are typically purchased by the husband with considerable input from the wife. Similarly, although appliance decisions are usually made by the wife, her husband may have substantial influence in the decision-making process.

4. **Joint influence — joint decision.**   These decisions are made jointly, with both parties contributing to the process and neither exerting a clearly dominant influence over the purchase decision. The two spouses may compromise, bargain, coerce, or persuade one another, but in the end both parties make the decision and agree more or less that it is the right one. Purchase decisions that often fall into this category include living room furniture and housing. Perhaps of greatest significance to us is that for most families, the decision to spend money on family vacation travel is typically arrived at jointly, with both husband and wife exerting nearly an equal influence over the decision.

Clearly, then, husband and wife roles will differ depending on the need confronting the couple and the type of product or service that might satisfy it. As we will see, the manner in which a particular family purchase decision is made affects how best to market and sell a particular product or service. Based on the foregoing discussion, the reader should be able to anticipate some of the important implications of family decision-making styles.

Family Travel Decisions

Our attention now focuses on specific family travel decisions and the mechanisms used by families to make them. Although only a limited amount of research has been conducted that relates to family travel decisions, some distinct patterns do emerge.

In Figure 3-7, nine travel decisions are identified along with the family decision style used to make them. Several important conclusions emerge from this summary. Interestingly, in only two of the decision areas — lodging accomodations and destination point(s) — is there a clearly dominant spouse. In most families, the husband seems to dominate these two important family travel decisions. For all other types of family travel decisions, the wife either makes the decisions jointly with her husband or exerts a significant influence on the decisions he ultimately makes.[22] Many of these decisions — whether to take the children along, actual dates of the vacation, transportation mode, kinds of vacation activities, and how long to stay on vacation — are usually made by one spouse, but the other has considerable influence over the resulting choice. In two areas — the vacation decision itself (should we take a family vacation?) and the amount of money to spend — there are strong inputs from both spouses who ultimately make a joint decision.[23]

Despite what is known about family travel decisions, it is a topic that clearly requires further study. For example, the reasons why husbands have such a decisive role in many travel decision areas are not entirely

---

FIGURE 3-7   Family decision-making styles.

Family Travel Decision	*Predominant Family Decision-Making Style*
Type of lodging accomodations	Husband Dominant
Vacation destination(s)	Husband Dominant
Whether to take children along	Joint Influence–Individual Decision
How long to stay on vacation	Joint Influence–Individual Decision
Dates of vacation travel	Joint Influence–Individual Decision
Mode of transportation on family vacation	Joint Influence–Individual Decision
Vacation activities	Joint Influence–Individual Decision
Whether to go on vacation	Joint Influence–Joint Decision
How much money to spend on vacation travel	Joint Influence–Joint Decision

Source: Adapted from data in Roger L. Jenkins, "Family Vacation Decision Making," *Journal of Travel Research,* Vol. 16, (Spring, 1978), pp. 2-7.

clear, and the available research yields few insights into this pattern. In several family decision areas — deciding how long to stay and the actual dates of the vacation — we suspect that the husband's job exerts substantial influence, requiring him to make the final choice. But, as the number of two-income families continues to increase, the husband's traditional dominance over decisions like these is likely to decrease.

It may be that the wife assumes a very active decision-making role when the family flies to a far-off destination, but plays a more passive role when the family takes a journey in an automobile. Yet the research thus far does not clearly point to why this is so.

In summary, it must be emphasized that a woman's role and the corresponding role played by her husband in making family travel decisions may depend on factors besides those already mentioned. In addition, any particular family will have its own travel decision-making style, and the general decision-making patterns discussed here may not apply to them.

Children's Influence on Family Travel

Up to this point, the children's role in family travel decisions has only been hinted at. Research indicates that the positive benefits of travel for children are one of the most important motivators for family vacation travel.[24] The value placed on travel for educational purposes has already been stressed. In addition, family travel provides an occasion for the strengthening of family bonds and for sharing important and memorable experiences.

Children, then, exert a strong although probably indirect influence over family travel. This is because travel is so often undertaken with their needs uppermost in mind. The needs of the children will determine the *types* of destinations selected, although perhaps not the specific choice. Children also influence the kinds of activities in which the family participates during a vacation, and their academic schedules affect the timing of the vacation as well.[25]

Research clearly indicates that children have very little direct influence over such decisions as vacation length, mode of transportation, and travel budget.[26] There is also evidence to suggest that once the family has left home, the children have minimal *direct* influence over specific enroute travel decisions. They may, of course, affect impulse decisions, as when the family interrupts its plans to spend an hour at a specific sightseeing attraction. Children may also have a strong voice in the types of travel firms that are patronized by the family during its journey. For example, motels with swimming pools are chosen because they give children a recreational outlet after spending a day in a car. Fast-food restaurants are popular — primarily for midday meals — because children like the food, and because fast-food prices help to keep the family travel budget under control.

In conclusion, children have a strong indirect influence over family travel decision-making, but their direct influence is probably minimal. In terms of the total decision-making process, children play a small role because they are rarely involved in the search for or evaluation of information; nor do they often make final decisions. Nevertheless, their important influence over the decision to travel itself must be recognized and taken into consideration by those who market and sell travel.

SUMMARY

As the first half of this chapter has emphasized, those who market and sell travel can have an effect on shaping individual travel decisions well beyond what one might first imagine. Travel decision-making is based in large part on what people learn, and what they learn depends to a large extent on what they are taught by the travel service firm as well as others. It is unwise to simply accept travel demand as an uncontrollable force, merely acting as an order-taker. Potential travelers' needs must be recognized and understood. Travelers must then be provided with necessary information, through personal selling contacts and promotional materials. From this information, potential travelers learn how best to solve specific travel problems and satisfy specific travel needs. The travel service firm can show the consumer how its product can help satisfy these needs, and it can help the consumer cope with the risk and uncertainty that accompany his travel decisions.

In the second half of this chapter, which focused on the process by which the consumer-traveler learns, we noted that learning takes place as a result of direct experience, and through information to which we are exposed. Not all learning, however, has an equal effect on eventual travel decisions and behavior. Information that we acquire from direct experience, or from people who we consider unbiased and trustworthy, undoubtedly has a greater impact than information acquired from the commercial environment.

Looked at in another way, information from the commercial environment is not likely to outweigh one's own unfavorable travel experiences or those reported by trusted friends. Consequently, it becomes all the more important to provide the traveler with a pleasurable experience that meets her expectations. This, of course, is the best assurance that favorable impressions will result and that positive word-of-mouth information will be transmitted to others.

The five stages of travel decision-making — problem or need recognition, information search, final decision, product consumption, and post-purchase feelings — suggest that the traveler's information needs differ over time. Firms that market and sell travel can use a variety of approaches to meet these needs at every stage. Problem or need recognition can be influenced by anticipating the consumer's needs and activating them (see Figure 3-4). During the information search, comprehensive literature can be of genuine help to the traveler (see Figure 3-5). The final decision can be affected when a travel firm demonstrates the advantages of its services over those of other alternatives (see Figure 3-6). At the time of product consumption, a travel firm can help to ensure that the traveler's experience will be a good one by providing friendly, helpful, and efficient service. Afterwards, to help eliminate feelings of postpurchase doubt, travel agents especially should maintain personal contact with their clients.

Discussions of travel behavior often focus on the individual consumer, leaving one with the impression that only one person moves through the decision-making process involved in these five stages. It is clear, however, particularly with respect to family vacation travel, that individual family members often specialize in performing various purchase roles. When a decision is clearly dominated by one family member, promotional messages that pertain to that decision should be targeted accordingly. For example, if the choice of vacation destination is dominated by the husband, he is the person to whom destination-oriented promotion should be directed. Two distinct marketing campaigns may be necessary, however, where both husband and wife influence and jointly decide the outcome. Attempting to influence the decision of whether or not to go on vacation may call for two promotional efforts, each aimed at a different spouse. A single promotional effort targeted only at one spouse will miss the opportunity to influence an individual who has an important impact on this decision. Moreover, a single campaign effort directed at both husband and wife may not be fully effective, because the appeals used to influence one spouse may not be meaningful to the other.

Finally, it is important to recognize that there may be a considerable span of time over which the purchase process takes place. Several months may pass between recognition that a problem or need exists and the multitude of decisions that accompany the vacation. The decision process to take a mid-winter Hawaiian vacation may begin six months prior to the desired departure date. Promotional efforts that hope to influence the destination and lodging decision must therefore commence at an early point in time. The choice of a car rental firm may be made only two weeks prior to departure, requiring a different timing of the promotional efforts that hope to affect this choice. In short, the length of time over which purchase decisions take place will affect the optimal timing for the promotional efforts of the travel services involved.

REFERENCES

[1] Hugh V. Perkins, *Human Development and Learning* (Belmont, California: Wadsworth Publishing Company, Inc., 1969), pp. 336-37.

[2] C.N. Cofer and M.H. Appley, *Motivation: Theory and Research* (New York: John Wiley & Sons, Inc., 1964), p. 572.

[3] Peter D. Bennett and Harold H. Kassarjian, *Consumer Behavior* (Englewood Cliffs, New Jersey: Prentice-Hall, Inc., 1972), p. 27.

[4] John A. Howard and Jagdish N. Sheth, *The Theory of Buyer Behavior* (New York: John Wiley & Sons, Inc., 1969) p. 106.

[5] Florence R. Skelley, "Outline of the Changing Consumer," *The 80s: Its Impact on Travel and Tourism Marketing,* Proceedings of the Eighth Annual Conference (Salt Lake City: Travel Research Association, 1977), pp. 201-03.

[6] "The Ms. Market," *Hotel and Motel Management* (March, 1979), pp. 27-29, 36.

[7] Raymond A. Bauer, "Consumer Behavior as Risk Taking," *Dynamic Marketing for a Changing World,* ed. R.S. Hancock, Proceedings of the 43rd Conference of the American Marketing Association (Chicago: American Marketing Association, 1960), pp. 389-98.

[8] Thomas S. Robertson, *Consumer Behavior* (Glenview, Illinois: Scott, Foresman and Company, 1970), p. 22.

[9] Donald E. Lundberg, *The Tourist Business,* third edition, (Boston: CBI Publishing Company, 1976), p. 134.

[10] W. Earl Sassar, R. Paul Olsen, and D. Daryl Wyckoff, *Management of Service Operations* (Boston: Allyn and Bacon, Inc., 1978), p. 15.

[11] Rom J. Markin, Jr., *Consumer Behavior* (New York: Macmillan Company, 1974), p. 531.

[12] Robertson, *Consumer Behavior,* pp. 22-23.

[13] Philip Kotler, *Marketing Management,* second edition (Englewood Cliffs, New Jersey: Prentice-Hall, Inc., 1972), pp. 134-35.

[14] Markin, *Consumer Behavior,* pp. 148-49.

[15] D. Ehrlich et al., "Postdecision Exposure to Relevant Information," *Journal of Abnormal and Social Psychology,* Vol. 54 (1957), pp. 98-102.

[16] "Tips on Closing the Sale," *Travel Agent* (July 25, 1979), pp. 44, 46, 48.

[17] Herbert A. Simon, *Models of Man* (New York: John Wiley & Sons, Inc., 1957).

[18] Jacob Jacoby, Robert W. Chestnut, and William A. Fisher, "A Behavioral Approach to Information Acquisition in Nondurable Purchasing," *Journal of Marketing Research,* Vol. 15 (November, 1978), pp. 532-44.

[19] William R. Burch, Jr., "The Play World of Camping: Research into the Social Meaning of Outdoor Recreation," *American Journal of Sociology,* Vol. 70 (March, 1965), pp. 604-12 at p. 605.

[20] Edward J. Mayo, *Regional Travel Characteristics of the United States* (Bedford Park, Illinois: 3M National Advertising Company, 1973).

[21] Harry L. Davis and Benny P. Rigaux, "Perception of Marital Roles in Decision Processes," *Journal of Consumer Research,* Vol. 1 (June, 1974), pp. 51-62.

[22] Family travel decision-making patterns have been studied by a number of different research organizations. Findings disagree somewhat with respect to the extent of joint husband-wife decision-making, but they more or less agree that

when decisions are not made jointly it is often the husband who makes final decisions. The interested reader is directed to the following sources: (1) 3M National Advertising Company, *Psychographics of the Automobile Traveler* (Chicago: 3M National Advertising Company, 1972). This study reported that destination-choice decisions are made 65 percent of the time by husbands and only 26 percent of the time by wives; moreover, this study reported that the husband is most often responsible for suggesting the family vacation and for suggesting changes in travel plans. (2) *Newsweek Magazine, "1970 Travel Study"* (New York: Newsweek Magazine, 1970). This study reported that husbands are responsible for making destination and travel mode decisions 40 percent of the time, while wives make these decisions only 22 percent of the time, and joint husband-wife decisions are also made just 22 percent of the time. (3) R.H. Bruskin Associates, *The Bruskin Report* (1970). This source also suggests the dominance of husbands in family vacation travel decision-making, noting that wives are more likely to want to spend family discretionary incomes on home improvements rather than family travel.

[23] Roger L. Jenkins, "Family Vacation Decision-Making," *Journal of Travel Research*, Vol. 16 (Spring, 1978), pp. 2-7.

[24] Behavior Science Corporation, *Developing the Family Travel Market* (Des Moines, Iowa: Better Homes and Gardens, 1972), pp. 5-6.

[25] See: C.K. Walter and Hsin-Min Tong, "A Local Study of Consumer Vacation Travel Decisions," *Journal of Travel Research*, Vol 15 (Spring, 1977), pp. 30-34. Also see Edward J. Mayo, *Restaurant Habits of the Long Distance Automobile Vacationer* (Chicago:National Restaurant Association, 1976).

[26] Jenkins, "Family Vacation Decision-Making," p. 4.

QUESTIONS FOR DISCUSSION

1. Describe stimulus-response learning and discuss its applicability to the travel decision-making process.
2. What is the relationship between learning and attitudes? Are attitudes learned, or are they simply feelings that one has about something? Can a traveler be taught to have positive attitudes toward, say, an airline? Toward a travel agency? Toward a destination area?
3. Learning can have a profound effect on how we view things (perception). Think of a perception you once had of a destination area and what you learned earlier in life about it. How did your perception of this destination area change when you visited it?
4. Which travel decisions do you make out of habit and which do you make by careful and deliberate decision-making? Can you explain why some decisions are routine or habitual while others are made only after careful deliberation?
5. How do people learn that certain destinations are more prestigious than others? Can advertising affect the degree to which a destination is viewed as prestigious?
6. A generation ago, family togetherness was an important value. To some extent, this has changed. What are the implications of this change for those who market and sell travel?

7. Discuss what you learned from your parents about how one should travel. Do you still practice what they taught you? Why or why not?

8. Why might a consumer perceive more risk when he is buying travel than when buying, say, an automobile or clothing? What does the consumer do to reduce this perceived risk? What can be done by those who market and sell travel to help the consumer reduce perceived risk?

9. Why might someone experience postpurchase dissonance after a vacation journey? Why is it important that dissonance be reduced? How can it be reduced? Can you recall from your own experience having felt dissonance after a vacation journey? What did you do about it?

10. When you are buying travel products and services, do you behave as a satisficer or as an optimizer? Explain.

11. Select some married couple you know. How do they make their family travel decisions? Are they joint decisions, or does one spouse dominate the travel decision-making? Does their travel decision-making style differ from trip to trip? If so, how? Would you consider their travel decision-making style typical of other married couples you know?

12. Some travel marketers use cut-out coupons for use in requesting more information when their ads appear in magazines like *Good Housekeeping* and *Better Homes and Gardens*. The same advertisers place ads in magazines like *Sports Illustrated* and *Newsweek* that do not include the request-for-more-information coupons. What might this suggest about the advertisers' assumptions concerning the family decision-making process?

4
PERSONALITY AND TRAVEL BEHAVIOR

In this chapter, we move closer to an understanding of the real reasons — the motivations — that explain why some people travel while others stay at home. We will provide some explanations of why some people prefer to fly to their destinations rather than travel by automobile, motorcoach, steamship, or train. We will continue to examine factors that help to explain why certain destinations, hotel chains, and leisure-time activites are more popular than others. And we will consider why some people use travel agents, along with a number of similar travel-related questions.

It is difficult to separate the concepts of motivation and personality. When one talks about motivation, it is impossible not to talk about personality at the same time. The reverse is also true. The topic of this chapter is personality and its relationship to travel behavior, but at many points throughout the chapter our discussion will deal with motivation as well. Chapter 5 — which focuses on specific travel motivations and identifies the basic or underlying reasons for traveling — may be seen as a continuation of our present discussion.

Personality is a composite of learning, perceptions, motivations, emotions, and roles. Perhaps the simplest way to explain the term *personality* is that it consists of those stable characteristics of an individual's behavior that distinguish him from others. An individual's personality characteristics are usually organized, patterned, and stable — in fact, this is why his personality can be described. Patterned personality characteristics are self-serving, meaning that they facilitate the attainment of an individual's needs and goals.

In the first section of this chapter, we will review several of the ways in which personalities can be described. Throughout this discussion, examples will be given to illustrate how an understanding of an individual's personality can help to explain his behavior as a traveler and tourist.

In the second section of the chapter, we will discuss the concept of *life style*. An individual's life style — her daily routines, activities, interests, opinions, values, needs, and perceptions — is a reflection of personality, and it can explain more about an individual's behavior than the personality characteristics that are measured by the psychologist's clinical personality tests. Here, too, several examples will be presented to illustrate how the life-style approach to personality analysis can provide valuable clues to understanding different types of travelers and different kinds of travel behavior.

It is said that one's personality is stable, but in fact such stability is only a tendency. We often respond to the same situations in different ways. The purpose of the third section of this chapter is to explain the instability and unpredictability of behavior by dividing the personality into its component parts and thereby showing how it functions and affects one's behavior. The emphasis, of course, will be on travel and leisure time behavior.

DESCRIBING PERSONALITIES

Personality is a complex psychological phenomenon, and the terminology used to describe it is sometimes ambiguous and obscure. As a result, numerous personality theories have arisen, dozens of methods have been developed to measure personality characteristics, and many different labels exist to describe specific personality characteristics. There are several approaches used to assess and describe individual personalities, and we will examine the most popular of these.

The Trait Approach to Personality Determination

The trait approach to personality focuses on the persistent ways in which an individual responds to recurring stimuli and events in his environment.

An overwhelming amount of the work on personality analysis and determination is based on trait measurement and evalution. Such personality tests as the Gordon Personal Profile and the Thurstone Temperament Schedule are designed to determine and measure personality traits. Another personality measurement tool, the California Personality Inventory, attempts to profile personalities by graphing traits such as dominance, sociability, self-acceptance, responsibility, socialization, self-control, tolerance, and achievement.

One of the most popular personality measurement tools is the Edwards Personal Preference Schedule, which attempts to measure a number of personality "needs" identified by Henry Murray. A portion of Murray's list of personality traits is presented in Figure 4-1. Murray, a clinical psy-

FIGURE 4-1   Murray's personality needs.

Personality Need	*Definition*
Abasement	To feel guilty or inferior
Achievement	To do one's best, to accomplish something
Acquisition	To acquire something of significance
Affiliation	To associate with other people
Aggression	To attack contrary points of view, to get revenge
Autonomy	To be able to come and go as desired, to speak freely
Blamavoidance	To avoid criticism or blame by inhibiting one's impulses
Change	To do new and different things
Cognizance	To observe and to find things out
Construction	To build something of significance
Defendance	To defend oneself against criticism or blame
Deference	To admire and follow someone superior
Dominance	To be a leader
Exhibition	To talk about personal achievements
Harmavoidance	To escape or avoid injury
Heterosexuality	To be in love with someone of the opposite sex
Infavoidance	To escape or avoid indications of inferiority or inadequacy
Intraception	To analyze motives and feelings
Noxavoidance	To escape or avoid unpleasant stimuli
Nurturance	To provide help and care to others
Recognition	To be noticed, acknowledged, and approved
Sentience	To receive physically or esthetically pleasant stimulation
Sex	To be gratified sexually
Succorance	To receive help and care from others

Note: The majority of the physiological needs on Murray's list and a few others that have been little used by psychologists are omitted.

Source: Henry A. Murray, *Explorations in Personality* (New York: Oxford University Press, 1938), pp. 76-83.

chologist, considered that measurement of these personality traits or needs was necessary to adequately describe an individual's motivational pattern.

Market researchers have attempted for some time to gather evidence that personality traits such as those listed in Figure 4-1 do, in fact, have an influence on consumer behavior. The evidence to date, however, is spotty and inconclusive. Some researchers have discovered important personality differences between owners of convertible cars, on the one hand, and owners of standard and compact cars on the other. They have also found significant personality differences between smokers and nonsmokers and between owners of savings accounts in commercial banks and in savings and loan associations. Significant statistical relationships have also been found between various personality traits and the use of headache remedies, vitamins, mouthwash, alcoholic drinks, chewing gum, and the acceptance of new fashions.

Despite research findings such as these, many authorities agree that research to date has yet to clearly demonstrate with a high degree of statistical accuracy the value of using personality as a key variable in explaining consumer behavior. Nevertheless the search goes on, primarily because intuition tells us that personality characteristics should normally have a very important influence on certain kinds of behavior.

One study of travel behavior did uncover some meaningful relationships between various personality traits and the vacation travel behavior of a large sample of adult Canadians. The personality traits measured in this study, as well as some of its findings, are summarized in Figure 4-2. These findings clearly demonstrate that the personalities of Canadians who travel on vacation are markedly different from those of their fellow Canadians who either stay at home on their vacations or who take no vacation at all. Canadians who travel on vacation are reflective: they like to think and constantly examine their own actions, along with those of other people. This trait distinguishes them most from other Canadians who do not take vacations at all. The vacation travelers interviewed in this study were also more active, more confident, more inquisitive, and more sociable and outgoing than those who did not take vacations. Thus, these personality traits can be linked to a person's interest in traveling, seeing different places, and meeting new people. His confidence and a corresponding sense of well-being will give him the courage to venture away from home and other familiar surroundings.

The research findings summarized in Figure 4-2 also shed light on the personality factors associated with the modes of transportation that the travelers use, where they go and what they do on their vacations, and the time of year that they choose for travel. It should be clear from this type of information that personality can indeed have an impact on travel behavior and can provide us with a better understanding of the kinds of decisions made by individuals in a travel environment. Although it is not

---

FIGURE 4-2   Personality traits and Canadian vacation travel.

Personality/Vacation Type	*Personality Characteristics*
Vacation Travelers	Reflective, active, sociable, outgoing, inquisitive, confident
Vacation Nontravelers	Reflective, passive, restrained, serious
Nonvacationers	Anxious
Auto Vacationers	Reflective, active, sociable, outgoing, inquisitive, confident
Air Vacationers	Very active, very confident, reflective
Train Vacationers	Reflective, passive, aloof, nonsocial, apprehensive, dependent, emotionally unstable
Bus Vacationers	Dependent, apprehensive, sensitive, hostile, belligerent, unrestrained
Domestic Vacationers	Outgoing, active, carefree
Foreign Vacationers	Confident, trusting, reflective, impulsive, brave
Male Vacationers	Reflective, brave
Female Vacationers	Impulsive, carefree, brave
Visit Friends/Relatives	Passive
Visit "Vacation Spots"	Active, sociable, reflective
Sightseers	Reflective, sensitive, emotionally unstable, unrestrained, passive
Outdoor Activities	Brave, active, asocial, apprehensive, moody
Winter Vacationers	Active
Spring Vacationers	Reflective
Autumn Vacationers	Emotionally stable, passive

Source: Canadian Government Travel Bureau, *1969 Vacation Trends and Recreation Patterns* (Ottawa, Canada: Canadian Government Travel Bureau, 1971).

possible to generalize based on a single study, some implications of this research seem appropriate to the Canadian travel market. Travel agents, for example, might more effectively promote their services among nontraveling Canadians who lack confidence by showing that professional travel planning takes the worry out of traveling. Resort destinations can appeal to passive nontravelers by stressing a quiet atmosphere conducive to rest and relaxation. Air carriers might attract those vacationers who normally travel by auto with an appeal to their outgoing and inquisitive personalities.

Only a very limited amount of research has focused on the relationship between personality traits and specific types of travel behavior. In part, this is probably due to a growing dissatisfaction among marketing researchers with the use of clinical personality measurement instruments to study consumer behavior.[1] One serious drawback to using instruments such as the California Personality Inventory and the Edwards Personal Preference Schedule is that they were not designed specifically for consumer behavior or travel research purposes. Rather, they were developed as aids to psychologists doing counseling and psychotherapeutic work.

The dissatisfaction with clinical personality measurement instruments led marketing researchers to an interest in what is called **psychographics.** Psychographics pertain to an individual's life-style characteristics — that is, his daily life routine, activities, interests, opinions, values, needs, and perceptions.[2] These characteristics reflect an individual's personality traits and attitudes, and their measurement can be tailored to specific activities, interests, and opinions. Using psychographics — instead of the standardized clinical personality measurement tools — a researcher interested in, say, how people come to select one air carrier over another can construct a life-style questionnaire that measures what are thought to be the most relevant personality traits and dispositions. Later in this chapter, several examples will illustrate how a psychographic or life-style approach to personality analysis can provide valuable clues to understanding certain kinds of travel behavior.

The Type Approach to Personality Determination

All of us characterize personality on the basis of both traits and types. Our friends are described as kind, generous, and warm. Enemies are seen as suspicious, greedy, and evil. We also tend to *type* our acquaintances as rational or emotional, introverted or extroverted, autonomous or dependent. There are many procedures for classifying personalities by types, and this section will discuss several of the more popular ones.

Karen Horney believed that a key determinant of behavior is **neurotic anxiety,** generated by the child's feeling of being "isolated and helpless in a potentially hostile world."[3] To cope with this anxiety and with the environment in which he lives, the child develops a set of dispositions that fall into three primary categories:

1. The **compliant** individual, as distinguished by the need to move *toward* people and the needs for love, affection, and approval.
2. The **aggressive** individual, as distinguished by the need to move *against* people and the need to excel and to achieve success, prestige, and admiration.
3. The **detached** individual, as distinguished by the need to move *away*

from people and the needs for self-sufficiency, independence, and unassailability.

The specific orientation adopted by an individual forms the basic structure of adult behavior, according to Horney's theory. The compliant person, for example, will go out of his way to conform to what he believes are approved forms of behavior, because many of his goals are concerned with finding an accepted place in society. The aggressive person needs people to confirm his self-image and to bolster his confidence; thus, he will go out of his way to be noticed, providing such notice implies admiration. The detached person desires emotional distance between himself and others and does not want to share experiences with them.

There is some research-based evidence to suggest that the three types of people identified by Horney behave in systematically different ways with regard to the purchase and use of various products and services.[4] There have not been any studies, however, that relate her personality types to various forms of travel behavior. Yet, such research would appear promising. It would seem, for example, that compliant and aggressive persons might be very interested in travel — although their primary motives for traveling would probably be different. The detached person, on the other hand, might be expected to take less interest in travel. When he does travel, however, his choices of transportation, destination, lodging, and other services would probably differ from the compliant and aggressive personalities.

Another popular typology of personalities was developed by sociologist David Riesman.[5] In his analysis of trends in the political and social history of Europe and the United States, Riesman made a case for categorizing personalities on the basis of **social character,** theorizing that the social character of people can be divided into three groups:

1. Through the Middle Ages and on into fairly recent times, much behavior was **tradition-directed:** a rigid set of rules, usually backed by powerful religious beliefs, prescribed what should be done under what circumstances, and why.
2. As the hold of religion weakened in the 18th and 19th centuries, and as greater value was placed on the rights and achievements of the individual, more behavior became **inner-directed:** each person had to decide for himself, in view of his own enlightened self-interest, the proper course to take in a world that was becoming increasingly complex.
3. In the United States today, the tradition-directed person is almost gone, existing only in a few small custom-bound communities that have managed to remain isolated from the cultural mainstream. Even the inner-directed person, the 19th century American ideal, is now being replaced by the **other-directed** person — the person who directs his behavior

toward securing the esteem and approval of his immediate peers. Thus, the definition of what is right is for many present-day Americans "That which is most popular."

Riesman went on to say that the shift from tradition-direction to other-direction has had a profound impact on consumer behavior. In tradition-directed societies, people wear, eat, and drink that which tradition says they should and little else, for even minor deviations are punished. In inner-directed societies, consumption of products and services is determined by the contribution this consumption makes to the long-term benefit of the individual. But in other-directed societies, consumption is determined by the contribution consumption makes to status and popularity.

Because the United States is in the very gradual process of shifting from inner-direction to other-direction, its population contains — and will continue to contain for some time to come — many people who follow one or the other of these two incompatible life styles. It is probably inevitable, therefore, that consumer choices made by the other-directed segment of the population will be determined by motives that the inner-directed segment regards as frivolous, superficial, and perhaps even ethically wrong.

Research has shown that Riesman's theory provides a useful perspective for studying various kinds of behavior. It has been found, for example, that younger people are significantly more other-directed than their elders,[6] that inner-directed people are less easily persuaded than those who are other-directed,[7] and that inner-directed individuals pay more attention to advertising that appeals to their own unique motives.[8] There have been no studies to date that investigate the relationship between inner- and other-direction and various forms of travel behavior. However, such research would also appear to have some promise. It would not be surprising, for example, to discover that the travel behavior of inner-directed and other-directed consumers differed in important ways. Travel-related decisions of the other-directed individual would probably be motivated more so by status and prestige, while the inner-directed individual would perhaps be motivated by educational, recreational, and cultural factors. Those travelers who could be described as tradition-directed would probably be most likely to visit the lands of their ancestors and destinations rich in religious significance or historical tradition.

One of the best known and most frequently employed type-casting approaches classifies people either as introverts or extroverts. **Introverts** are people who are normally preoccupied with themselves and their own subjective world. **Extroverts** are people oriented primarily toward others and the external, objective world.

Most of us, looking at the people we know, could find some whom we would confidently label introverts and others whom we would label extroverts. We could then speak of the introverts and extroverts as two *types* of people. Picking the first one or two people for each category would probably be fairly easy. Later, however, less obvious choices would probably be quite difficult to make. "Well, he's partly introverted and partly extroverted. He doesn't really belong in either category," we would be likely to say. This problem could be solved by adding a third, in-between category of people who do not clearly belong to either type. The term **ambivert** has been suggested for such people. Adding this third category of ambiverts would make the classification task easier, but still other difficulties could develop. "Mary is sort of introverted, but not nearly as much as Jane," we might say. "Should she be considered an introvert or an ambivert?" Such borderline cases would soon lead us to conclude that what we are dealing with is neither two types nor three, but a *continuum* extending from the most introverted to the most extroverted. The three-type classification is only a rough division of this continuum into three categories: those at the introverted end, those at the extroverted end, and those in the middle, as illustrated in Figure 4-3. Just as it is much more useful to know someone's IQ than merely to know that he is bright, dull, or in between, so it is more useful to say *how* introverted someone is on a scale of numbers than merely to say that he is or isn't in the category of introverts. Thus, we proceed from a set of types to a trait on which each person has a score, ranging from the most introverted to the most extroverted.

Despite the problems of classifying people into two or three types,

FIGURE 4-3   Extroversion–introversion scale.

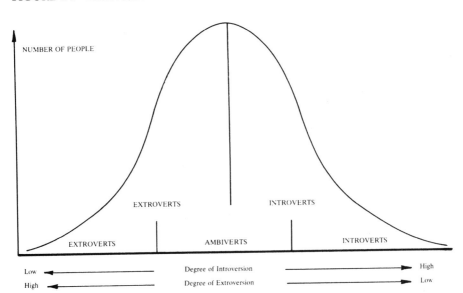

this approach to personality analysis can be very useful — particularly when we can be satisfied with broad and general descriptions of personality rather than precise and very specific ones.

A very similar classification system categorizes people as either psychocentrics or allocentrics. **Psychocentric** people are concerned with little problems and with themselves, and they are generally anxious, somewhat inhibited, and nonadventuresome. **Allocentric** persons are adventurous, self-confident, curious, outgoing, and eager to reach out and experiment with life. Clearly, there is a great deal of similarity between an introvert and a psychocentric person and between an extrovert and an allocentric person.

In a study designed to explain why destination areas rise and fall in popularity, it was found that the travel behavior of psychocentrics and allocentrics differs significantly in important ways.[9] Some of these differences are summarized in Figure 4-4. The psychocentric personality apparently has a strong need for predictability in his life. Thus, he typically visits familiar destinations to which he can drive. Being something of a passive personality, rest and relaxation are among his strongest travel motives. Much of his ideal vacation — including the destination itself and

FIGURE 4-4   Travel characteristics of psychographic types.

Psychocentrics	*Allocentrics*
Prefer the familiar in travel destinations	Prefer non-tourist areas
Like commonplace activities at travel destinations	Enjoy sense of discovery in new experiences, before others have visited the area
Prefer sun 'n' fun spots, including considerable relaxation	Prefer new and unusual destinations
Low activity level	High activity level
Prefer destinations they can drive to	Prefer flying to destinations
Prefer heavy tourist accommodations, such as heavy hotel development, family type restaurants, and tourist shops	Tour accommodations should include adequate to good hotels and food, not necessarily modern or chain type hotels, and few tourist attractions
Prefer family atmosphere (e.g., hamburger stands), familiar entertainment, absence of foreign atmosphere	Enjoy meeting and dealing with people from a strange or foreign culture
Complete tour packaging appropriate, with heavy scheduling of activities	Tour arrangements should include basics (transportation and hotels) and allow considerable freedom and flexibility

Source: Stanley Plog, "Why Destination Areas Rise and Fall in Popularity," a paper presented to the Southern California Chapter of the Travel Research Association, October 10, 1972.

the activities, hotel accommodations, restaurants, and entertainment available to him there — can be described as consistent and predictable.*

The allocentric personality, on the other hand, apparently has a strong need for unpredictability in her life. She typically visits out-of-the-way, less well-known destinations. She prefers to fly to her vacation destinations. She is an active individual, and she enjoys traveling to foreign lands and meeting people with different cultural backgrounds from her own. Much of her ideal vacation can be described as unpredictable or complex. She does not have the psychocentric's need for predictability. She is flexible and she welcomes the opportunity to visit unknown destinations, to have new experiences, to escape from predictability and sameness.

Figure 4-5 illustrates the influence of the key personality characteristics of psychocentrics and allocentrics on the vacation destination areas to which they are attracted. Figure 4-5 indicates that few people are either entirely psychocentric or allocentric. Between the two extremes on the

FIGURE 4-5   Psychocentric–allocentric scale.

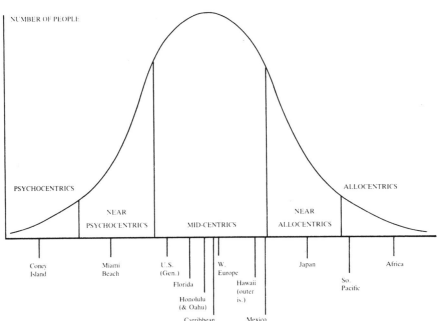

Source: Stanley Plog, "Why Destination Areas Rise and Fall in Popularity," a paper presented to the Southern California Chapter of the Travel Research Association, October 10, 1972.

*The psychological concepts of consistency and complexity mentioned here are discussed in detail in Chapter 5.

scale in Figure 4-5 are three in-between categories for those people who belong to neither extreme.

Figure 4-5 suggests that people with strong psychocentric personalities will normally be attracted to destinations like Coney Island, Miami Beach, and Monterey — destinations that are well known, have been visited by millions before, and are consistent and predictable. Individuals with strong allocentric personalities — being adventurous, curious, energetic, and outgoing — will normally be attracted to novel destinations like Cuba, the South Pacific, Africa, and the Orient. The so-called mid-centrics — who are neither really adventurous nor fearful of travel — represent the mass market for travel. They are attracted to destinations like Hawaii, the Caribbean, Europe, and Mexico — destinations that are foreign and unfamiliar, but not completely so. Many Americans have already traveled to these destinations, brought back their stories and their slides, and made these foreign places much less unpredictable as a result. Mid-centrics represent the mass market for pleasure travel. Not surprisingly, the destinations to which they are attracted are among the most popular tourist destinations today.

For several reasons, Figure 4-5 should be viewed as a picture of travelers and the destinations to which they are attracted at a single point in time. People change, sometimes becoming more adventurous and active. Travel itself serves to make psychocentric persons less so, and makes mid-centric persons more allocentric. This is one reason why people who have visited Miami, Honolulu, the Caribbean, Great Britain, and Western Europe will later depart for South America, Eastern Europe, Japan, Russia, the South Pacific, and Africa. The attitudinal change that brings about such a difference in behavior is normally a long-term process. Psychocentric people do not become brave, adventurous, and outgoing overnight.

Over time, however, some people will move from left to right across the psychocentric-allocentric scale in Figure 4-5. Another way of explaining why this happens was discussed earlier in terms of inner- and other-directedness in a society like the United States. As people become less inner- and more other-directed, as they have in most western industrialized countries, they tend to be more open to new experiences, people, and cultures. The other-directed person, as noted earlier, is also more interested in status — and a trip to an exotic destination like the South Pacific or the Orient would provide more of it than a two-week family vacation to Asbury Park or Myrtle Beach.

Over time, not only people but destinations too will change and move across the psychocentric-allocentric scale in Figure 4-5. Over time, a successful destination area will attract tourists in greater numbers. At first, it is the allocentric personalities who are attracted to a little-known destination. Later on, people of a more psychocentric nature arrive, their numbers increase, and the destination is forced to commercialize. More hotels are needed to accommodate the visitors, who show an increasing preference for the standardized lodging facilities of large hotel chains. Once the mass market arrives, travel to the area is marketed in earnest. Complete tour packages are developed and offered to this market. The atmosphere becomes more familiar. Family-type restaurants open. Tourist shops blossom. The cuisine, the entertainment, and the activities become Americanized. Finally, when the near-psychocentric arrives, not much more than the climate is likely to differ from home.

Countless destination areas have evolved in this way. Hawaii is an excellent case in point. It is a vacation destination markedly different from what it was fifteen years ago and radically transformed from the Hawaii known to American servicemen during World War II. Today's visitor to Honolulu may spend a week in a Holiday Inn or Sheraton not too different from those he might find along I–80 in Pennsylvania or Iowa. He may watch a few people try to surf at Waikiki Beach, but will spend a great deal of time lying on the sand or at poolside. He can sip a Mai Tai or two at a bar on the top floor of his hotel; or order seafood from a menu not unlike that of any good seafood restaurant in San Francisco or New York. And, along with a hundred other people, he may journey to the U.S.S. Arizona memorial with his instamatic camera. His entire visit may be prepackaged, so to speak, unless he wanders off to one of the outer islands or farther into the South Pacific. Only then is it likely that he will discover anything dramatically new, unusual, or surprising.

These changes are a source of concern to the permanent residents and natives of Hawaii and similar tourist destination areas. The uniqueness of the homeland disappears when it commercializes in order to attract and accommodate larger groups of tourists. The point here, however, is that the current masses of tourists are themselves different from those who came first. The mass market would not be attracted unless the accommodations, food, activities, and entertainment were not to some degree Americanized, standardized, and packaged for it. This is the inevitable price that destination areas pay for the dollars that tourists bring and the jobs that they create. For some destination areas — particularly the island resorts like Hawaii, Bermuda, Antigua, the Bahamas, the Virgin Islands, and Trinidad — there is no choice. Of course, the economic development that results from tourism can be planned and managed better than it has been in many of these areas. It seems inevitable, nevertheless, that the destination area will change as the types of tourists attracted to it begin to change.

The Self-Concept Approach

Still another way of explaining how personality influences behavior is referred to as the **self-concept approach.** Personality theory based on the self-concept approach is an outgrowth of Freudian psychoanalytic theory. Each of us has a unique view of himself, called a self-concept or self-image. The self-concept is an integral part of one's personality. It develops on the basis of the individual's interaction with his social environment and with various reference groups. Reference groups — such as the family, classmates, professional colleagues, fellow parishioners, and others — can exert an enormous influence upon an individual, and they are used as a point of reference in determining his own judgments, preferences, beliefs, and behavior. The most important judgment an individual will make involves the evaluation of his self-worth, based on his perceptions of himself and on how he perceives that others view him.

At almost all costs, we safeguard and protect our self-images. When possible, we try to enhance them. It is no wonder, then, that so much of our behavior is ego-defensive and self-enhancing. One writer states boldly that the basic purpose of all human activity is the protection, maintenance, and enhancement of the self-concept.[10] One thing does appear fairly certain: an individual's evaluation of his *self* will greatly influence his behavior. Important needs and goals emerge that are related to the enhancement and defense of the self.

A concern with self-image leads people to perceive many products that they own or would like to own in terms of their meaning to themselves and others. Many of the goods and services we purchase are symbols intended to enhance or complement our self-images. At the heart of many of our buying decisions is an urge to identify with the image of a product, a service, a brand, a store, or even a company. When the symbolic image of a product corresponds to the image we have or would like to have of ourselves, we are more likely to want that product.

Considerable research-based evidence demonstrates the importance of certain products as symbols that enhance the individual's self-concept. One product that has always had great symbolic potential is the automobile.[11] Someone who perceives himself as fun-loving, for example, would probably choose to own a car that reinforces this image —a Corvette, perhaps, instead of a Cadillac. Someone who perceives himself as sophisticated and conservative would probably choose the Cadillac over the Corvette. Other products found to have significant symbolic potential include cigarettes, beer (premium vs. regular), air conditioners, instant coffee, and princess telephones.[12]

Some products, of course, do not have much, if any, symbolic potential. These might include salt, canned peaches, laundry soap, and radios. Such products are not socially conspicuous. As a general rule, it can be said that the more visible a product, the more likely that it might serve an important symbolic function. Examples would include automobiles, clothing, and furniture. These products help an individual to prove to himself, as well as to others, that he is indeed this or that kind of person.

Travel presents a very interesting and almost unique situation. It is, first of all, an intangible product. It is invisible; it cannot be held in the hand or parked in the driveway; and after it is "consumed," there is nothing left to show for it except some snapshots, perhaps, or a suntan and a pleasant smile on one's face. In another sense, however, travel is highly visible. Some of its paraphenalia — motor homes, travel trailers, golf clubs, tennis rackets, snow skis, luggage, cameras, credit cards, postcards, and so forth, is not only visible but highly symbolic as well.

Travel is a conspicuous and symbolic product because people make it so. Business travel is a good example. The fact that a high level corporate executive flies frequently to trade centers throughout the world, stays in the very best hotels, dines in the finest restaurants, sometimes flies first class, and has a liberal expense account symbolizes a great deal. Family, friends, secretaries, junior executives at the company, and others are all aware and probably somewhat envious of this corporate life style. The airplanes, the passport, the credit cards, and all the rest remind everyone, including the executive himself, that he is important and successful.

In a similar fashion, company salespeople and others who receive all-expense-paid trips through incentive travel programs are reminded of their worth. They, too, are part of a group whose members are clearly identified as productive and successful.

Pleasure travel, too, is a visible and highly symbolic product. Before undertaking any significant journey, we plan it, save for it, and perhaps make our acquaintances envious or even bored as we talk about it. There might be a bon voyage party. A relative or friend or two may drive us to the airport. Perhaps our neighbors watch, wave goodbye, and assure us that they will tend to our mail as the overloaded family station wagon or motor home backs out the driveway. During our travels, friends are again reminded of how fortunate we are when the mailman delivers our postcards. And upon our return, we sometimes find it very difficult to refrain from telling everyone and anyone about our journey. Mom and Dad show their slides. The children brag to their comrades, and at school they write essays about the trip. And everyone talks about next year's vacation.

Clearly, travel can be one of the most symbolic of all products and services. As a symbol, travel can communicate a great deal about an individual: success, achievement, sophistication, worldliness. The opportunity to travel, therefore, can be extremely important in reinforcing certain types of self-images.

One other important point needs to be made about the self-concept approach to personality. It is that a person actually holds two images of himself. One of these images is called the **real self**, and the other the **ideal self.** The real self is what we actually perceive ourselves to be. The ideal self is what we would like to be. To the extent that there is a gap between these two self-concepts, this gap serves as a key motivational force. Suppose that someone thought of herself as an average, "plain Jane" kind of person, although ideally she would like to be modern, sophisticated, and worldly. To close the gap between her real and ideal self images, she might be motivated to improve her looks and wardrobe, move into a modern apartment, read the best books, and take an enriching course or two. She might also be interested in taking a yearly trip overseas.

All of us need evidence of who and what we are, and evidence that we are becoming what we want to become. As already suggested, travel for some people symbolizes movement toward an ideal that many of us value. In addition, people express who they are and what they aspire to be through their leisure-time activities. In short, the self-concept approach provides yet another valuable perspective for understanding why people travel.

LIFE STYLES AND TRAVEL BEHAVIOR

Psychographics, we have said, pertain to an individual's life-style characteristics — to his daily routine, activities, interests, opinions, values, needs, and perceptions. These characteristics reflect an individual's personality traits, and they can explain more about consumer behavior than the measuring devices of clinical psychology. Here we present several examples that illustrate how the psychographic or life-style approach to personality analysis can provide valuable clues to understanding different types of travelers and their behavior.

The Peace-and-Quiet Traveler.   William Wells, a leading authority on psychographics, demonstrated the usefulness of life-style research in understanding travel behavior by analyzing the life styles of different types of travelers.[13] One type of traveler, for example, agreed with the following statement: "A cabin by a quiet lake is a great place to spend a summer." By linking specific life-style information to this statement, Wells illustrated the ability of psychographic research to produce useful information concerning the needs, values, interests, and personality of this type of traveler.

The person who said, "A cabin by a quiet lake is a great place to spend the summer" was easily described as an outdoors-oriented individual drawn to camping, hunting, fishing, fresh air, and the great outdoors. This person was also described as child-oriented because he tended to agree with statements like:

"My children are the most important thing in my life."
"Our family is a close-knit group."
"I spend a great deal of time with my children trying to teach them good habits."
"Part of every vacation should be educational."

A theme of Puritanism runs through the life style of the quiet-lake person and is reflected in his attitudes toward the family — especially with respect to the roles played by women and young people. The quiet-lake man agreed with statements like:

"The father should be the boss in the house."
"A woman's place is in the home."
"Young people have too many privileges today."
"If people would work more and complain less, this would be a better country."
"The Army is a good career for young men."

The quiet-lake person was devoted to cleanliness. He had an unusual interest in health. He was distrustful of advertising — especially advertising in newspapers and magazines. He was against taking risks. And he thought that every family should have a dog.

This composite picture of the quiet-lake person suggests many ideas for products and promotions designed to satisfy his needs, values, interests, and attitudes. A resort area that offers the atmosphere of "a cabin by a quiet lake" should promote the occasion for family togetherness, the benefits of teaching children to enjoy the great outdoors, and the opportunities to hunt and fish. It might also stress the benefits of fresh air, cleanliness, and health.

The Overseas Traveler.   In contrast to the profile of the quiet-lake person, Wells provides a description of the person who says, "I would like to take a trip around the world." The people who agreed with this statement were likely to portray themselves as:

Active and Aggressive
"I like to be considered a leader."
"I am influential in my neighborhood."
"I often influence what my friends buy."
"I like danger."
"I would do better than average in a fist fight."
Interested in New Experiences
"I like to try new and different things."
"When I see a new brand, I often try it just to see what it is like."
"On a vacation, I want to do more than just rest and relax."
"I would like to spend a year in London or Paris."
Interested in Clothes
"I buy at least three suits a year."
"When I must choose, I dress for fashion, not for comfort."
"I like to shop for clothes."
"I enjoy looking through fashion magazines."

Actively Social

"I do more things socially than do most of my friends."

"I like parties where there is lots of music and talk."

"I would rather go out to a party than spend a quiet evening at home."

Self-Confident

"I am happier now than ever before."

"I expect my income to be a lot higher in the next five years."

"I think I would be a good politician."

"I like to take chances."

"It shouldn't be hard to get a good job these days."

When the around-the-world person is contrasted with the quiet-lake person, it becomes evident that life-style research can add much to what is known about different types of travelers. Some of the life-style and attitudinal differences between around-the-world persons, quiet-lake persons, and other types of travelers are easily predictable — but some of them are not. The around-the-world person is active, outgoing, confident, and open to new experiences. These traits explain her interest in traveling to far-off destinations, and they suggest that benefits other than rest and relaxation must be stressed in order to promote foreign travel to this personality type.

It may come as some surprise to know that, when choosing between the two vacation alternatives described here, about two out of every three American adults stated that they would prefer a quiet-lake to an around-the-world vacation.[14] This suggests that a majority of adults view their vacations as an opportunity to relax, recuperate, and escape from the demands of the clock and fixed itineraries. In contrast to the quiet-lake vacation, the around-the-world trip offers greater stimulation and complexity. But for many of those who can manage to leave home during the summer months, there may be enough stimulation, complexity, and unpredictability at home and at work during the bulk of the year.

Woodside and Pitts shed additional light on the overseas vacation traveler.[15] They note that in contrast to domestic vacation travelers, overseas travelers have a much stronger interest in cultural experiences. They are attracted to art galleries and museums, and they attend classical concerts and plays. The average domestic vacation traveler, as a general rule, has much less interest in such attractions.

In an extensive study of the life styles of overseas travelers, Bernay contrasts two groups she calls the **movers-and-shakers** and the **homebodies.**[16] The movers-and-shakers are so-called because they are actively involved, in one way or another, in trying to change the world in which they live. Compared to other people, they are more active in civic and political affairs. They give speeches, they write essays for publication, and they write often to elected representatives. They are active sports participants, they attend concerts, they own original paintings, and they read sophisticated magazines like *Saturday Review* and *The New Yorker.* They watch little television, listen to FM radio, and often drink wine with dinner. It should not be too surprising that, in contrast to other groups of people, movers-and-shakers travel more. They travel by air and travel overseas more. They rent cars more often. They take more winter vacations.

The homebodies, on the other hand — even though they might live next door to the movers-and-shakers and have the same income, education, and jobs — have very different life styles. Their homes mean more to them. They spend more money on furnishings and more time on repairing and painting their homes. They have a strong interest in automobiles. They own more fishing gear, shotguns, rifles, camping equipment, bowling balls, and outboard motors. They watch more television and read more newspapers — but fewer "highbrow" magazines. Their activities and interests clearly indicate that they are, as Bernay says, "nest-oriented." Unlike the movers-and-shakers, the homebodies more or less sit back and wait for the world to happen to them.

The contrasts between these two life-style groups easily explain why one group is much more travel-oriented than the other. Table 4-1 summarizes some of the travel-related life-style differences between these two different types of people.

The Historian Traveler. One motivation for travel of importance to a significant number of people stems from a keen interest in history — an interest in historical figures, places, and events. Each is, in a sense, a means of communicating with the past. The urge to mold oneself with the past, to understand it, and even to relive it must run strong, says one authority, in millions of people.[17]

FIGURE 4-6   Travel-related life-style differences.

	Movers-and-Shakers	Homebodies
Travel by airplane	84%	56%
Trip to another continent	20%	5%
Rented a car	43%	19%
Off-season vacation	43%	37%
Valid passport	30%	7%
Own a vacation home	13%	7%

Source: Elayn K. Bernay, "Emerging Life-Styles and their Effect on the Travel Market," *Proceedings of the First Annual Conference* (Salt Lake City : Travel Research Association, 1970), pp. 19-31.

In a study of domestic travel during the American Bicentennial, psychographics was used to contrast historian travelers with those who had very little, if any, interest in historical places and events.[18] Psychographic analysis was used in part because both groups were similar in terms of several traditional demographic factors — sex, marital status, occupation, education, and family size. Although the historian traveler was no better educated than others, his interest in historical vacations was strongly motivated by a belief that vacations should be educational. Fun is actually a secondary motivation for this type of traveler. A vacation is a time to learn about other people, their customs, and their cultures. It is a time to enrich one's understanding of historical figures and events that shaped the world as we know it today.

The historical traveler's interest in educational experiences was linked to a strong commitment to his children and family. Vacations, he said, should be planned for one's children, and he believed that families that vacation together are happy families. He counted his family and children as among the most important things in his life, and he believed that his key parental responsibilities included contributing to the education of his children. An element of Puritanism influences the historical traveler's attitudes and motivations. As we shall see later, the notion that a vacation should yield positive and useful benefits is a factor which affects other travelers as well.

The implications of these findings are of great importance to destination areas interested in attracting the historical traveler. To appeal to this type of traveler, the vacation should be promoted as an educational opportunity and as an occasion for family togetherness. Travel service businesses can easily join together in an effort to produce integrated, historical tourist attractions. An entire community, in fact, can join together in such an effort. This approach has been used with dramatic results in Colonial Williamsburg, where an entire colonial city — over a long period of time and through masterful planning — was restored and reconstructed to present an authentic and living picture of what it was like to live in another century. The visitor to Colonial Williamsburg sees the city nearly as it was 200 years ago. Its features include colonial taverns, lovely gardens and greens, colonial guest homes, miniplantations, craft shops, horse-drawn carriages, and a charming general store. Its restaurants feature popular 18th century fare served in a genuinely historic atmosphere by waiters and waitresses attired in period costumes. Colonial Williamsburg is an outdoor museum and a unique demonstration of how history and educational tourism can be successfully marketed.

The Recreational Vehicle Traveler. Life-style analysis has also helped to identify a unique set of personality characteristics that describe the traveler who makes his journeys in a recreational vehicle (RV). These vehicles include camping trailers, travel trailers, motorhomes, and truck campers. Once again, traditional demographic characteristics — income, education, marital status, and so forth — do not effectively explain why someone might be attracted to the kind of travel made possible by the RV.

A study of RV owners showed that those who had no interest in the RV and the type of travel it affords had little interest in the outdoors.[19] Instead, they preferred to spend their time and money on what can be called gracious living — dining out, attending concerts and plays, entertaining friends, going to cocktail parties, and so forth. These people preferred to spend their leisure time indoors, and when they did travel they preferred to spend their vacation time in big cities. They considered vacations a time to rest and relax. Perhaps the most distinguishing and important life-style characteristic of those who had no interest in recreational vehicles was their deep commitment to their work. They derived a great deal of satisfaction from work, and one of their primary goals in life was to advance professionally. They worked long hours and saw little reason to take too much time off from their jobs. The RV would normally demand more time and a greater commitment than these individuals were willing or able to make.

Those who owned recreational vehicles provided a predictable contrast. They were not as outgoing or socially active. They preferred a quiet evening at home to a cocktail party. They dined out only occasionally. Curiously, while they believed that one should avoid purchasing expensive luxury products, many of them spent thousands of dollars on their recreational vehicles. In general, the RV owners were much more conservative and tradition-oriented than those who did not own recreational vehicles. Their life styles were much more home-centered and family-oriented — and they may have viewed the RV as an extension of the home, around which family activities could be focused. They maintained strong beliefs in the leisure-ethic and felt that people spend too much time working. They cherished the great outdoors, and they were physically active and athletic.

One demographic characteristic that does distinguish RV owners from those who do not own RV equipment but would like to is age. Those who do not own RV equipment but want to tend to be younger than present RV owners, suggesting that the single largest barrier to the ownership of the RV is an inability to finance the purchase of one. Younger families are typically too heavily in debt to be able to incur the monthly payments for an expensive RV. To more effectively market recreational vehicles, then, more liberal financing plans would need to be developed. The renting of recreational vehicles might also be more effectively promoted.[20]

The Travel Now/Pay Later Traveler.   It is just as easy today to use credit to purchase travel services as it is to purchase clothing, furniture, new automobiles, appliances, and many other products. There are, of course, many people who are willing to do so. At the same time, however, there are many more who are reluctant to use credit when they travel.

Attitudes that encourage people to use credit for travel and attitudes that discourage them are actually reflections of two fundamental viewpoints of travel: it is either a luxury — sometimes a relatively expensive one — or it is as much a necessity as an automatic dishwasher, a new wardrobe, a set of encyclopaedias, or a second family automobile. Some people experience little anxiety when buying a $4,000 motorboat or a $10,000 motorhome on credit, but these same people may think they would have to win the Irish Sweepstakes before they could seriously think about purchasing a $4,000 family vacation to a foreign destination on credit. There are some important differences, of course. The motorboat and recreational vehicle are tangible products. Even after they have been used, they will have some resale value. The foreign vacation, however, is an intangible. After it has been consumed, it has no monetary value. In this sense, travel is no different from any perishible good. Americans may have little trouble justifying the use of credit to purchase luxury items like jewelry, expensive sports cars, and vacation homes. It is a different matter, however, when one talks of using installment credit to purchase an intangible and perishable item like travel, especially when it is viewed as a luxury.

Earlier it was stated that the Puritan Ethic is still alive and well in the United States and that its impact on travel behavior is significant. One reflection of this is the general opposition among Americans to the use of installment credit for purchasing travel. Hawes estimates that better than 90 percent of all Americans share this attitude.[21] Many people will use credit as a convenience when they travel, but will avoid using it to purchase travel services on an installment basis. Many will use credit to buy gasoline and oil on their vacations, and a significant number will use it for lodging and some meals when they are away from home. Business men will use their credit cards extensively when they are away from home. The general attitude among pleasure travelers, however, is that credit cards make it too easy to buy things that are not really needed, and there is a general reluctance to use installment credit to purchase big-ticket items like airline travel or steamship passage.

As Hawes points out, it takes a special kind of personality to be comfortable with using credit for the purchase of travel services. Credit is used more often by those who travel to big cities on their vacations. This may have something to do with the higher risk that cash will be stolen and with the generally higher prices of goods and services in big-city destinations. Credit is also used more often by those who travel to foreign destinations. As discussed earlier, these travelers are active, outgoing, confident, and open to new experiences. They are not afraid to spend money, and, when possible, they prefer to travel first class. In addition, they do not like to plan their vacation travels in great detail. They tend to be relatively young and financially optimistic about the future.[22] It would seem logical that such a personality would have a positive attitude toward the use of credit during journeys away from home.

Nevertheless, most Americans are reluctant to use credit for purchasing travel services other than gas and oil. Hawes estimates that these people outnumber those who will travel on credit by better than two to one.[23] Credit is viewed more favorably when it is used to purchase products that are perceived to serve a "practical" purpose. A business man might buy an airline ticket with a credit card — but he may find it more psychologically difficult to purchase an airline ticket for a golfing holiday in Arizona on credit. Psychologically, it appears to be much easier to use a credit card for convenience purposes (that is, paying all monthly charges immediately upon receipt of a statement) than for the installment purchase of luxury items.

What all this suggests is that promoting credit card usage by travelers might best be accomplished by positioning it as a *convenient* way to pay for the purchase of all travel-related services — gas, oil, lodging, food, airline tickets, and car rentals, as well as clothing and various other items — rather than as a means of paying for such items over a long period of time. What is also suggested is that travel should be positioned in more utilitarian terms. This would include an emphasis on such benefits as the strengthening of family ties, recuperating from work, providing cultural and educational experiences for one's children, and the opportunity to gain or renew friendships. Effective travel promotions would also stress the glamour, romance, and fun of travel. These points will now be discussed in considerable detail.

THE STRUCTURE AND FUNCTIONS OF PERSONALITY

It should be clear by now that personality can influence behavior in a multitude of ways. Most people, however, do not display absolute consistency in their behavior. Sometimes we are manipulative and domineering; at other times, submissive. Sometimes we are friendly and outgoing, but we can be withdrawn, shy, and antisocial as well. Sometimes we are understanding and patient, while at other times we are intolerant. It is said that one's personality is stable, but the fact of the matter is that such stability is only a tendency. Our personalities and behavior are not completely predictable. It would be a dull world indeed if they were. We often respond to exactly the same situations in several different ways. The purpose of this section is to explain this instability and unpredictability by dividing the personality into its component parts. In this way, we will see how it functions and affects behavior — particularly travel and leisure-time behavior.

Freud and Personality

Sigmund Freud viewed man as an energy system regulated by the same kind of physical laws that regulate the soap bubble and the movement of planets. Freudian psychology is based on theories regarding the transformation and exchange of energy between different components of the personality. According to Freud, the three major components of the personality were what he called the *id,* the *ego,* and the *superego.*

The Id.   The main function of the id is to release quantities of energy. In doing so, it is governed by a basic principle of life that Freud called the **pleasure principle.** The id is not controlled by the laws of reason or logic and knows nothing of values, ethics, or morality. It is compulsively driven by one basic goal: to obtain satisfaction for instinctive needs in accordance with the pleasure principle.

The Ego.   The individual requires a mechanism other than the id to behave in harmony and cope with reality. Freud called this mechanism the ego. The ego, in a well-adjusted personality, acts very much like a thermostat. It enables the personality to maintain an equilibrium between its external environment and the impulsiveness of the id. The ego performs the executive functions of the personality. It determines goals, evaluates alternatives, and makes decisions. Whereas the id impulsively pursues the pleasure principle, the ego is governed by the **reality principle.**

The Superego.   The third dimension of personality, according to Freud, is the superego, and it serves as the moral and judicial branch of the personality. The superego represents the ideal rather than the real. Its goal is to strive for perfection rather than pleasure or reality. The superego houses the individual's moral code. It tells the person what is good and virtuous, and what is bad and sinful.

Freud believed that the real motives underlying our behavior are largely unconscious. He was also concerned with the idea that behavior is determined by heredity, and past environment. Although a pioneer of much that we know about psychology today, Freud was also narrow-mindedly convinced that human life centered around a basic desire for sexual gratification. He reasoned that society's taboos on free and unlimited sexual gratification resulted in frustrations and anxieties that influenced behavior. He argued that sexually aggressive instincts were channeled into apparently nonsexual and nonaggressive forms of behavior. Strict Freudian psychologists would argue today that consumer behavior is triggered by subconscious sexual motivations and that many products and services are sexually symbolic. It has been suggested, for example, that consumer attitudes toward flashy automobiles, cake mixes, airplanes, clothing, and many other products are based in large part upon unfulfilled sexual drives.[24]

Freud was a deep and complex thinker, and it is easy to misinterpret his theories or carry them to extremes. What these theories contribute to our present discussion is the division of personality into separate but related components that can provide a useful perspective for understanding how personality functions and directs travel behavior.

Ego States: The Three Voices

Freudian personality theory provided much of the ground work for Transactional Analysis, a relatively new branch of psychology. Popularized by Eric Berne, the author of *Games People Play*, and Thomas Harris, author of *I'm Ok–You're OK*, Transactional Analysis — or T.A. — provides us with a new and simplified language and an uncomplicated approach to understanding travel behavior.[25]

One of the basic T.A. concepts is called the **ego state.** An individual's personality is said to consist of three important parts, each of them called an ego state. These three ego states are termed the **Parent,** the **Adult,** and the **Child,** * and they correspond roughly to Freud's superego, ego, and id. Each of the ego states is a separate source of thoughts, feelings, and behavior. And in any given situation, an individual's behavior can be directed by any of these personality parts or ego states:

> You can feel things, smell things, touch things . . . you can talk to people, listen to them, look at them, and act toward them with separate and quite distinct behavior from each one of your ego states. And, because your Parent, Adult, and Child each have their own programming, each one of them can respond to exactly the same experience in different ways.[26]

The Parent and Child ego states are said to develop from permanent recordings in the brain. They are mental recordings of events, thoughts, images, and feelings experienced by an individual almost from the time of birth. Everything is recorded and constantly replayed within the individual's mind. Almost all of these replays occur unconsciously when a

---

*To distinguish them from actual parents, adults, and children, the three ego states — Parent, Adult, and Child — are capitalized.

new situation is encountered and the individual seeks information and guidance from previous but similar experiences. The individual can respond to new experiences in three different ways, depending upon the ego state recording he listens to.

The Child.   Psychologists believe that the first of the ego states to develop in an individual is the Child. The Child ego state is comprised of natural feelings, thinking, and behavior. It also contains information a person needs to adapt to emotional situations. A person acting from his Child ego state would behave as he wanted to act (the *Natural Child*) or as he was trained to act (the *Adapted Child*) when he was a child.

The Child is that part of one's personality which experiences feelings of frustration, inadequacy, helplessness, and joy. In addition, the Child is the source of curiosity, creativity, imagination, spontaneity, impulsiveness, and the excitement born of new discoveries. The Child is responsible for completely uninhibited and seemingly ridiculous behavior, for playfulness, and for natural statements and acts.

The Child is that part of one's personality responsible for **feelings** and **emotions.** And it is the Child that is responsible for most of one's **wants, needs,** and **desires.** Whenever a person feels that she wants something, it is her Child which expresses her desires:

"I want another piece of cake!"
"I want to buy a Corvette!"
"I want to go to Hawaii!"
"I want to have fun!"

In *I'm OK–You're OK*, Harris lists a number of physical and verbal clues to behavior directed by the Child ego state. These clues, reproduced in Figure 4-7, clearly indicate that the Child ego state is responsible for an individual's needs, wants, desires, sensuality, feelings, and emotions.

The Parent.   The second ego state to develop in an individual is the Parent. It is the source of behavior and attitudes usually copied from the individual's own parents, or from some other parental figure. The Parent ego state is the *main source of an individual's opinions and prejudices, "how-to" information, and right-wrong information:*

"You ought to save for a rainy day."
"Good girls don't stay out all night."
"Big boys don't cry."
"You're doing it all wrong. Let me show you."
"No! You can't go to Florida."

An individual's Parent lectures, moralizes, points its finger righteously or accusingly, teaches, and lays down the law. The Parent is in command when the individual scolds, when he lectures about what's wrong (or right) about today's youth, and when he corrects someone's grammar or manners.[27] Other verbal and nonverbal clues to Parent-directed behavior are listed in Figure 4-7. These clues indicate that there are two sides to the Parent ego state. One side is sympathetic and comforting, while the other is critical, directive, and appraising. The Parent tells the individual about the way things ought to be, and it also tells the individual what is right and wrong.

The Adult.   The third ego state to develop in an individual is the Adult. The Adult is the part of one's personality that directs rational thinking and the objective processing of information. The Adult directs behavior which is rational, unemotional, and relatively objective. It is that part of the personality which directs problem solving. The Adult also tests the data stored in the Parent and Child ego states for its appropriateness to specific situations.

Everyone, even the small child, has an Adult capable of assessing external reality. Thus, the Adult ego state is not related to age. Rather, it is oriented to current reality and the objective gathering of information. It is organized, adaptable, intelligent, and functions by testing reality, estimating probabilities, computing dispassionately, and making judgments based on facts. Figure 4-7 also provides a number of verbal and nonverbal clues to Adult-controlled behavior.

Ego State Balance

Each of the three ego states — Parent, Adult, and Child — functions in an emotionally healthy individual. In a normal, well-adjusted person, there are times when his Parent will and should be in charge of his behavior. There are also times when his Adult should be and is in charge of his behavior, and still other times when his Child is in charge.

When a loved one needs sympathy, for example, or when a youngster needs discipline, it will normally be the Parent that gives both. When someone is working on the family budget or trying to solve a complex problem at work, his Adult will normally be in command. A person's Child will normally take charge when he is in active pursuit of pleasure — on a vacation trip, during an inter-office softball game, or on a visit to a theme park. A "balanced life" really refers to giving a fair share of one's time and emotional energy to each of these three parts of the personality.

A person whose behavior is controlled almost exclusively by just one ego state may have a serious enough personality problem to warrant professional help. A person who operates primarily from the Parent ego state — the Constant Parent — often treats everyone around her as if they

FIGURE 4-7 Clues to Parent, Adult, and Child ego states.

	Words	*Tone of Voice*	*NonVerbal*
P	Ought, should, never,	Loud = Critical	furrowed brow, pointing
A	don't ever, No!, always,	Soft = Nurturing	index finger, head
R	don't, let me show you		wagging, horrified look,
E	how.		foot-tapping, hands on
N	Evaluative words: stupid,		hips, arms folded,
T	disgusting, ridiculous,		wringing hands, tongue-
	naughty, shocking,		clucking, sighing, patting
	nonsense.		another on head.
	Not again! Now what!		Stiff, West Point-like
	How many times have I		posture.
	told you! Now always		
	remember, there there,		
	sonny, honey, poor		
	thing, poor dear.		
A	Why, what, where,	Almost computer-	Straightforward face
D	when, who, how much,	like	Comfortable
U	in what way, true, false,		Little enthusiasm
L	possible, I think, in my		Unexcited
T	opinion, I see, I think.		Dull
C	Baby talk: I wish, I want,	Excitement	Delight
H	I dunno, I gonna, I don't	Enthusiasm	Laughter
I	care, I guess, when I	High-pitched	Giggling
L	grow up, bigger, biggest,	whining voice	Charming
D	better, best.	Joy	Tears
		Anger	Quivering lip
		Sadness	pouting
		Fear	temper tantrums
			rolling eyes
			shrugging shoulders
			downcast eyes
			teasing
			nail-biting
			squirming

were children. The Constant Adult usually qualifies as a bore; her relationships with others are likely to be sterile because the caring Parent and the fun-loving Child are not allowed to function. The Constant Child is the perpetual little boy or girl who, like Peter Pan, does not want to grow up. This person does not think for herself, make her own decisions, or take responsibility for her own behavior. In summary, an individual's three ego states can be likened to three different voices, each of which must be allowed to speak at the right times.

Ego States and Travel Decisions

The viewpoint that our personalities consist of three separate and distinct components provides a valuable perspective for analyzing various travel decisions. Each of the three parts of the personality — Parent, Adult, and Child — is responsible for directing different kinds of behavior, and, as we shall see, each part will have different things to say about whether the individual travels or not, where he will go, how much he will spend, how long he will stay, and so forth. When the individual leaves home, he takes with him his Parent, his Adult, and his Child — each of which must be catered to in some way or other. All three functions of the personality must be convinced that a journey away from home makes sense. Otherwise, no sort of trip is likely to take place.

Many of the primary motivations for pleasure travel are clearly motivations which reside in the Child ego state. Remember that the Child represents the "I want" part of the personality, and that the Child is responsible for most of the feelings that an individual has. If a person is bored and needs the kind of stimulation that travel can provide, it is probably the Child that will seek escape through travel. If travel is motivated by curiosity and the need to explore and discover, it is the Child that says, "Let's go." If travel is motivated by the need to play — to ski the slopes of Aspen, to fish the waters of the Bahamas, or to enjoy the fantasies of Disney World — it is the Child's voice that urges, "Do it." If the motivation for travel is fun — no matter what that may mean to the individual — it is the Child which is responsible for the desire to get up and go.

The Child is easily attracted to travel because, first and foremost, travel usually promises a lot of fun. It does not take much more than the thought of sandy beaches, swaying palm trees, sleek airplanes, championship golf courses, fine restaurants, comfortable hotel rooms that are cleaned by someone else, beautiful scenery, novelty, and excitement to hook the Child in the potential traveler — no matter what his age. Travel advertising, memories of last year's vacation, and the first-hand reports of friends who have traveled here and there help the Child to form these mental images.

While the Child is instinctively attracted to travel for the fun it promises, the Parent and the Adult will usually have reservations and questions about any journey away from home. The Parent ego state, in particular, is likely to have serious doubts about the Child's desire to indulge itself with a trip away from home. Remember that the Parent ego state is the main source of an individual's opinions and prejudices, of "how-to" information, and right-wrong information. Remember, too, that there are two sides to the Parent ego state. One side is protective and nurturing, while the other is critical and hands out a lot of instructions. The second side of the Parent, the so-called Critical Parent, is likely to possess opinions and beliefs that oppose the idea of leaving home and spending time and money on fun alone. Some of the more important of these Parent ego state recordings might include, but are certainly not limited to, the following:

"Work before pleasure."
"Work hard and get ahead."
"Duty first."
"Be productive."
"Don't be lazy."
"Make sure you've got all your work done."
"Don't spend more than you can afford."
"Don't spend what you don't have."
"Live within your budget."
"Don't waste money."
"Save for a rainy day."
"A penny saved is a penny earned."
"Don't get ripped off."
"Don't waste time."
"Waste not, want not."
"Plan ahead."

Many of these Parent messages are likely to be expressed in the frequent "conversations" that take place between Parent and Child. Everyone talks to himself — and does so more often than he probably realizes. If one listens closely to these internal discussions, it should be easy to see that the dialogue is usually between different ego states. Most frequently the internal dialogue takes place between Parent and Child while the Adult serves as arbitrator, because the conversation between Parent and Child often involves conflict.

Remember that the Child ego state is that part of the individual's personality which says — and usually says with great determination: "I want what I want when I want it — and I want to have fun now!" At the same time, the Parent ego state is usually prepared to answer the Child as follows: "No! Duty before pleasure. Let's get some more work done, and then maybe we can talk about having some fun." The following internal dialogue would not be an unusual one:

Child: Gee, I'd sure like to go to Europe this summer!
Parent: Yes, I know you would, but we can hardly afford to take that kind of a vacation.
C: You always say we can't afford it! Take the money out of the bank.

P: Out of our savings account?! Are you crazy?

C: Well, what have we been saving for?

P: Not to blow it on a trip to Europe, that's for sure.

C: Why not? We never go anywhere!

P: What do you mean we never go anywhere? We went to Florida last year.

C: That was two years ago. We didn't go anywhere last year.

P: We couldn't take off from work last year. You know that. And we sure can't take off three weeks to go to Europe this year.

C: We never have any fun! All you do is work, work, work!

P: The trouble with you is that all you ever think about is having fun, fun, fun! Honestly! You must think that money grows on trees!

To illustrate how this kind of internal conflict between Parent and Child ego states can be resolved, let us consider the impact of effective travel advertising.[28] To help settle the dispute, creative advertising would speak to each of the individual's three ego states. The first job is to "hook" the Child ego state. Destination advertising, for example, would clearly demonstrate that what the destination offers is the opportunity to have fun. This can be accomplished easily, by presenting pictures of people sailing, golfing, scuba diving, playing tennis, dancing, gambling, fishing, hunting, surfing, and sunbathing — pictures of happy people with big smiles, having fun.

The second task for the creative advertiser is to appease the Parent ego state and encourage it to grant the Child permission to indulge itself. There are several ways to achieve this objective. The most effective is to address various leisure-time motives that reside in the Parent ego state. Education is a good example. Stored somewhere in the Parent ego states of many people is the prescription that "education is one of the most important things in life." To the extent that this Parent message is replayed while an individual contemplates a journey to a particular destination area, and to the extent that he is aware that the destination area offers educational benefits, the Parent is likely to grant permission to his Child to indulge itself with such a trip.

Educational benefits, in fact, play a key role in travel behavior in general. Washington, D.C., Amish Country, Yellowstone National Park, Greenfield Village, and many other tourist attractions are popular in no small part because they promise an educational experience. The same is true of many foreign destination areas. Trips to such destinations are not easily classified as frivolous because the Child, although amused and entertained, stands to learn things of lasting importance. Such journeys will be productive in the truest sense of the Protestant Ethic.

The modern theme parks of America provide an excellent example of one travel business that has profited from offering educational attractions and benefits. Its forerunner, the old-time amusement park, offered little besides unadulterated amusement and fun. The modern theme park is a different story. The visitor to Disney World is not only amused and entertained, but is also given a refresher course in American history when she visits the Hall of Presidents. At Busch Gardens in Williamsburg, Virginia, and at several other major theme parks, the visitor is treated to a day in a foreign land. The Sea World parks teach their guests about marine life, while Knott's Berry Farm acquaints its guests with the laser. At Marriott's Great America in Santa Clara, California, at Opryland in Nashville, at Six Flags Over Texas, and elsewhere, one learns something about the history of music in America. Kings Island treats its guests to the history of college football through the College Football Hall of Fame. Educational attractions like these can appeal to the Parent in any potential visitor and convince it that a theme park visit can be something more than roller coaster rides, bumper cars, and cotton candy.

Other destinations have employed similar appeals. New York City points to its night life but also emphasizes its museums. The state of Virginia points to its beaches but also to Colonial Williamsburg. Mexico promises the sun and fun of places like Acapulco and Puerto Vallarta, but it also boasts the oldest culture in the Americas.

Education is not the only motivating factor that can encourage the Parent ego state to say yes when the Child wants to travel. If, for example, the Parent feels an obligation to permit the Child a periodic change-of-pace from the routines of home and work, then it will be more likely to say yes. If the Parent senses that travel will somehow promote solidarity within the individual's family, then it will be more likely to say yes. If the Parent believes that a particular trip will not result in the outlay of an unreasonable amount of money, then it will be more likely to say yes. If the Parent perceives that there is some measure of prestige or status attached to a particular trip, then it will be more likely to say yes.

In short, educational and cultural benefits, family togetherness, recuperation from work, obligation, economy, status, and prestige are some of the travel motives that usually reside in the Parent ego state. They are motives which, if activated, can encourage the Parent to grant permission to the Child to indulge itself through travel. Travel advertising can be used to help activate these motives.

Even after the Parent has given its permission for the Child to indulge in travel, it may still insist on setting guidelines such as how much to spend or how long to be away. These instructions may be as general as "Don't be extravagent" and "Don't get ripped off." Or they may be as specific as "Stay in budget motels," "Fly supersaver," or "Don't buy any cheap souvenirs."

Once the Child and Parent ego states have been satisfied, effective travel advertising must then address the Adult. There are some travel motives which reside primarily in the Adult ego state — travel that is

motivated by health considerations, for example. Effective travel advertising might address motivations of this kind.

As indicated earlier, the Adult is also responsible for reconciling conflicts between the Parent and Child ego states. The Adult will weigh both
sides of the argument about travel and attempt to make rational, objective
decisions. It will ask questions like:

> "When was the last time we went on a trip?"
> "How much will it cost?"
> "Can we really afford it?"
> "How would we pay for it?"
> "Is there any way we could spend less?"
> "How long will we be away from home?"
> "Can we afford to be gone that long?"
> "How badly do we need to go?"

The Adult, in other words, serves to *rationalize* the travel decision. If it
decides that a journey should be undertaken the Adult will, in effect,
explain to the Parent why a trip may be a good idea at this point in time.
It may activate, so to speak, that side of the Parent called the Nurturing
Parent — the side most likely to see and understand the need for travel.
The Nurturing Parent might be activated by travel advertising messages
like: "Take a break — you've been working too hard," or "You deserve
to take a winter trip to sunny Acapulco."

The Adult is also responsible for gathering factual information that
will allow the individual to plan a journey away from home. Here, too,
the Adult acts as arbitrator, trying to please the Child — which would like
to leave right away, stay perhaps forever, and spend all the money in the
world — and trying to accommodate the Parent — which really might not
wish to go at all but will at least insist that a reasonable expenditure of
money and time be maintained. The Adult will need information about
how to get to the destination, how long a journey it is likely to be, how
much money to bring, what lodging facilities are nearby or available and
what they cost, and other information that will allow it to make sensible
travel plans. It is not unlikely that the Adult would postpone the journey
until necessary factual information becomes available. Interestingly, travel
advertising which says "Call Your Travel Agent" attempts to get the potential traveler to turn over a good portion of the Adult decision-making
to a professional travel planner.

In summary, it is useful to think of each traveler not just as one person
but as an individual with three separate and distinct personality components. Each personality component — Parent, Adult, and Child — must
be appeased in some way if the individual is to travel and enjoy it. Each
component has, in the first place, a different predisposition to travel, and
each component has different needs or motivations that travel can satisfy.

All of these predispositions, needs, and motivations must be taken into consideration when explaining travel behavior, and they must be accommodated in some way when various travel products and services are being marketed.

SUMMARY

The point is emphasized throughout this book that human behavior is a complex phenomenon that sometimes baffles even the best of psychologists. Rarely are there easy explanations of why people behave as they do. This is especially true when one's interest is travel behavior. A number of psychological factors must be considered — including personality, which can influence travel behavior in a multitude of ways.

Personality consists of those stable characteristics of an individual's behavior that distinguish him from others. These characteristics help to explain how the individual goes about satisfying specific needs and goals.

Personality is a complex psychological phenomenon, but by examining some of the popular ways of analyzing personality, we can better understand how it functions and influences travel behavior. The trait approach describes personality by focusing on the persistent ways in which an individual responds to recurring stimuli in his environment. Personalities are also classified into broad types, an approach which seems to offer more promise for better explaining travel behavior. One application of this approach classifies travelers as either psychocentric or allocentric. These two personality types exhibit markedly different predispositions and attitudes toward travel. This approach helps to explain, among other things, why destination areas rise and fall in popularity, and what kinds of travelers will be attracted to a specific destination area at a given point in time.

Another way of explaining how personality influences travel behavior is referred to as the self-concept or self-image approach. Our self-images are developed and enhanced in no small way by the products and services we purchase. Travel can play a very important symbolic role in enhancing our self-images by communicating to others, as well as to ourselves, that we are a certain kind of person.

Life-style or psychographic research represents still another way of analyzing personality and other factors that influence travel behavior. This approach evolved when researchers recognized the limitations of using clinical personality measurement tools to analyze consumer behavior. Travel behavior is part of an individual's overall life style, and one can better explain travel behavior by understanding how travel fits into an overall life-style pattern. In this chapter, a number of life-style studies were reviewed that provided valuable clues for understanding travel behavior and motivations.

It becomes easier to understand why we often respond to the same experiences in different ways when we divide personality into three separate but related components. Transactional Analysis is essentially a new branch of Freudian psychology which provides useful labels for these components: Parent, Adult, and Child. Each of these three ego states, as they are called, is responsible for different kinds of behavior. Each ego state is likely to house different attitudes about travel, and understanding these attitudes helps us to better understand travel behavior. Moreover, each of these ego states must be catered to by those who market travel products and services.

REFERENCES

[1] James Engel, David T. Kollat, and Roger D. Blackwell, *Consumer Behavior* (New York: Holt, Rinehart, and Winston, Inc., 1978), p. 201.

[2] See: William D. Wells, *Life-Styles and Psychographics* (Chicago: American Marketing Association, 1974).

[3] Karen Horney, *Our Inner Conflicts* (New York: W.W. Norton & Company, Inc., 1945).

[4] Joel B. Cohen, "The Role of Personality in Consumer Behavior," in H. Kassarjian and T. Robertson, eds., *Perspectives in Consumer Behavior* (Glenview, Illinois: Scott, Foresman and Company, 1968), pp. 220-234.

[5] David Riesman, *The Lonely Crowd* (New York: Doubleday Anchor Books, 1953).

[6] W. M. Kassarjian, "A Study of Riesman's Theory of Social Character," *Sociometry*, Vol. 25 (September, 1962), pp. 213-230. Also: R. Centers, "An Examination of the Riesman Social Character Typology: A Metropolitan Survey," *Sociometry*, Vol. 25 (September, 1962), pp. 231-240.

[7] H. Linton and E. Graham, "Personality Correlates of Persuasability," in I. Janis et al., *Personality and Persuasability* (New Haven: Yale University Press, 1959), pp. 69-101.

[8] Harold Kassarjian, "Social Character and Differential Preference for Mass Communication," in Kassarjian and Robertson, *Perspectives in Consumer Behavior*, pp. 261-269.

[9] Stanley Plog, "Why Destination Areas Rise and Fall in Popularity," a paper presented to the Southern California Chapter of the Travel Research Association (October 10, 1972).

[10] S.I. Hayakawa, *The Semantic Barrier* (Providence, Rhode Island: Walter V. Clark Associates, Inc.), a speech by Hayakawa at the 1964 Conference of Activity Vector Analysis at Lake George, New York.

[11] Al E. Birdwell, "A Study of the Influences of Image Congruence on Consumer Choice," *Journal of Business*, Vol. 41 (January, 1968), pp. 76-88.

[12] See: Francis S. Bourne, "Group Influence in Marketing," in Kassarjian and Robertson, *Perspectives in Consumer Behavior*, pp. 289-296.

[13] William D. Wells, "Life-Styles in Selecting Media for Travel Advertising,"

The Values of Travel Research, Proceedings of the Third Annual Conference (Salt Lake City: Travel Research Association, 1972), pp. 63-74.

[14] Douglass K. Hawes, "Psychographics are Meaningful . . . Not Merely Interesting," *Journal of Travel Research,* Vol. 15 (Spring, 1977), pp. 1-7.

[15] Arch G. Woodside and Robert E. Pitts, "Effects of Consumer Life-Styles, Demographics, and Travel Activities on Foreign and Domestic Travel Behavior," *Journal of Travel Research,* Vol. 14 (Winter, 1976), pp. 13-15.

[16] Elayn K. Bernay, "Emerging Life-Styles and their Effect on the Travel Market," *Proceedings of the First Annual Conference* (Salt Lake City: Travel Research Association, 1970), pp. 19-31.

[17] Donald E. Lundberg, *The Tourist Business,* third edition (Boston: CBI Publishing Company, Inc., 1976), p. 138.

[18] Paul J. Solomon and William R. George, "The Bicentennial Traveler: A Life-Style Analysis of the Historian Segment," *Journal of Travel Research,* Vol. 15 (Winter, 1977), pp. 14-17.

[19] Douglass K. Hawes, "Empirically Profiling Four Recreational Vehicle Market Segments," *Journal of Travel Research,* Vol. 16 (Spring, 1978), pp. 13-20.

[20] Ibid.

[21] Douglass K. Hawes, *Uses of and Attitudes Toward Consumer Credit as a Means of Financing Leisure-Time Products and Pursuits* (Laramie, Wyoming: Division of Business and Economic Research, University of Wyoming, 1975), p. 8.

[22] William R. Darden and Donna D. Darden, "A Study of Vacation Life-Styles," *Marketing Travel and Tourism,* Proceedings of the Seventh Annual Conference (Salt Lake City: Travel Research Association, 1976), pp. 231-236.

[23] Hawes, "Psychographics are Meaningful. . ," p. 4.

[24] See: Rom J. Markin, Jr., *Consumer Behavior* (New York: Macmillan Company, 1974), p. 67.

[25] Eric Berne, *Games People Play* (New York: Grove Press, 1964); Thomas Harris, *I'm OK–You're OK* (New York: Harper & Row, 1967).

[26] *I Win–You Win* (Eden Prairie, Minnesota: Wilson Learning Corporation, 1975), p. 28.

[27] Lyman K. Randall, *P-A-C At Work* (New York: American Airlines, 1971), p. 5.

[28] The main points in this discussion were first developed by Dr. John Kennedy at the Transactional Analysis and Travel Behavior Workshop at the University of Notre Dame during the Spring of 1977. See: John J. Kennedy, "A Transactional Analysis Model for Understanding Travel Decisions," *The 80s–Its Impact on Travel and Tourism Marketing,* Proceedings of the Eighth Annual Conference (Salt Lake City: Travel Research Association, 1977), pp. 159-162.

QUESTIONS FOR DISCUSSION

1. What do you believe to be some of the dominant personality characteristics of people who travel during their vacations as opposed to those who do not travel at all while taking vacations?
2. Select a friend and, based on your knowledge of this person's character, guess

what type of destination(s) he or she would want to visit during an ideal vacation. Then ask your friend, "Where would you want to go on an ideal vacation?" Is the answer pretty much what you expected? If not, why not?

3. Some of the things people purchase and own are highly symbolic. Such things as automobiles, homes, and clothing are "socially conspicuous" — they are highly visible and can communicate a great deal about a person to those around him. Travel, however, is an invisible item, an intangible. How is it, then, that travel comes to be a very symbolic product, a product that can communicate a great deal about a person to those around him?

4. What are some of the key personality characteristics of the historical traveler?

5. The attitude that a vacation should produce some positive utilitarian benefits is a factor which affects many leisure travelers. In what ways does this attitude affect your own vacation behavior?

6. What are some of the key personality characteristics of people who own recreational vehicles versus those who do not and don't wish to?

7. How might you describe the personality and attitudes of someone who is opposed to purchasing travel on an installment credit basis? (Remember that purchasing something on an installment credit basis is not the same thing as using a credit card for convenience purposes — that is, paying for all monthly charges immediately upon receipt of a statement.) How might a travel firm persuade more people to purchase travel services on an installment credit basis?

8. Let's say that you considered attending the most recent Rose Bowl in Pasadena, California. Describe the dialogue that might have taken place among the three parts of your personality as you considered this trip.

9. Choose one of your favorite vacation destinations and assume that you have to make a sales presentation to someone in order to persuade him to visit this destination. What key sales messages would you communicate to this person's Parent, Adult, and Child?

5
MOTIVATION: WHY PEOPLE TRAVEL

Why do people travel? At first, this would appear to be a simple question. They travel to broaden their horizons. To see the world. To learn about, and to understand, other people. To visit friends and relatives. To relax and have a good time. To visit the places from which their ancestors came. To escape winter weather, or boredom.

To those interested in understanding why people *really* travel, these answers are superficial. They mask the deeper psychological reasons why travel is undertaken. Why do we want to see the world? Why do we want to visit friends and relatives? Why do we want to visit the places from which our ancestors came? And why do we want to get away? What does Acapulco have over sitting in front of the television with one's feet up? Dr. Joseph Smith, a psychologist who has spent a number of years analyzing travel behavior, states:

> Most of you know the reasons you get . . . if you ask people why they took a trip. 'I went home to see Grandma' or 'I had it at home — we decided it was time for a holiday.' Somehow, there is something not quite satisfying about a roster of answers of that sort.[1]

Why *do* people travel? There are many answers, depending upon the individual and his cultural conditioning. The answers are psychological and sociological. Lundberg suggests that what the traveler says are his motivations for traveling may be only reflections of deeper needs, needs which he himself does not understand, may not be aware of, or may not wish to articulate.[2]

Perhaps an even more interesting question is why some people choose not to travel at all. Can they simply not afford to? Or are there barriers — other than time and money — that keep these people in their armchairs? Despite the fact that the travel industry in the United States and throughout much of the industrialized world has grown rapidly during the past two decades, millions of people remain who rarely wander too far from their homes. Less than one-half of one percent of the world's people travel outside of their homelands in any given year. Eighty percent of the travel in the United States is accounted for by just 20 percent of the population. About 50 million Americans have never flown in an airplane. Approximately 80 million spend their weekends and vacations in their own back-yards.

Travel is such a widespread and complex phenomenon that Erik Cohen, a well-known sociologist, expresses astonishment that social scientists have paid but scant attention to it. He notes that, despite the social scientist's concern with geographic mobility, a comprehensive understanding of travel remains undeveloped.[3] The same observation was voiced by William Prigge, vice president of Hilton International: "We know practically nothing about what motivates the decision to travel . . . or who may have been instrumental in making the decision."[4] Lundberg observes that little research has been done on travel motivations, and that which has been done is not sufficiently related to a well-established theory of human motivation.[5]

Learning, perception, and personality, as we have seen in previous chapters, *influence* a person when he makes decisions — decisions like whether or not to travel, what destinations to visit, how to travel, what airline to use, whether or not to use a travel agent, and so forth. These factors however, provide only a limited understanding of why the individual travels in the first place. What are the forces that compel one person to fly his family to Florida for a week's vacation, while another person stays at home, burns some logs in his fireplace, reads a book, and sends his children to the movies? What are their motives?

Motivation may be thought of as the driving force behind behavior. It is guided by learning and perception, as well as by group and cultural influences. Motivation is also strongly related to the individual's personality. In fact, as we mentioned earlier, it is difficult to make a sharp distinction between motivation and personality. Motivation influences how the individual reacts to the world around him, and we describe his personality in terms of his consistent reactions to this world. Thus, personality is described in terms of habitual patterns and qualities of behavior, while this behavior is influenced in large part by the individual's motivations.

This chapter discusses motivation and shows how it influences travel behavior. The first section discusses the purpose of motives, different types of motives, and how motives serve to direct behavior. The second section describes basic human needs and shows how they can be useful in explaining travel behavior. If there is one factor that best explains why people travel, it is the human need for variety — and the last section of this chapter provides a detailed discussion of how travel functions to satisfy this need.

MOTIVATION AND TRAVEL BEHAVIOR

Motivation is often thought to be the ultimate driving force that governs travel behavior. The purpose of a motive is to protect, satisfy, or enhance the individual. Some psychologists define a motive as an active, driving force that exists to reduce a state of tension. When one is hungry, for example, he experiences physiological tension (hunger pains) and is motivated by this tension to seek food. In fact, if he is starving, the tension will be so intense and the corresponding motivation so strong that he will give attention to no other need. Feelings of loneliness or rejection create psychological tension, and the individual is motivated by this tension to seek love, affection, or companionship. When one is bored by the day-in-day-out routine of everyday living, another kind of psychological tension develops that motivates the individual to get away from where he is or to do something different.

Motives are often classified as either physiological or psychological in nature. Physiological motives stem from biological needs. These are the physiological tensions which must be reduced if the body is to survive. They arise from the need for oxygen, water, food, and waste elimination; relief from pain and fatigue; and protection from the elements. Motives arising from these needs are not learned; they are innate primary drives that originate in some physiological condition within the body. Although biologically determined, physiological drives are sometimes subject to social and cultural influences. Warm clothing, for example, will provide protection from the cold, but the type of clothing actually worn may be prescribed by a variety of social and cultural factors.

In earlier times, before the emergence of tourism and travel for its own sake, travel was undertaken to satisfy physiological motives: nomads wandered in search of food and water; soldiers stalked their enemies to prevent sudden attacks on their own homelands; and others sought protection from the elements or from despotic rulers. Only after the emergence of a large middle class — whose discretionary incomes could be spent on things other than food, clothing, and shelter — and after technological developments in the area of transportation — enabling large numbers of people to travel long distances in relatively short periods of time — would tourism begin to resemble its present-day form. It was only after World War II, when America was described as the "affluent society," that the large mass of people undertook travel simply for its own sake. Then millions of Americans journeyed to far-off destinations, to places of which their parents and grandparents might never have heard. And all of this travel took place not to satisfy physiological drives — but to satisfy psychological motives and needs.

Psychological motives stem from needs created by an individual's social environment. These motives are generally learned, and the learning begins shortly after birth. The infant's need for comfort and security emerge. Various social institutions — the family, schools, clubs, and churches, for example — demand the growing child's conformity to specific values and patterns of behavior. He learns the need to succeed and to attain a reputable place in society; the need for a college education, a nice home, an expensive car, an attractive spouse. In rare cases, some psychological motives become strong enough to overcome physiological survival needs.

Few psychologists agree on how many basic needs actually exist. Some have constructed inventories of human desires consisting of basic needs by the dozen. Others, such as Freud, are careful to distinguish between biological necessities and other, psychological sources from which our motives derive. Thus, their lists of basic human needs are shorter and more selective.

One travel researcher suggests 18 important motives that compel people to travel. These motives are listed in Figure 5-1. There is some doubt, however, about whether these motives are truly basic in the sense of *causing* behavior. Do they really explain why people travel? Do they answer the types of questions posed in the beginning of this chapter? It seems more likely that this list provides only intermediary answers that lead us to seek the deeper causes of travel behavior.

McIntosh suggests that basic travel motivations can be divided into four categories:[6]

1. **Physical Motivators:** physical rest, sports participation, beach recreation, relaxing entertainment, and health considerations.
2. **Cultural Motivators:** the desire for knowledge of other countries — their music, art, folklore, dances, paintings, and religion.
3. **Interpersonal Motivators:** the desire to meet new people; to visit friends or relatives; to escape from routine, family, or neighbors; or to make new friendships.
4. **Status and Prestige Motivators:** the desire for recognition, attention, appreciation, and a good reputation.

McIntosh also stresses that we should rarely expect that travel behavior will involve a single motive. Travel is a complex, symbolic form of behavior through which the traveler is usually striving to satisfy multiple needs.

To demonstrate how travel satisfies multiple needs, it is helpful to examine the different types of rewards or satisfactions people seek when they travel. Consumers may expect any of four different types of rewards: rational rewards, sensory rewards, social rewards, and ego-satisfying rewards.[7] Moreover, they may achieve these rewards in different ways: as the direct result of traveling, during the act of traveling, or as an incidental result of the travel experience.[8] These four types of rewards and the three ways to achieve them suggest twelve ways in which travel motivations can be analyzed. These are illustrated in Figure 5-2, along with advertising messages that stress different kinds of rewards and recognize that these rewards are achieved under different circumstances. Airline advertising, for example, emphasizes time savings (a rational reward), relaxation (a sensory reward), friendliness (a social reward), and flight attendants who pamper the traveler (an ego-satisfying reward). These rewards are promised as either the direct result of flying a particular airline, as an in flight benefit, or both.

THE BASIC HUMAN NEEDS

One of the best-known theories of human motivation is Abraham Maslow's **hierarchy of needs.**[9] Maslow suggests that man has five sets of basic needs:

1. **Physiological needs:** food, water, oxygen, sex, etc.
2. **Safety needs:** security, stability, order, and protection.
3. **Love needs:** affection, identification, belonging (family and friends).
4. **Esteem needs:** self-respect, presitge, success, and achievement.
5. **Self-Actualization needs:** self-fulfillment.

The relationships between these needs and how they influence behavior is illustrated in Figure 5-3.

Physiological Needs.   This group of needs encompasses the physiological motives discussed earlier in this chapter: food, water, oxygen, sleep, and so forth. Maslow felt that the physiological needs are the most prepotent of all needs. Thus, a starving man (need 1) is not likely to be interested in his unfinished paintings (need 5), or in how he is seen or esteemed by others (need 4), or even in whether he is breathing clean air (need 2). In a very poor society, people will be primarily concerned with lower-order physiological needs. The next meal normally takes precedence over social and psychological needs and will rule behavior in such a society. In an affluent society, where most people do not have to be concerned with

FIGURE 5-1 Eighteen Important Travel Motivations.

Education and Culture	Relaxation and Pleasure	Ethnic Heritage	Other
To see how people in other countries live, work, and play	To get away from everyday routine	To visit places one's family came from	Weather
To see particular sights			Health
	To have a good time	To visit places one's family or friends have gone to	Sports
To gain a better understanding of what goes on in the news	To achieve some sort of sexual or romantic experience		Economy
			Adventure
To attend special events			One-upmanship
			Conformity
			Participation in history
			Sociology, a desire to get to know the world

Source: John A. Thomas, "What Makes People Travel," *ASTA Travel News* (August, 1964), pp. 64-65.

FIGURE 5-2   Examples of twelve types of appeals.

Types of Potentially Rewarding Experience	Potential Type of Reward			
	Rational	*Sensory*	*Social*	*Ego-Satisfying*
Direct-Result Experience	Northwest: fastest way to the Orient	Arrive relaxed and refreshed	Pleasant people await you in Mexico	Virginia is for lovers
In-Use Experience	You'll never wait in line at Hyatt	Escape the winter's cold in warm sunny Florida	Fly the friendly skies of United	Equatoriana's attractive, multilingual stewardesses are chosen and trained to pamper and please you
Incidental-to-Use Experience	Coming or going nobody gets you out of the airport faster than Hertz	Just to dig a toe into the soft sand of Bermuda is to feel young	You'll want to be seen in Barbados	A tour for the discriminating traveler

Note: The peak of an earlier main class of wants must be passed before the next "higher" want can begin to assume a dominant role. Generally, as psychological development takes place, the number and variety of wants increases.

Source: David Krech, Richard S. Crutchfield, and Egerton L. Ballachey, *Individual in Society* (New York: McGraw-Hill Book Company, 1962), p. 77.

physiological needs because they are generally satisfied, behavior is governed by higher-order needs.

Safety Needs.   This group of needs refers to the individual's concern with physical survival, safety, and security. If these needs are unfulfilled, the individual's behavior can be totally dominated by her search for safety and protection. Again, she would not be likely to care about love, esteem, or self-actualization.

It is probably useful to take a broader view of safety needs beyond those pertaining simply to physical survival. For example, safety needs

FIGURE 5-3   Progressive changes in wants as described by Maslow.

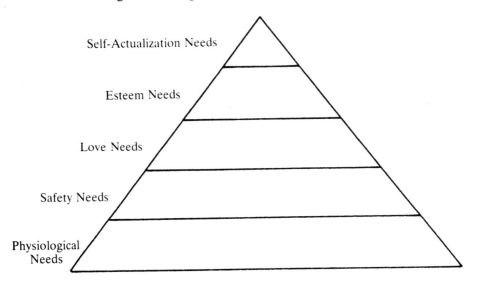

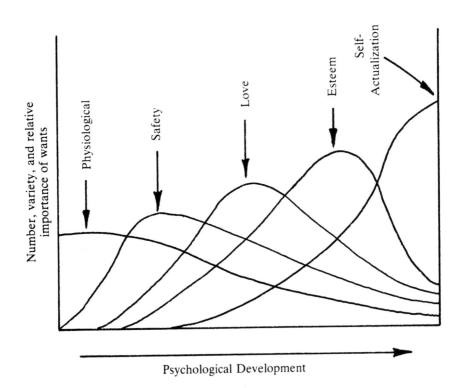

might also be thought to include a preference for familiar rather than unfamiliar things, for the known rather than the unknown. If this is true, then the individual caught in an unfamiliar environment would search for something familiar and known. In the area of travel, however, people often search for the unfamiliar, the unknown. What this clearly suggests is that the travel environment is indeed something different. People behave differently in the travel environment. Moreover, it is apparent that there is often some basic need at work when people travel — the need to explore the unfamiliar and the unknown — and that this need is not as strong when they are at home. This basic need to explore is not recognized in Maslow's hierarchy of needs model, a point discussed in depth later in this chapter.

Love Needs.   When a person has unfulfilled love needs, he may feel the absence of friends, a spouse, children, and a place in a group. At this stage, memberships in organizations may become important to the individual. Marriage and parenthood may also become urgent.

   Some authorities believe that the physiological and safety needs are generally met for most Americans, but that for many, the love needs are not fulfilled.[10] Mass advertising, it is felt, reflects this. Clothing, soap, perfumes, automobiles, deodorants, and countless other products are promoted with promises of a place in the group, love, affection, and sexual companionship. And travel advertisements — especially for destination areas — make the same kinds of appeals. The travel advertisement shown on page 154 illustrates this point.

Esteem Needs.   As love needs are more or less fulfilled, the needs for esteem, prestige, self-respect, reputation, and status emerge. Esteem needs also include the desire for achievement, independence, mastery, and self-confidence — in addition to recognition or appreciation and esteem in the eyes of others. These needs relate to the individual's feeling of usefulness in the world. Many products — clothes, automobiles, education, and travel are examples — help to satisfy these needs by serving as symbolic reflections of their fulfillment.

   It is quite clear that some forms of travel — to a foreign destination, for example — are very prestigious and help to satisfy an individual's need for esteem. Travel, in such cases, becomes a symbol of success and achievement. This is not to suggest that a trip to some highly prestigious foreign destination cannot be taken for other reasons. One of the several important motives for such a trip, however, might be to satisfy an unfulfilled need for esteem.

Self-Actualization Needs.   The need for self-actualization refers to the need to develop one's potentialities to their fullest. The exact meaning of this

FIGURE 5-4

Copyright © United Airlines, Chicago, IL. Reprinted by permission.

need will vary from person to person, because our potentialities differ. For some, self-actualization could mean achievement in literary or scientific fields. For others, it might mean leadership in politics or the community. For still others, it might mean merely living one's own life fully, without bowing to social conventions.

As Figure 5-3 indicated, the emergence of this higher-order need depends on the prior satisfaction of lower-order needs. Travel, however, might represent an exception. For many, travel provides an escape from everyday routine. This change prompts some travelers to alter their basic need structures. Unfulfilled lower-order needs temporarily lose their urgency while the individual travels away from home. Intellectual needs become important and take precedence over some of the lower-order needs. The traveler seeks to see things she has never seen, to better understand the world in which she lives, to satisfy aesthetic needs, and to learn. In fact, there may be a need to travel and explore the unknown that, for some people at certain times, is as basic and as powerful as their needs for safety, love, and esteem.

This is not to suggest that the motivation for all travel arises from the need for self-actualization. Indeed, there is reason to believe that this need motivates only a small number of travelers to any great extent. Many authorities, including Maslow himself, feel that few people experience self-actualization. There are signs, however, that more people are learning how to self-actualize as American society moves farther away from the Great Depression and Protestant Work Ethic and concerns itself more with the quality of life.

The Basic Intellectual Needs

The words *curiosity* and *exploration* need to be discussed when one asks why people travel. Maslow's theory of human motivation alludes only vaguely to human intellectual needs. Acquiring knowledge, for example, is presumed to be a technique for achieving the basic safety of an individual. Maslow's hierarchy of five basic needs, however, does not explain what can be termed the intellectual activities of women and men. Curiosity, exploration, the desire to learn, the desire to understand — these are sometimes pursued even at great cost to the individual's safety.

To explain man's intellectual activities, Maslow suggested that the hierarchy of five basic physiological-psychological needs coexist with a separate hierarchy of intellectual needs. These needs consist, first, of "a basic desire to know, to be aware of reality, to get the facts, to satisfy curiosity — or . . . 'to see rather than to be blind'."[11]

Even after we know, however — even after we have collected the facts, so to speak — we are impelled to know more, to discover the finer details. At the same time, says Maslow, we are impelled to organize the facts we have gathered, a process he describes as *the search for meaning*. This process can be explained by the desire to understand.

Thus, people exhibit two basic intellectual needs: first, the need to know, and, second, the need to understand. As with the physiological and psychological needs, the fulfillment of these two intellectual needs are governed by the principle of prepotency. In other words, the need to understand does not emerge and dominate behavior until the individual has satisfied her need to know by collecting some of the facts.

It should now be easy to see that travel can be explained in terms of both psychological and intellectual motives. Travel can provide us with a way of satisfying unfulfilled needs for love, esteem, and self-actualization. Travel to the right destination can provide us with prestige, recognition, self-respect, and status, along with feelings of independence, mastery, self-confidence, and of being all that we can become. Travel can assure us of a place in some important reference group. It can assure us of love, affection, and companionship.

Travel can also help to satisfy unfulfilled intellectual needs. It is a means of fulfilling the need to know, allowing us to collect facts about the world around us in a way that books or magazines cannot. Just reading about the world is not enough. We must see it for ourselves.

Intellectual Needs in the Travel Environment.   Based on the hierarchy of intellectual needs, an important distinction can be made between **sightseers** and **vacationers.** Sightseers can be defined as tourists. They tend to visit a variety of places during a single trip. Vacationers, on the other hand, usually visit one destination area and return home from there. This distinction between the two types of travelers suggests that sightseers may in large part be motivated by the prepotent intellectual need to know, while vacationers might be motivated moreso by the intellectual need to understand.

The sightseer is the traveler who takes the seventeen-day tour of twelve European countries. He collects countries, so to speak. Or, as Maslow might phrase it, he collects facts and impressions that satisfy his curiosity about Europe. Very likely the trip is the sightseer's first to Europe, and he scurries around collecting quick impressions of everything that his tour operator has determined he should see.

The vacationer, on the other hand, is the traveler who chooses to spend his seventeen days in a single destination area. It is likely that he collected quick impressions during a previous sightseeing tour through the area, found something intriguing about it, and decided to return for a longer stay at some later time. As Cohen observed, tourists tend to behave as sightseers primarily during their first visit to a particular destination area.[12]

The sightseer can be likened to the window shopper, who quickly passes through a store full of destinations. If he is fortunate enough to be able to return, the chances are greater that he will choose to spend his time more leisurely, exploring those countries or destination areas that most interested him. The first trip satisfies his need to know. It allows him to collect the facts, so to speak. On a subsequent trip, he is more likely to want to satisfy his need to understand. This will require more time and greater leisure if he is to absorb the detail necessary to understand a specific destination area, its people, and its culture.

All of this helps to explain why the individual who has spent a day or two sightseeing in each of a dozen different European countries is probably the best prospect for a long stay — a vacation — in just one of them at some later point. Accordingly, the travel marketer should learn which of those dozen countries most interested the traveler. On the other hand, the person who has never traveled abroad probably represents a poor prospect for the more leisurely vacation to a single destination. It is much more likely that he would be attracted to a tour package that exposes him to as many countries as possible during his journey abroad.

The Need to Explore

As suggested earlier, the words *curiosity* and *exploration* must be considered when explaining why people travel. Maslow, as we have seen, explains human curiosity in terms of the basic intellectual needs to know and understand — needs which are distinct from the basic physiological and psychological needs. Human curiosity can cause psychological tensions with which people must somehow cope. These tensions and how they are dealt with in a travel setting can help to explain a great deal about travel behavior.

According to one leading authority on the subject, curiosity and the urge to learn must be innate because they appear so soon after birth.[13] An infant demonstrates curiosity and begins to find outlets for it as soon as the necessary motor skills develop. And for many, curiosity continues to grow well into adulthood, and finds new and different kinds of outlets.

In 1960, H.G. Hasler and Francis Chichester raced each other across the Atlantic. A few years later, Chichester raced himself, or the ghosts of the masters of the old clipper ships, singlehanded around the world. Chichester is not alone in demonstrating that there is some motivation in man which prompts a few individuals to attempt things that seem almost purposeless. There is a little — and, in a few cases, a great amount — of Chichester in most of us. It is a deep need to explore ourselves and the world in which we live. For some, this need finds expression in mountain climbing, hang gliding, sky diving, scuba diving, ballooning, and sailing. For most of us, in one way or another, it finds expression in travel —

discovering new destinations, meeting different people, and understanding foreign cultures.

This deep need to explore appears to be a special characteristic which man shares with many other animals. Animals are most likely to explore when they have no emergencies with which to deal. There are times, however, when the urge to explore overrides what one would expect to be more urgent considerations. A hungry cat may spend time investigating some strange object before settling down to eat. A bird may approach a foreign and potentially threatening object at the risk of its life. Human beings, too, risk life and limb because of a desire to explore the unknown. Men and women have beggared themselves deliberately in order to build boats to cross an ocean for no apparent purpose. Travelers had always looked first for an easy pass before climbing a mountain, but there came a time when a few looked at great peaks and felt that they had to be climbed simply because they were there.

The Ulysses Factor. The word **adventure** is important to our discussion here. Webster defines it as an exciting and sometimes dangerous undertaking. An adventure is a stirring and often romantic experience, full of wonderful and extraordinary events that have no apparent practical value and that almost seem unreal.

Most healthy human beings have a taste for adventure in them. It sends little boys up trees. It makes people want to change jobs. It sends college students to Ft. Lauderdale each spring. It sends American tourists to Europe and European tourists to America. Without some sense of adventure, without some need to explore, we would not get much past our nurseries or our backyards.

Anderson calls the need for exploration and adventure the **Ulysses Factor.** It is a motivational force that prompts a person to do something which, for him, may be extraordinary, and which also contains some degree of risk. The action may seem utterly purposeless. But the fact of the matter is that this action, or some suitable replacement for it, is probably essential for the survival of the individual in a crowded, urbanized society.[14]

Ulysses is the hero of Homer's epic poem, *The Odyssey. The Odyssey* is an adventure story about Ulysses' travels over a ten-year period between the fall of Troy and his homecoming in Ithaca, an island off the west coast of Greece. In the story, Ulysses angers the sea god Poseidon, who sends a gale to wreck his ship and besets him with troubles on his journey home. He is befriended, however, by the goddess Athene, who in the end persuades Zeus, the most powerful of gods in the Greek pantheon, to permit him a safe homecoming.

An individual motivated by the Ulysses Factor strives to satisfy his curiosity about the world and about himself. Physical boundaries and limitations are not accepted as insurmountable. The need to explore is both a physical and an intellectual need. This is what is meant when it is said that travel appeals to the competitive instinct in us — especially travel to remote places that involves hardship or requires ingenuity. The Ulysses type is driven by a need to know, but his journeys cannot be solely intellectual. There must be some physical action. Thus, the Ulysses Factor represents an intellectual *and* a physical search for knowledge. The Ulysses type is driven by a deep need to experience the world with all his senses. He is not looking for anything in particular and is not greatly concerned with what he discovers. It is in this sense that he is a true explorer. He is interested in everything.

There would seem to be at least a bit of the Ulysses Factor motivating nearly all of us. Few of us, of course, would find it possible to accept all of the risks that Chichester faced when he sailed around the world, or the risks faced by various mountaineers, certain fliers, and others who force cars across roadless deserts. There are those who can tolerate only the most modest amounts of risk and uncertainty. Their travels are made relatively risk-free by travel agents, tour guides, standardized lodging chains, and Americanized hotels in foreign countries. Nevertheless, they still feel the need to leave the warmth and safety of their homes and to travel.

The Ulysses Factor is a powerful force driving us to seek adventure, whatever that may mean to us. At the same time, an opposing and equally powerful force motivates us to seek security and predictability in our lives. Shortly, we will turn to explaining how these two opposing forces are reconciled by the individual traveler. First, however, we need to develop more fully our understanding of why multiple motivations exist — indeed, why multiple motivations often have to exist before travel takes place.

Travel and the Puritan Ethic

Earlier we noted that travel and tourism as they are known today did not really begin to emerge until after World War II. Then, for the first time, masses of people had the time, money, and means to travel great distances away from home — and they needed no real excuse for travel other than the pleasure of travel itself. But many people, even today, are not far enough removed psychologically from the Great Depression or the Protestant Work Ethic to indulge without guilt in something that promises nothing but pleasure. As Walter Kerr points out in a masterfully written book titled *The Decline of Pleasure,* Americans and others living in affluent, industrialized western societies have a compulsive need to find a useful purpose for whatever they do. It seems, Kerr states, that nearly every activity must have a well-defined objective. Whether we are at home, at work, or at play, every activity is expected to achieve something, if only an arbitrary goal:

> The man who asks you to join him in a day's outing no longer suggests that you get into the car and see where the wheels go, poking at random into unexplored roadways. He picks a point on the map which may have no other charms than that it is a point on the map; he picks it because it is at a sufficient distance away to require him to maintain a certain relatively high speed; and, having decided upon a predetermined speed toward a predetermined goal, he is free to work steadily at the task. He may become angry at more casual drivers; he may sweat out the risk of passing other cars on curves; he may arrive at his destination with no real desire to do anything but get back into the car and forge his way home. But he will have invited you on a trip and taken one himself; he will have mileage on his speedometer to show for it.[15]

Kerr's final words are very instructive. We not only drive for mileage but, as travelers, we also collect postcards, bumper stickers, decals, suntans, motel towels, restaurant menus, and matchbooks. The domestic traveler collects national parks, museums, motel swimming pools, and states. The overseas traveler collects foreign countries. Both shoot rolls and rolls of film, and all of it proves — if only to the traveler himself — that he did not take a trip to nowhere.

The hold of the Puritan Ethic runs deeper, however. Historically, pleasure alone was not considered a fully legitimate reason for travel. Even today, it is clear that some people still believe that travel for its own sake is something of an idle whim. Thus, they search for more purposeful reasons to justify a trip. Although travel strictly for the pleasure it provides is more fully legitimate today, there are many forms of what can be called *partial tourism*, in which at least part of any given journey has useful purpose. Student travel is justified by formal or informal course work. Pilgrims justify their travels on religious grounds, although their travels may take them to many destinations of no religious significance. Conventioneers travel ostensibly to conduct business or to upgrade their professional skills. People travel to Florida to see a retired relative but spend as much time visiting Disney World.*

The point here is a simple and yet a very important one: all other things being equal, a journey is more likely to take place if it serves some instrumental purpose other than the pleasure that it promises. Although we deceive ourselves at times, it is a psychological game that helps us to rationalize the decision to travel. Moreover, it is a game that helps to remove any subconscious guilt that we may feel about doing something that promises to be a lot of fun.

---

*The fact that pleasure travel is more likely to take place if it can also serve a practical purpose was discussed in Chapter 4. The pleasure motive, it was stated, resides in the Child ego state of one's personality, while the instrumental or practical motive resides in the Parent ego state of the personality (see pages 130–131).

Most of us living in an affluent society should be free to squander our leisure, and we should be free of the necessity to invest it in some meaningful and useful endeavor. But we aren't. As Kerr explains, the utilitarian philosophy dictates that every activity should achieve *something*. We identify pleasure with profit, happiness with usefulness, and we work hard even at play to ensure that our leisure hours are productive hours. Often we suspect that we should feel guilty when a single hour or activity fails to yield something tangible and useful.

This utilitarian ethic dates from a time when people worked six days a week all year long just to survive. There was no time for idle pleasures. Today the situation has changed, but our values and attitudes still lag behind. Less than forty hours of work each week ensures not only the necessities of life but many of its luxuries as well, and the average worker is blessed with three or four weeks of paid vacation time each year, along with a dozen or so long weekends. Discretionary income and free time, however, are not spent easily by all. From the past we have inherited an attitude dictating that we spend our time and money wisely, and that even our leisure is productive. It is not surprising, therefore, that we often search for motives that will help to justify indulging in travel and other activities that we are tempted to consider idle pleasures. Nor is it surprising that we often choose not to travel — even when we have the time and money to do so — because the house, the yard, and our jobs all call out for more time and promise to yield something tangible, useful, and meaningful.

TRAVEL AS A SOURCE OF VARIETY

During a recent summer, three young school teachers, all women, spent part of their vacations traveling. We will refer to them here as Ann, Barbara, and Cathy. What follows is a brief description of their travels.

Case #1 Ann spent 17 days traveling through Europe with one of her close friends. Their trip was planned by a travel agent, who arranged for them to join a tour group that flew from Chicago to London during the fourth week of June. In London, the group stayed at the Sheraton Park Tower Hotel. After three days, they flew to Paris. During the next two weeks, the group kept up a busy schedule as it traveled from Paris to Geneva by train, and from there by bus to Milan, Genoa, and Rome. After three days in Rome, the group was flown to Madrid where it spent the last days of the journey. The group bid farewell to its tour guide, climbed aboard a 747, and returned home.

Case #2 Barbara also traveled to Europe, but she set out on her journey alone. From Chicago, she rode amtrak to New York and spent two days there waiting to board a Laker DC–10 for London. In London, she rented a car and spent five days driving leisurely through the Scottish Highlands and tried, without any luck, to locate a friend of her high school principal. She returned to London, flew to Amsterdam, purchased a Eurailpass, and spent the next two weeks getting on and off trains in Dusseldorf, Frankfurt, Stuttgart, and Zurich. She then flew to Paris, where she spent a week. Finally she returned to London and managed to catch a Laker jet back to New York.

Case #3   Cathy flew from Chicago to Seattle and on to Fairbanks, Alaska. She had registered for a six-week anthropology course at the University of Alaska, and after a three-day orientation at the university she flew to Bethel, Alaska. During the next five weeks, she traveled — mostly aboard small airplanes — to a number of Aleut Indian villages in southwestern Alaska. She usually spent three days in each village, living with the Aleuts and eating their food. She was scheduled to return home by air through Seattle, but on an impulse she accepted the invitation of a fellow student to return to Seattle by car via the Alaska Highway and the Inland Passage.

Obviously our three subjects took very different vacations. Two of them traveled to Europe, but one traveled alone and one traveled in a tour group with a friend. They visited different destinations. One itinerary was highly organized while the other was very flexible. The third vacation seems as much related to an educational purpose as to travel per se.

If we assume that each individual enjoyed her summer travels and returned home equally satisfied, how can we explain how they came to choose such different vacations? Obviously, the first answer to this question is that their vacations served different sets of needs. Accordingly, each woman acted on a different set of motivations. If motivations were the same for everyone, many of us would travel to the same destinations, do the same things, stay in the same types of hotels, and use the same kinds of transportation. There are, of course, wide individual differences in travel motivations and preferences — and these differences are what we now want to examine. We also want to identify and discuss one important common denominator that probably underlies all forms of pleasure travel.

The Need for Consistency

Psychologists have debated for years over whether people strive to maintain logical ("psychological") consistency in all areas of their lives or whether it is primarily inconsistency and variety that they strive for. Both sides of this argument can contribute to our understanding of the basic reasons why people travel and the kinds of decisions they make when they do.

The essential message of consistency theorists is that people nearly always seek balance, harmony, sameness, the absence of conflict, and predictability — what we refer to here as consistency. Any inconsistency is viewed as psychologically uncomfortable. In other words, inconsistency produces psychological tension in much the same way as thirst or hunger would. Under such circumstances, an individual is expected to seek out things which are predictable and consistent in order to reduce the tension.

In a travel setting, an individual, according to consistency theory, would visit only reasonably well-known vacation destinations like Disney World, Washington, D.C., and Yellowstone National Park. The overseas traveler would visit popular sites like England and France, or other well-known destinations in western Europe. The automobile vacationer would drive only on major Interstate highways and patronize only well-known chain restaurants like Howard Johnsons and McDonalds. And the traveler searching for consistency and predictability would patronize national lodging chains offering standardized accommodations and services. These well-known destinations, highways, restaurants, and lodging facilities offer the traveler consistency. Because they are predictable, there is little risk that the traveler will have an undesirable experience during his journey away from home.

It is clear that the concept of consistency can explain much of what happens in the travel environment. Disney World, Washington, D.C., Yellowstone National Park, and western European countries are among the most popular tourist destinations. Well-known chain restaurants are popular among away-from-home travelers. Most auto vacationers have a preference for standardized, brand-name chain motel accommodations, while many overseas travelers seek out American hotels in the foreign countries they visit.

In summary, consistency theory holds that people, expecting a particular thing to happen, do not want to be confronted by something unexpected. Freud argued that behavior is essentially directed toward reducing the type of psychological tension brought on by inconsistency. If people are threatened with the experience of inconsistency, they will take whatever action is necessary to ensure that the threat does not materialize. If they should be unfortunate enough to actually experience something unexpected, they will feel considerable discomfort and anxiety. From these feelings they will learn to be more careful to avoid inconsistency in the future. The traveler may learn, for example, to make advance reservations or to use a travel agent, to fly only on scheduled air carriers, or not to travel again.

The Need for Complexity

An equally plausible explanation of a great deal of human behavior and motivation — and also much of what happens in the travel environment — is referred to as complexity theory. The essence of complexity theory is that novelty, unexpectedness, change, and unpredictability — what we refer to here as complexity — are pursued because they are inherently satisfying. One of the leading authorities in this field, Salvatore Maddi of the University of Chicago, states that life is much too complex to be properly lived and understood through a reliance on easy consistencies. To insist, he says, that behavior can be explained largely in terms of the need for consistency is to trivialize life unnecessarily. To suggest that the pursuit of consistency is the major psychological activity in life is to underestimate people. One cannot ignore the fact, says Maddi, that consistency theory fails to explain how people cope with the unpleasant experience of boredom.[16]

In a travel setting an individual, according to complexity theory, would visit destinations that he had never visited previously. He might choose to drive on back roads and to patronize local eating spots instead of popular chain restaurants. He might decide to take a cruise ship to the Caribbean rather than fly. And he might choose to patronize independent lodging facilities instead of brand-name chains offering standardized or Americanized accommodations and services. To the traveler interested in avoiding the consistent and the predictable, the well-known highways and restaurants, the popular destinations, and the most-used lodging facilities offer too much consistency and predictability. They are boring. This traveler seeks a change from what he is accustomed to at home or what he experienced during his last vacation.

Clearly both concepts — consistency and complexity — can explain much of what happens in the travel environment. Although this may seem contradictory, we shall soon see that these concepts in combination can provide an invaluable perspective for understanding travel motivations and behavior. First, however, we need to examine in more detail the need for variety — a common denominator that probably underlies all forms of pleasure travel.

Travel as a Source of Variety

The central nervous system of a human being is designed to cope with the influx of stimulation. It will not perform at its best, however, when the stimulation is excessive or prolonged. At the same time, prolonged exposure to an inordinately monotonous environment is detrimental to a variety of psychological functions. Thus, a person will suffer when he is over-stimulated, and when he is under-stimulated as well. Prolonged overstimulation produces excessive tension and stress that can lead to ulcers, heart attacks, and premature death. Under-stimulation produces boredom which, if prolonged, can lead to depression, paranoia, hallucinations, and other genuine illnesses. Let us first examine the condition we call boredom.

A bored person is one who takes little interest in the small portion of the world in which he finds himself. His disinterest may be due to any number of factors. A useful way to describe his corner of the world is that it is too consistent — meaning that it is much too predictable for him. This predictability bores him because he is not stimulated. His environment presents no challenges. It is always the same.

Everyone, at one time or another, suffers from boredom. It is part of the human condition, so to speak. At one time or another our jobs, our acquaintances, the cities and homes in which we live, the schedules which govern our lives, the food we eat — all become boring because in some ways they grow too predictable, too consistent. Containing too few surprises, they fail to stimulate us. In response, we sometimes have to go out of our way to introduce variety into otherwise consistent and repetitive lives. At the one extreme, we change jobs, move to different cities, or walk away from boring marriages. Fortunately, less extreme measures usually provide the stimulation we seek. We search for new acquaintances, change our eating habits, and rearrange the living room furniture.

Judging from any number of indices, it is clear that travel represents one of the most popular forms of stimulation for people seeking to escape boredom. It provides a change of environment, calls for a change of pace, allows one to do something different.

Travel can also be described as an escape from reality. Joffre Dumazedier, a French social scientist, refers to travel as a kind of game that allows us to escape temporarily into a *secondary reality*. There we play for a time at being rich, primitive, or daringly brave — things which may be utterly at variance with our everyday lives.[17] Looked at in this way, it can also be said that travel allows us to live out our fantasies.

Two important points are emphasized here. One is that travel, more so than most other forms of escape, frees us from boredom because it allows us to leave behind the attitudinal and behavioral restrictions that prohibit us from "playing" at home. There are no jingling phone messages from callers reminding us to do this or that. There are no occupational roles to act out. There are no household jobs crying to be done.

Secondly, getting away from home brings welcomed variety to a consistent life. Life in an urbanized and industrialized society is especially predictable because it requires that so much be reduced to organized routine. The pace of life is sometimes much too hectic. The routine and the frenzy produce a monotonous tension that can only be reduced by seeking stimulation in the novel, the surprising, the unpredictable. Travel is an effective antidote to the stresses of urbanization and industrialization. In this sense, says Dumazedier, it is more a necessary escape than a voluntary exploration of the world in which we live. One might say that the need for variety is among the most basic of travel motivations.

Balancing Consistency and Complexity

It should be clear that well-adjusted people need a mixture of consistency and complexity in their lives. This need is usually fulfilled by seeking consistency in certain domains of experience and complexity in others. Consistency is generally provided by the organized routine that one finds at home and sometimes at work. Most people probably prefer a considerable amount of consistency and predictability at home. At home, the individual may prefer to eat at precisely the same time each day, and to prepare his eggs, steaks, and martinis always in the same way. He may prefer to mow his lawn at the same time each week, and he may like it best when his wife does not change her hair style or rearrange the living room furniture every week. Domestic life is built around routine and predictability. It is, in large part, consistent. It is psychologically comfortable to know that the daily newspaper will be delivered at five o'clock each afternoon, that the trash will be collected on the same day each week, and that the children will always be well-behaved and bring home good grades from school.

Work environments differ widely in the amount of consistency or complexity they provide. An assembly-line worker, for example, may find his work environment consistent to the point of boredom. He performs the same tasks five days a week, fifty weeks a year. This extreme consistency, as we shall see shortly, can have a tremendous influence on how he spends his leisure time. By contrast, the top-level corporate executive works in an environment of considerable unpredictability, variety, and complexity. No two work days are exactly alike. Each day presents problems that are unlike any others faced on other days. He deals with different people all the time, and may carry on his work in the office, in the factory, at home, in high-priced restaurants, in airplanes, and perhaps in a dozen cities throughout the world. The executive life can be a very stimulating, complex, and unpredictable one — and this can have a tremendous influence on how the executive spends his or her leisure time.

The amount of consistency and predictability that the homemaker finds in her life will depend on the extent to which her time and energy are spent on activities centered in and around her home and family. The homemaker who has few outside activities and interests generally leads a very consistent life, and it should not be surprising to learn that she normally has no strong preferences as to how she spends her leisure time. Research evidence clearly suggests that for this type of individual any change is a welcome one as long as it promises a change of scenery and some degree of complexity.

The consistency, predictability, and sameness that people find in their lives at home and at work must be balanced with some degree of complexity, unpredictability, novelty, and change. No individual can live sanely in a totally predictable world. At some point, the organized routine and consistency one finds at home and at work becomes boring. The individual needs the stimulation brought on by novelty and change to counter the psychological tension produced by boredom. The amount of novelty and change that is optimal will vary from one individual to another. Most of us welcome the unpredictable if it is not too drastic or demanding. But some require a great deal of novelty and change, while others can tolerate only minimal amounts. The need for variety as it exists in a population like that of the United States can probably best be described by the bell-shaped curve in Figure 5-5.*

In Figure 5-5, some of the major distinguishing values of people are identified and categorized on the basis of the need for variety in their lives.[18] These values include:

> **Adventure**   Those people with the strongest need for variety in their lives are adventuresome. They like to try new and different things, even at some risk.
>
> **Respect**   The next group of people, whose need for variety is not

FIGURE 5-5   Need for variety scale.

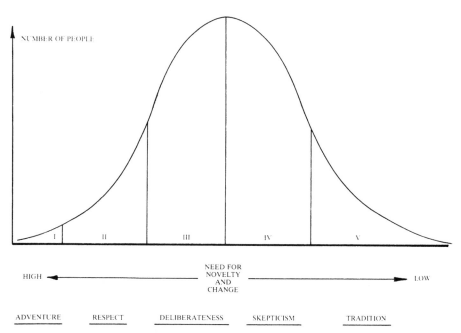

*After examining Figure 5-5, the reader may quickly recognize that there is some similarity between what is discussed here and in Chapter 4, where allocentric and psychocentric personalities are described.

quite as strong, attach a great deal of importance to respect. They, too, like to try new and different things, but they are more apt to exercise some discretion before they do so. They do not value adventure as much as they value the respect of others who admire them for the new and different things they do.

Deliberateness One of the dominant values of the third group of people is deliberateness. These people like to try new and different things before the average member of the social system, although they are rarely among the first to experiment with anything new and different. It is unlikely, for example, that they would be among the first to travel to novel destinations or to experiment with new leisure-time activities.

Skepticism People who value skepticism do not usually try anything new and different until the weight of majority opinion legitimizes it. These people may travel to places like Florida and California, but it will probably be some time before they would venture to destinations in eastern Europe, Asia, or Africa.

Tradition Those who place a high value on tradition are suspicious of anything new and different. The travels of people in this group are more likely to take them back to the same destinations year after year. They might return every year, for example, to the same lake cottage — indicating that they travel because of a need for change, rather than a need for novelty.

It can be said that the need for variety, which varies from one individual to another, is related to and perhaps even explained in part by each individual's personality and the values that he considers important. The person who values adventure and who is willing to assume the risks often associated with it is one who has a strong need for variety. Things do not have to be all that predictable for such an individual. In fact, there is a certain pleasure that comes from new and different experiences precisely because of the uncertainty involved. The person who avoids any real adventure does so in large part because he fears the unknown. Unpredictability, for this person, produces too much tension. It is too risky. This individual still experiences the tension brought on by boredom, but he reduces it by seeking out change, rather than novelty. Change presents much less risk than does novelty, a fact that influences the travel behavior of this type of individual. He is more likely to return to the same kinds of destinations when he travels, and from one year to the next his vacations are apt to "BE" nearly alike.

Figure 5-6 reproduces a questionnaire used by psychologists to estimate the strength of an individual's need for variety. It requires that an individual indicate for each of 31 pairs of statements that statement, A or B, with which he or she most strongly agrees. The more "A" statements that are selected, the stronger is the need for variety. Some pairs of statements apply only to males, and these are indicated by the letter "M". Other pairs of statements apply only to females, as indicated by the letter "F". Statements which apply both to males and females are indicated by "MF".

Figure 5-7 shows how an individual manages to achieve an optimal balance of the consistent and the complex in life. It illustrates that some things — for example, staying home all the time — can sometimes produce a great deal of psychological tension. To reduce psychological tension to an optimal level, the individual may decide to travel. The destination to which she travels, however, will have an influence on whether the tension is actually reduced to an optimal level. Travel to some set of destinations say, in Africa, might be too novel for this person, thereby producing a different kind of tension (i.e., panic). Travel to a destination like Hawaii, however, would probably be far less threatening. Hawaii would be novel and different, yet not so much that the prospect of what awaited her there would cause psychological discomfort. For another person, a trip to Hawaii might not be sufficient to achieve an optimal level of tension. It might not be novel or different enough, perhaps because the individual has already been there or else envisions it to be like other destinations she has visited in the past.

A destination is not the traveler's only potential source of consistency or complexity. We must also consider the stimulation potential of the hotels, the restaurants, modes of transportation, and activities that contribute to the total travel experience. Take, for example, an individual who seeks a moderate amount of novelty through travel. Suppose that for his first trip abroad he chooses, for one reason or another, to visit several eastern European countries. Such destinations are likely to represent a considerable amount of complexity and unpredictability for this traveler. He has few, if any, acquaintances who have visited these countries, and he is unfamiliar with the languages, cultures, and customs that he is likely to encounter during his travels. By itself, eastern Europe would seem to promise this individual too much complexity and unpredictability. But if he has chosen to travel there, it is likely that his decision would have been influenced by the promise of sufficient consistency and predictability derived from other factors. One such factor might be the prospect of traveling with a large group of other first-time visitors to eastern Europe and being escorted by a professional tour guide. The group itself might consist of a large number of acquaintances — of fellow workers, perhaps, or fellow members of a church group or fraternal organization — and this would promise even more consistency and security. In short, it would be highly unlikely that people like this individual would choose to travel to a strange destination area without the familiarity and support afforded by the company of a group of acquaintances.

In another instance, suppose that the Smith family spends a three-

---

FIGURE 5-6 Need for variety questionnaire.

---

1. (MF) A. I would like a job which would require a lot of traveling.
         B. I would prefer a job in one location.
2. (MF) A. I am invigorated by a brisk, cold day.
         B. I can't wait to get into the indoors on a cold day.
3. (M)   A. Although it is sometimes necessary, I usually dislike routine kinds of work.
         B. I find a certain pleasure in routine kinds of work.
4. (MF) A. I often wish I could be a mountain climber.
         B. I can't understand people who risk their necks climbing mountains.
5. (MF) A. I like some of the earthy body smells.
         B. I dislike all body odors.
6. (MF) A. I get bored seeing the same old faces.
         B. I like the comfortable familiarity of everyday friends.
7. (MF) A. I like to explore a strange city or section of town by myself, even if it means getting lost.
         B. I prefer a guide when I am in a place I don't know well.
8. (F)   A. I sometimes take different routes to a place I often go, just for variety's sake.
         B. I find the quickest and easiest route to a place and stick to it.
9. (MF) A. I would have preferred living in the unsettled days of our history.
         B. I would prefer living in an ideal society where everyone is safe, secure, and happy.
10. (MF) A. I sometimes like to do things that are a little frightening.
         B. A sensible person avoids activities that are dangerous.
11. (F) A. I like to try new foods that I have never tasted before.
         B. I order the dishes with which I am familiar, so as to avoid disappointment and unpleasantness.
12. (F) A. I sometimes like to drive very fast because I find it exciting.
         B. I can't stand riding with a person who likes to speed.
13. (M) A. If I were a salesman, I would prefer working on a commission if I had a chance to make more money than I could on a salary.
         B. If I were a salesman, I would prefer a straight salary, rather than the risk of making little or nothing on a commission basis.
14. (MF) A. I find people who disagree with my beliefs more stimulating than people who agree with me.
         B. I don't like to argue with people whose beliefs are sharply divergent from mine, since such arguments are never resolved.
15. (MF) A. I would like to take off on a trip with no preplanned or definite routes or timetables.
         B. When I go on a trip, I like to plan my route and timetable carefully.
16. (F) A. Most people spend entirely too much money on life insurance.
         B. Life insurance is something that no man can afford to be without.
17. (MF) A. I would like to learn to fly an airplane.
         B. I would not like to learn to fly an airplane.
18. (MF) A. I would like to have the experience of being hypnotized.
         B. I would not like to be hypnotized.

19. (MF) A. The most important goal of life is to live it to the fullest and experience as much of it as you can.
    B. The most important goal of life is to find peace and happiness.
20. (MF) A. I would like to try parachute jumping.
    B. I would never want to try jumping out of a plane.
21. (MF) A. I like to dive or jump right into a cold pool.
    B. I enter cold water gradually, giving myself time to get used to it.
22. (F) A. I like to listen to new and unusual kinds of music.
    B. I do not like the irregularity and discord of most modern music.
23. (MF) A. I prefer friends who are excitingly unpredictable.
    B. I prefer friends who are reliable and predictable.
24. (MF) A. When I go on vacation, I prefer the change of camping out.
    B. When I go on vacation, I prefer the comfort of a good room and bed.
25. (MF) A. I often find beauty in the clashing colors and irregular forms of modern paintings.
    B. The essence of good art is in its clarity, symmetry of form, and harmony of colors.
26. (F) A. The worst social sin is to be a bore.
    B. The worst social sin is to be rude.
27. (F) A. I wish I didn't have to waste so much of the day sleeping.
    B. I look forward to a good night of rest after a long day.
28. (MF) A. I prefer people who are emotionally expressive even if they are a bit unstable.
    B. I prefer people who are calm and even tempered.
29. (MF) A. A good painting should shock or jolt the senses.
    B. A good painting should give one a feeling of peace and security.
30. (M) A. When I feel discouraged, I recover by going out and doing something new and exciting.
    B. When I feel discouraged, I recover by relaxing and having some soothing diversion.
31. (MF) A. I would like to own and drive a motorcycle.
    B. People who ride motorcycles must have some kind of an unconscious need to hurt themselves.

Source: Adapted from: E.A. Kolin, L. Price, and I. Zoob, "Development of a Sensation-Seeking Scale," *Journal of Consulting Psychology,* Vol. 28 (1964), pp. 477-82.

week holiday each Christmas at a family-owned condominium in Ft. Lauderdale. Suppose that they have done this every year for the past six years and that they normally travel by car from their home in Maryland. For the seventh annual journey to Florida, the Smiths decide to travel to Florida by train. Why? One possible answer to this question is that, after six years, the journey itself has become boring. There is nothing new or different about hopping in the family car and driving for eighteen or twenty hours from Maryland to Florida. And the three weeks spent in Florida, though

FIGURE 5-7   Consistency — complexity and psychological tension.

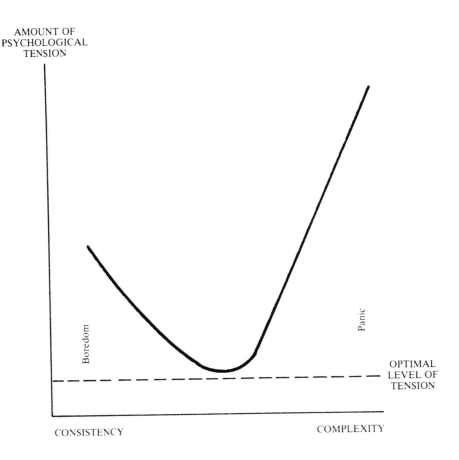

perhaps still very enjoyable, may have also become very predictable and consistent. In an effort to balance the increasing consistency of the holiday trip, the Smiths decide to change the annual routine by taking a train to Florida. The journey on Amtrak promises a change, an antidote to the increasing consistency and predictability of the annual journey south.

Alternatively, consider the business traveler who journeys frequently to the same destination and who regularly stays at the same hotel or motel when he arrives. It is a known fact, and one that is disturbing to many of the leading full-service lodging chains, that many business travelers consistently avoid eating their evening meals in the dining rooms of the hotels or motels at which they stay. There are perhaps several factors that explain this behavior, one of which is the traveler's need to balance consistency and complexity. He may be attracted to the Holiday Inn, the Sheraton, or the Hilton because they offer him consistency. He is more or less guaranteed a comfortable bed, pleasant surroundings, air conditioning that will not malfunction, and a good night's rest — things which are very important to him. For the very same reason, however, he may not be attracted to the hotel restaurant. It offers him consistency — but too much of it. The destination is already familiar to him. The airplane that brought him there was like every other airplane he flies. And the Holiday Inn or Hilton at which he stays is like nearly every other Holiday Inn or Hilton in which he has ever stayed. To counterbalance all of this sameness and consistency, the business traveler seeks out local restaurants where the atmosphere and the menus are at least slightly different.

Each of the examples discussed here helps to demonstrate how an individual traveler will mix sameness and predictability with novelty, change, and unpredictability in order to achieve an optimal balance of consistency and complexity. Figure 5-8 provides further support for the notion that each of five different elements of vacation travel offers a range of alternatives — from the very consistent to the very complex — that assist the traveler in blending consistency and complexity to achieve an optimal balance of the two. Figure 5-8 is based on a pilot study of the relationship between the individual's need for variety and his attitudes and preferences toward various destinations, modes of transportation, lodging alternatives, dining facilities, and leisure-time activities.[19] Research findings like these can help identify the types of travel and leisure-time services that can be blended together in order to appeal to the members of a particular group of travelers. It was found, for example, that the cruise ship represents a complex (novel) mode of transportation for many people — if only because they have much more experience with travel by airplane and automobile. The cruise line, therefore, must offer travel packages that include some measure of consistency — a mixture of activities and amenities that are not foreign to the traveler. These can include escorted shore excursions in well-known ports, movies, swimming pools, live entertainment, bridge tournaments, and a variety of other group and shipboard activities.

FIGURE 5-8   Consistency-complexity and five travel decisions.

Decision	*Consistency*		*Complexity*
Destination	Miami	Western Europe	Southeast Asia
Transportation	Air	Auto	Ship
Lodging	Holiday Inn	Best Western	Independent
Restaurant	Howard Johnson	Stouffers	Independent
Activities	Guided Tour	Deep Sea Fishing	Hang Gliding

Americans traveling overseas need to balance consistency and complexity. This need can be easily appealed to through advertising by a U.S. hotel organization. An ideal advertisement would tell Americans traveling abroad, through words and pictures, that their travels are likely to be disorienting (i.e., complex). The ad would then suggest that to counterbalance this complexity, they would be wise to plan on staying in the firm's overseas hotel properties, which offer a number of familiar and comforting "American" services: clean, spacious rooms; private baths; swimming pools; hamburgers; and English-speaking employees. In other words, the hotel firm can promise to balance the complexity of overseas travel with the consistency of many of the creature comforts Americans are used to at home.

The need to balance consistency with complexity also suggests that the standardized lodging chain should add novelty to the dining facilities at each of its hotels or motels. The restaurant's atmosphere should be unique, conveying a theme that plays perhaps upon some aspect of local history. Its menu should provide novelty with a representative sample of local fare. Of course, the traveler must be assured of dependable food, service, and cleanliness, and the chains should continue to maintain these qualities. Resorts should offer a variety of activities, from golf and tennis to backpacking or river rafting. Air carriers can counterbalance the routine and boredom that air travel represents for many travelers with distinctive inflight cuisine and entertainment.

The inclination to attain an optimal level of stimulation by mixing consistency and complexity raises an important question about the concept of close-to-home vacations. The close-to-home vacation became a popular idea during the Arab oil embargo of 1973. The prospect of even higher gasoline prices in the not-too-distant future has fostered the belief that close-to-home vacations will become even more popular in the years ahead. This prospect cannot be ignored — but neither can one ignore the motivations for travel that have been discussed throughout this chapter.

Some people travel merely for the change it provides. For them, a trip to the corner saloon or to the classroom of a local university is sufficient. A vacation at a motel ten miles away may be all that is needed. But for many others, change alone is not enough. They need, in addition, something entirely new — what we have called complexity. For many, this means a complete change of environment — sunshine and warm weather instead of cold weather and snow, mountains or seashore instead of an urban landscape, people who dress and speak differently and who eat different foods. For some, it is just the realization that they are a thousand miles away from the office and the kitchen sink.

As mentioned earlier, there is an attraction about the journey to a distant destination simply because it is far off. Psychologically, the far-off destination promises not only more change, but more of the novelty and variety that we need as well. For all of these reasons, we are led to suspect that — barring astronomical and unimaginable economic costs — close-to-home pleasure travel will never replace the desire to travel to far-off and exotic vacation destinations.

Finally, it is useful to consider that consistency and complexity are also sought through different domains of experience. It was suggested, for example, that the high-level business executive might experience a great deal of consistency at home and substantial complexity at work. His work may be so stimulating, however, that his need for the type of stimulation provided by pleasure travel and other leisure-time pursuits may be very weak. The tension experienced by this person might very well be the tension of over-stimulation that arises from his job. Accordingly, his leisure time is spent in search of rest and relaxation — which he can find very easily in the chaise lounge in his own backyard. This would explain why, as *Fortune* magazine reported, many successful business executives do not take much time off to travel for pleasure.[20] The high-level corporate executive will spend money on family pleasure travel, but one of his primary motivations for doing so is a sense of obligation to his family rather than a need to get away himself. This suggests that travel agents and others can promote substantial expenditures on family pleasure travel by appealing to the corporate executive's sense of obligation to his family. Such appeals could be made when he is planning a business trip to an attractive destination area.

SUMMARY

Why do people travel? Many of the usual answers to this question can seem rather superficial. They mask the deeper psychological reasons why people travel. What the traveler says are his motivations for traveling may be only reflections of deeper needs, needs which he himself does not understand, may not be aware of, or may not wish to articulate.

Motivation may be thought of as the ultimate driving force governing travel behavior. It would be a mistake, however, to assume that simple explanations of travel behavior are adequate. Travelers are usually striving to satisfy multiple needs. Moreover, people behave differently in a travel environment — in part because they are motivated by different needs that are not as strong when they are at home. In fact, some basic human needs seem to lose their potency temporarily when an individual travels away from home.

Leisure travelers are driven by curiosity, along with a basic need to explore themselves and the world in which they live. At the same time, leisure travelers are also influenced by a utilitarian ethic which dictates that one's leisure be productive. This pushes people to search for motives that will help to justify indulging in travel and other activities that they are tempted to consider idle pleasures.

A common denominator that probably underlies all forms of leisure travel is the need for variety. Boredom is part of the human condition, especially in urbanized and industrialized societies where so much of life is reduced to organized routine. Travel represents one of the most popular ways of escaping from boredom and the tension it produces. More so than most other forms of escape, travel permits us to leave behind the attitudinal and behavioral restrictions that prohibit us from "playing" at home. Travel frees us physically from many of the consistencies of everyday life and allows us to experience change, novelty, and unpredictability — what the psychologist calls complexity. There can be too much novelty, however, and a traveler must find ways of balancing consistency and complexity. A journey to a totally novel foreign destination, for example, would produce less psychological tension if the traveler stays at Americanized hotels and travels with a group of friends or acquaintances.

REFERENCES

[1] Travel Weekly, *What Makes Some People Travel and Others Stay at Home?* (New York: Travel Weekly, 1972), p. 3.

[2] Donald E. Lundberg, *The Tourist Business*, second edition (Boston: CBI Publishing Company, 1974), p. 118.

[3] Erik Cohen, "Who is a Tourist? — A Conceptual Clarification," *Sociological Review*, Vol. 22 (1974), pp. 527–55.

[4] William F. Prigge, "Environment and the Accommodations Industry," *The Travel Environment of the 70s*, Proceedings of the First Annual Conference (Salt Lake City: Travel Research Association, 1970), p. 7.

[5] Lundberg, *The Tourist Business*, p. 101.

[6] Robert W. McIntosh, *Tourism Principles, Practices, Philosophies*, second edition (Columbus, Ohio: Grid, Inc., 1977), p. 61.

[7] John C. Maloney, "Marketing Decisions and Attitude Research," in G.L. Baker, Jr., ed., *Effective Marketing Coordination* (Chicago: American Marketing Association, 1961), pp. 595-618.

[8] Philip Kotler, *Marketing Management*, second edition (Englewood Cliffs, New Jersey: Prentice-Hall, Inc., 1972), p. 678.

[9] Abraham Maslow, "A Theory of Human Motivation," *Psychological Review*, Vol. 50 (1943), pp. 370-96.

[10] Peter D. Bennett and Harold H. Kassarjian, *Consumer Behavior* (Englewood Cliffs, New Jersey: Prentice-Hall, Inc., 1972), p. 63.

[11] Maslow, "A Theory of Human Motivation," p. x.

[12] Cohen, "Who is a Tourist? . .," pp. 544-47.

[13] D.E. Berlyne, "Curiosity and Exploration," *Science*, Vol. 153 (1966), pp. 25-33 at p. 26.

[14] J.R.L. Anderson, *The Ulysses Factor* (New York: Harcourt Brace Johanovich, Inc., 1970), pp. 17-18.

[15] Walter Kerr, *The Decline of Pleasure* (New York: Simon and Schuster, 1962), p. 37.

[16] Salvatore R. Maddi, "The Pursuit of Consistency and Variety," in R.P. Abelson et al., eds., *Theories of Cognitive Consistency: A Sourcebook* (Skokie, Illinois: Rand McNally and Company, 1968), pp. 267-74 at p. 268.

[17] Joffre Dumazedier, *Toward a Society of Leisure* (New York: The Macmillan Company, 1967), p. x.

[18] The following is based on: Everett M. Rogers, *Diffusion of Innovations* (New York: The Free Press, 1962), p. 168.

[19] Edward J. Mayo and Lance P. Jarvis, "The Travel Decision Maker: In Search of Consistency or Variety?", a paper presented at the Tenth Annual Conference of the Travel Research Association, San Antonio, Texas (June 5, 1979).

[20] H.E. Meyer, "Boss Ought To Take More Time Off," *Fortune*, Vol. 89 (June, 1974), pp. 140-42.

QUESTIONS FOR DISCUSSION

1. As a result of the Industrial Revolution which began in the mid-1800s in the United States, two important things happened which led eventually to the emergence of tourism as it is known today. What were these two developments?
2. A traveler is usually striving to satisfy multiple needs. Think about your own last major vacation trip. How many different needs motivated the trip? What were they?
3. There are four different types of rewards or benefits that can be achieved through leisure travel and three different circumstances under which these rewards can be achieved. Thus, there might be as many as twelve different factors that would motivate travel, to a specific destination. Choose one of your favorite vacation destinations and see how many different advertising messages or themes you can think of that would stress different types of rewards and the different circumstances under which one might achieve them.
4. Identify six of your favorite ways of saving time when you travel.
5. When you are on a pleasure trip, do you ever feel the need to be productive? Discuss.
6. How would Freud explain the behavior of a tourist who always tried to make advance reservations at hotels and motels?
7. On one half of a sheet of paper, list a half-dozen or so things about one of your recent vacation trips that were consistent. On the other half of the paper, list a half-dozen or so things about the same trip that were complex. Then think about how you would change the trip if you were to take it again. Would you make it more or less consistent? Why?
8. How might a vacation trip to South America be promoted most effectively to people who have never been abroad?
9. How might leisure travel be sold to high-level business executives who indicate that they prefer to spend what time they do take off in their own backyards? What key motivating factor would have to be tapped?

6
ATTITUDES AND TRAVEL BEHAVIOR

In this chapter, we turn our attention to the influence that **attitudes** have on individual travel behavior. This chapter should make clear that each of the psychological factors already discussed — perception, learning, personality, and motivation — contribute to the development of attitudes. Attitudes, in turn, often have a very strong influence over actual behavior.

WHAT ARE ATTITUDES?

Almost everyone has an intuitive understanding of what attitudes are. We are often asked questions like:

"How do you feel about the job the President has done during the past year?"

"How would you feel about taking a train to the West Coast?"

"How well do you like Ramada Inns?"

"What do you think about gasoline prices?"

We understand from these kinds of questions that our attitudes are being sought. Our attitudes, in turn, indicate how we might act in a specific type of situation. Very often a second set of questions is implicit in the first:

"Who would you vote for in the next national election?"

"What is the likelihood of your buying tickets to ride on an Amtrak train?"

"Would you stop at a Ramada Inn or some other lodging facility when you are away from home?"

"What is the likelihood that you would take a long-distance automobile trip?"

Attitudes, then, are most commonly thought of as predispositions to act. More specifically, they are the individual's predisposition to evaluate some symbol, object, or aspect of the world in a favorable or unfavorable manner.

Almost everyone, regardless of the nature of their occupation, is concerned with the concept of attitudes. The politician and the political scientist are interested in attitudes regarding taxation, housing, military spending, and voter appeal. Business managers are concerned with employees' attitudes as they might affect morale and productivity. Marketing managers are interested in consumers' attitudes regarding competing brands of products and services. Attitudes are of great interest to everyone because they often serve as reliable indicators of how people will act under a given set of circumstances in many different walks of life.

This chapter consists of three major sections. In the first section, attitudes are more clearly defined and the way in which they form and develop is discussed. The second section provides an explanation of the travel decision-making process itself. The discussion should help clarify how attitudes affect the decisions made by travelers. The third section explains how attitudes change and how such changes can be stimulated to encourage changes in individual travel behavior.

THE CHARACTERISTICS OF ATTITUDE

Although attitudes vary from person to person and often seem wholly unalike, there are several characteristics that all attitudes have in common. All attitudes are composed of the same basic elements. The intensity and stability of all attitudes can be influenced by specific factors. And the impact of all attitudes on behavior tends to be greatest when they are anchored to strong personal values. A discussion of these main characteristics of attitudes will help us better understand how attitudes actually influence travel behavior.

Components of Attitude

Words such as **beliefs, opinions,** and **feelings** are often used interchangably with the word *attitude*. While an attitude is any predisposition, each of the above terms denotes a particular type of attitude, and they can be differentiated on the basis of their duration and intensity.

Beliefs are predispositions accepted as truth and supported by strong facts or other information. Most beliefs are reasonably permanent, but they may or may not be important. A consumer may have a strong belief about Motel 6 based on its low prices for reasonably comfortable accomodations," and a strong belief about Hertz because it "primarily rents Ford automobiles." These beliefs, however, may not be equally important, since low-priced accommodations may be of greater importance to the consumer than the make of car rented from Hertz.

Opinions differ from beliefs in that they are predispositions not based on certainty. There may be some facts involved, but they only suggest a conclusion that might be drawn by the individual. Opinions often but not always relate to current questions, and they are relatively easy to change. Easterners planning a trip to the West may be of the opinion that the scenery throughout Idaho is characterized by endless fields of potatoes, but a few facts and pictures could change a lot of minds.

Feelings are predispositions of an essentially emotional nature. They can be quite durable and sometimes very intense, but they are not always supported by relevant facts. The feeling that it is a woman's job to keep the children in line during a family vacation, is somewhat chauvenistic but, nevertheless, deeply entrenched in many minds.

We can think of feelings as sentiments, opinions as impressions, and beliefs as reflections of personal values. Attitudes, then, can be any type of conviction — weak or strong, long-lasting or temporary — based on fact or emotion.[1] It should also be remembered that an attitude can center on anything. We have attitudes toward people, places, events, situations, experiences, actions, ideas, concepts, objects, and ideals. All of these things are referred to as **attitude objects.** Attitudes can involve general categories such as presidents, magazines, motels, and skiing. Or specific objects such as *The New Yorker*, Holiday Inns, and Sun Valley. Anything about which we have information and feelings can be the focus of an attitude.

Psychologists often divide an attitude into three different components. As Figure 6-1 indicates, there is (1) a knowledge component, (2) a feeling component, and (3) a behavioral component.

The Knowledge Component refers to the beliefs or opinions that an individual holds about some aspect of an object in his personal environment (another person, a place, an event, an idea, a situation, an experience, etc.). These beliefs or opinions are based on tangible evidence perceived as fact by an individual at a given point in time. Someone may hold the opinion that New York City, for example, is an exciting, cosmopolitan, urban center with a tremendous range of things for a tourist to see and do. He may also hold the opinion that New York can be a dangerous place for a visitor, a place where one can lose his wallet and even his life if he

FIGURE 6-1   Components of attitudes.

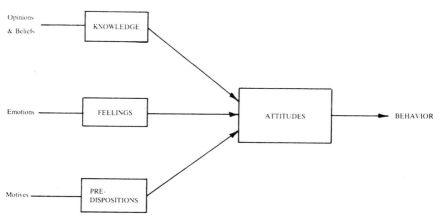

Source: Adapted from: Milton J. Rosenberg et al., *Attitude Organization and Change* (New Haven: Yale University Press, 1960), p. 3.

wanders into the wrong place at the wrong time. These are opinions and beliefs about various facets of New York City that serve as the foundation for the feelings one has about it.

The **Feeling Component** of an attitude refers to the emotional judgments an individual makes about an object. An object can be judged to be either good or bad. A person, for example, can be liked or disliked, loved or hated. Although someone may hold both positive and negative beliefs about New York, he may, on balance, conclude that he likes the city. It would not be possible to have feelings about some object without also holding some beliefs about it, for attitudinal feelings cannot exist in a vacuum. On the other hand, however, one can have a belief or opinion about some object that involves little or no emotion. Airline inflight meals might serve as an example. An individual who dines inflight could have no particular feelings about the food one way or another. The food, in his opinion, might be mediocre, but he will not join a conspiracy to have it improved or write letters about it, because, in his feelings about this particular object, he is indifferent.

The **Behavioral Component** of an attitude is usually defined by psychologists as the tendency to respond favorably or unfavorably to certain objects, persons, or situations. If a person holds a negative attitude toward an object, he is potentially ready to attack, destroy, punish, ignore, or otherwise reject the object and those things associated with it. If his attitude is positive, he is potentially ready to help, reward, purchase, or otherwise embrace it. The tendency to act toward some object, in either a negative or positive way, is referred to as a predisposition. There is, for example, some potential for a person with a positive attitude toward travel and also toward Miami to travel there some day. This person has a predisposition to travel and a predisposition to travel to Miami.

People generally try to harmonize the knowledge, feeling, and behavioral components of the attitudes they hold. If someone detests large crowds of people and believes that Disney World is overrun with them throughout the year, it is unlikely that he would have strong positive feelings about Disney World or that he would freely choose to travel there. His need to avoid large crowds and his belief that Disney World is almost always crowded would lead to a negative attitude and a predisposition to avoid this destination.

Despite this tendency toward consistency among the knowledge, feeling, and behavioral components of attitudes, examples of inconsistency abound. Perfect attitudinal and behavioral consistency would be uncharacteristic in human beings because nearly everyone, to one extent or another, is curious, whimsical, and impulsive — qualities that push us toward inconsistent behavior. Human beings are not like computers. We make decisions on the basis of imperfect information, sometimes we forget important information, and sometimes we do something different just for the sake of variety. It is not at all unusual to find that consumers who state their preference for a given brand will often buy another brand in an actual purchase situation.

This might happen on an automobile trip, for example, because the preferred lodging chain at a particular location had no vacancies. Or another chain may have offered a particularly attractive deal at that location (teens stay free). Alternatively, another lodging chain may have displayed its sign more prominently, attractively, and conveniently. A family member may have insisted that the travel party stay at the motel with the largest swimming pool. Or perhaps, out of curiosity and in the interest of variety, a non-preferred lodging chain was selected.

In a recent study of travel decision making in the lodging market, it was found that only 10 percent of those auto vacationers who normally stay in commercial lodging facilities regularly patronize chain motels and hotels about which they hold strong positive attitudes. In fact, 55 percent of the auto vacationers surveyed in this study regularly patronized chain motels and hotels about which they held less than positive attitudes.[2]

Similarly, despite a strong negative attitude toward Disney World, the individual described earlier might travel to Orlando just to "get it over with," because his children insist. It seems likely that the same sort of phenomenon would also affect, to a greater or lesser extent, the carrier-choice decisions of air travelers. A business traveler, for example, may express a strong liking for Continental Airlines but fly with Continental only infrequently because it does not serve many of the cities to which he travels, because it does not offer the most convenient departure times, or perhaps because someone else is making the carrier-choice decision for the traveler. A degree of inconsistency is an integral part of human nature, and while weak or negative attitudes predispose people to avoid some situations, they do not preclude them from making unexpected choices.

Another source of inconsistent behavior can arise when one must play two different social roles at the same time.[3] An excellent example of **role conflict** might occur when a business man takes his family along on a trip with the intention of combining business and pleasure. Tension can result from the need to play the roles of executive and family man simultaneously. The role conflict in this type of a situation can be lessened by splicing, so to speak, the business and pleasure parts of the journey together. A travel agent, for example, might encourage this person to finish his business in a specified amount of time, and to join his family afterwards at a place some distance away — in Palm Springs, for example, after two or three days of work in Los Angeles.

A final source of inconsistency between attitudes and behavior arises in what are called **forced compliance** situations. In this kind of situation, an individual who is predisposed to fly first class would be forced to comply with his company's policy that employees always fly coach.

Despite the numerous inconsistencies that exist between our attitudes and behavior, a knowledge of attitudes remains essential to an understanding of travel decisions. When the traveler is free to make a decision, it is generally believed that his behavior will be consistent with his attitudes. Where inconsistencies are found, it is generally because "something else" has entered the traveler's decision framework.

Intensity of Attitudes

In addition to the components of knowledge, feeling, and behavior, attitudes can also be characterized by their intensity. The intensity of an attitude refers to its strength — to its degree of favorability or unfavorability. Normally it is not enough to know merely that an attitude is positive or negative. Attitudes involve degrees of feeling, no matter which direction the attitude takes. Usually, the more intense an attitude, the more difficult it is to modify.

Stability of Attitudes

Another important characteristic of an attitude is its stability. The stability of an attitude pertains to its tendency to resist change over time. Many attitudes are stable only in the short run, although some grow stronger with time. There are at least three factors that encourage attitude stability.[4]

1. *Attitude Structure.*   Each person holds thousands of attitudes, some of which pertain to similar objects. A business traveler could have separate attitudes about each of several different major air carriers. And while these attitudes might not be exactly the same, most of them are likely to be very similar. As a general rule, people hold similar attitudes toward objects that they consider to be in the same class.

As psychologists view it, there is a certain structure to the groups of attitudes that we hold about similar objects, and this structure causes one attitude to reinforce others in the same group. Thus, an individual's attitude toward American Airlines will reinforce her attitude toward United and other major air carriers. Attitudes toward United Airlines and Hughes Air West, on the other hand, might be dissimilar if they are considered to belong in different categories. A traveling salesman's attitude toward, say, Motel 6 will to a degree reinforce his attitude toward Day's Inn and other economy motels.

The tendency to resist attitudinal change is particularly apparent when we view one attitude as part of a group. As one researcher discovered, a consumer's attitudes toward products or stores of the same type will affect each other if one of these attitudes is strengthened or weakened.[5] If a housewife's negative attitude toward a new cold-water detergent is weakened by new information, her attitude toward all other detergents in the same class may be changed in either of two ways: (1) the negative attitude toward all cold-water detergents in the same class may be weakened, or (2) she may disassociate the new product from all others in the same class. Both of these alternatives involve the often psychologically uncomfortable job of restructuring a whole group of attitudes. It is for this reason that people resist attitude changes. For the same reason, new information that might lead to a restructuring of attitudes is often distorted, forgotten, or both.

Suppose that a traveler has a very pleasant experience with Days Inns. He might then develop a stronger attitude toward all economy motels as a result. Alternatively, he might begin to view Days Inn in a different category, positioning it in the group reserved for full-service lodging chains like Holiday Inns and Ramada Inns.

This, in fact, is what Days Inns has tried to encourage with its national advertising, which attempts to position Days Inns in the full-service lodging chain category. This advertising will have succeeded if people disassociate Days Inns from economy lodging chains and attach the attitudes reserved for full-service lodging chains to Days Inns.

The same principle would support the wisdom of the institutional advertising program recently considered by the American Society of Travel Agents. If the overall image of travel agencies can be improved, then attitudes toward the individual agency will change as well.

2. *Cause-and-Effect Relationships.*   Our attitudes also tend to strengthen and

stabilize when we clearly perceive one thing as the direct cause of another. When this is the case, a consumer's attitudes toward a particular business, its personnel, and its products are likely to be the same. Exploratory research on this issue in the airline industry indicates that people develop attitudes toward air carriers on the basis of their dealings with inflight personnel, reservation agents, and other customer-contact employees. An airline with friendly, courteous, helpful, and competent employees is usually described in exactly these terms by its customers.[6] Furthermore, each encounter with an employee of this description will strengthen the customer's attitude toward the airline itself. The same principle applies to any travel industry firm and underscores the critical importance of effective customer-contact personnel.

3. Attitudinal Agreement. An attitude is also strengthened and stabilized when people find others who share the same attitude. People compare attitudes in the same way that they compare other things — and when we find others who agree with us, this reinforces and strengthens our own attitudes. In fact, we often search out people who share our attitudes. The power of attitudinal agreement is particularly evident in personal selling situations. If a sale is to take place, there must usually be attitudinal agreement between the salesperson and customer.

Instability of Attitudes

Although there is a tendency for some attitudes to remain stable, many of them do change later, if not sooner. There are at least three reasons why attitudes change:

1–Conflict of Attitudes. Because a person holds thousands of attitudes, it would be too much to expect complete consistency among all of them. A person with a very positive attitude toward riding motorcycles might prohibit his teenage children from owning or riding them. When attitudes are in conflict, a person may have to compromise. It is a question of which attitude is more important or powerful. In an example discussed earlier, it was suggested that a man might visit Disney World despite strong negative attitudes toward it. If so, he would seem to be acting against his attitude. We seldom really overstep our attitudes, however. What might actually happen in this example is that the father also has a favorable attitude toward his children, who want to visit Disney World. Holding both positive and negative attitudes, the father compromises in favor of pleasing his children. Similarly, a traveler may have very favorable attitudes toward foreign travel, but may never travel overseas because of an even stronger positive attitude toward thrift.

2–The Situation Affects Attitudes.   Because situations differ from one to another, there is considerable variation in our behavior. Although we expect behavior to reflect attitudes, it must be remembered that our behavior is influenced by many different factors, and not by attitudes alone. An individual's behavior is influenced not only by his background and experiences — which help shape his attitudes — but also by what he perceives in any given situation.

A consumer might purchase a motorhome because the salesman was very persuasive, because his family put great pressure on him, or because he did not take enough time to deliberate over the purchase. The consumer's attitude about motorhomes is not necessarily changed because he buys one; it is merely not as strong as other conflicting attitudes at the time of purchase. There are many situations, like this one, in which mitigating factors have a decisive influence on an individual's behavior. In addition, some attitudes may become lost, so to speak, among the thousands of others that we keep stored in our minds.

Allowance must also be made for simple impulse decisions. Sometimes decisions are made on the spur of the moment, without enough time for a relevant attitude to surface and influence one's judgment. Impulsive decision making appears to be prevalent when people travel.[7] This could be because, unless a decision involves hundreds of extra dollars, most travel decisions do not have many long-term repercussions. Vacations represent an escape from the anxieties of living according to organized routines that are cluttered with appointments, schedules, and long-term commitments and plans. This appears to be one of the attractions of automobile vacationing, which provides the individual with a maximum amount of flexibility.

Figure 6-2 indicates the extent to which auto vacationers purposely build flexibility into their travel plans. Flexibility and the freedom to make enroute impulse travel decisions are probably important to most pleasure

---

FIGURE 6-2   Unplanned decisions of auto vacationers.

73%	Do Not	Plan specific stop-over locations
61%	Do Not	Make advance motel/hotel reservations
50%	Do Not	Plan number of days to be spent at each location
49%	Do Not	Plan specific destinations
38%	Do Not	Plan approximate amount of money to be spent
22%	Do Not	Plan routes to be driven
80%	Do	Allow for unplanned side-trips
21%	Do	Allow for extending the duration of trips

Source: Edward J. Mayo, *Regional Travel Characteristics of the United States* (Bedford Park, Illinois: 3M National Advertising Company, 1973).

travelers. This suggests that it is wise for the professional travel planner to incorporate sufficient flexibility into the itineraries and travel plans they develop for their clients. It also underscores the potential power of advertising aimed at the enroute traveler to stimulate impulse decisions, be he traveling in his own automobile or via commercial carrier.

3–Traumatic Experiences.   Attitudes can change dramatically as a result of a traumatic experience involving a great deal of emotion. One's attitude toward air travel might change from positive to negative very quickly after a frightening emergency landing or a great deal of high-altitude turbulence. An attitude can be shaken by news of a commercial aircraft crash, or after being involved in an automobile accident. As a general rule, attitude changes that result from traumatic experiences are not believed to be as lasting as those that take place more slowly.

Attitudinal Importance

The degree of consistency between attitudes and behavior also depends on the **centrality** of the attitude. The centrality of an attitude refers to how strongly it is related to deep personal values — values rooted in an individual's concept of self. Strong, professed personal commitments are likely to generate more consistent patterns of behavior than non-central or peripheral attitudes. People sometimes hold strong attitudes toward God, family, democracy, self-reliance, and any number of other things. These attitudes are usually extremely stable, so much so that a person's behavior is sometimes perfectly predictable when one of these attitudes is involved. In addition, any attempt to change central, value-oriented attitudes is likely to fail, because it would amount to a substantial restructuring of an individual's self-concept — the very person he is.

Social anchoring is concerned with the extent to which our personal attitudes about objects and events are widely held or "anchored" within the groups to which we belong. Somewhat related to the concept of centrality, the concept of social anchoring can also indicate the degree to which attitudes and behavior will correspond. The various groups to which we belong — church groups, fraternal organizations, civic and business organizations, neighborhoods, and other formal and informal organizations — have a significant impact on attitude formation and change. When a given attitude is well-anchored, then behavior, especially when it is subject to the scrutiny of a group that is important to us, is likely to be very consistent with the attitude itself.

Most people's attitudes toward travel play a central role in their value systems, and it is clear that these attitudes are socially anchored as well. Positive attitudes toward travel are reinforced by the attitudes of friends, relatives, neighbors, fellow workers, other acquaintances, and society at large.

A number of research studies have assessed the intensity of attitudes toward travel in general and have found them strong. Given an imaginary windfall of $1,000 and directed to spend it on something, a majority of people in one study stated that they would spend it either on household improvements or on travel. Few people stated that they would spend the unexpected money on a new automobile, home entertainment, new clothes, hobbies, or local recreation.[8]

Strong general attitudes toward travel are also evidenced by the fact that during recent downturns in the economy, people have generally reacted by changing the style or scope of their travel activities, rather than cutting out travel altogether. One segment of the travel market — presumably a higher income segment — does not change its travel behavior in any way at all. Others have reacted to economic downturns by becoming more receptive to package deals and economy accommodations.[9] More adults have come to view annual vacation travel not as a luxury but as an essential part of life — something on which time and money will be spent almost no matter what.[10] A recent survey of single adults between the ages of 18 and 40 disclosed that 82 percent of these people rated travel as either a moderately or highly important part of their lives.[11] Clearly, the ability and freedom to travel is valued highly by most Americans, and by people of other industrialized nations as well. Changing these attitudes — the beliefs and feelings people have about the value of travel — would seem to be next to impossible for people who are accustomed to traveling wide and far and freely. This is one of the most perplexing aspects of the problem created by fuel shortages.

The motivation to travel is so strong that it is hard to imagine that people would ever willingly stop. A long-term solution is not immediately clear. Much, of course, depends on the development of new crude oil reserves, alternative sources of energy, and other factors. Meanwhile, important questions need to be answered. Will people find substitute activities that satisfy their travel needs? This seems unlikely for the most part, since the attitude toward travel has strong psychological and social roots. Will they adjust their travel behavior so that close-to-home, one-tank-of-gas journeys replace the two-week auto vacation sightseeing tour? Perhaps — if there is no other choice. Will people turn more and more to buses, trains, and planes? Possibly — if there is no other choice and if the costs are perceived as reasonable. Will people rearrange their priorities, spending a greater percentage of their disposable incomes on travel? Quite possibly they would, given the high value placed on travel. But this also depends on real income growth and inflation. Might people exert more pressure on government leaders to develop long-term solutions to the energy problems that affect travel? At the moment, this is much more likely than a wholesale restructuring of our attitudes. To discount the value and importance that most of us attach to travel would be difficult indeed.

ATTITUDES AND TRAVEL DECISION-MAKING

We turn our attention now to a detailed explanation of the travel decision-making process itself. Our discussion should help clarify how attitudes affect the decisions that travelers make. By examining the relationship between attitudes and travel decisions, we are in a better position to understand how an attitude change can be encouraged and thereby lead to a change in behavior. This topic should be of great interest to those who market and sell travel services.

Travel decision-making, like most other forms of consumer decision-making, often requires that the decision maker pass through a number of mental steps. One way of viewing this decision-making process is illustrated in Figure 6-3. This conceptual model of the relationship between attitude and behavior shows that an attitude consists of beliefs and opinions, feelings, and a predisposition to act. The attitude, once formed, leads to either a preference or an intention to act in a certain way. Social factors of one type or another can now have a significant impact on whether this preference or intention actually leads to specific behavior. For example, the minister who would like to spend some time and money in Las Vegas some day may never do so if he fears that his congregation would not approve. He may prefer to visit Las Vegas, but his intention to do so would be affected by social factors — the disapproval of his congregation. We see from this example that there can be a very important difference between preferences and intentions.

The Attitude–Preference Relationship

Attitudes can be a very good predictor of preferences, if not of actual behavior. In fact, dozens of research studies confirm a very strong predictive relationship between the two. There are at least two features of attitude that have significant bearing on the attitude–preference relationship. Again, we are reminded that our interest in this section — and, indeed, for the rest of this chapter — is on clearly understanding how attitudes can influence travel behavior and how travel behavior can be influenced by encouraging appropriate changes in attitudes.

The Complexity of an Attitude.   The complexity of an attitude refers to the amount and variety of information possessed by the individual regarding the attitude object. Attitudes toward travelers' checks, for example, are

FIGURE 6-3   Attitudes and the travel decision-making process.

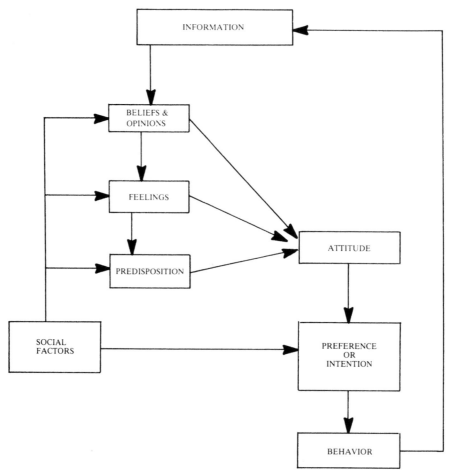

likely to be quite simple. Perhaps the only distinguishing characteristic between competing checks is the number of places where they are sold and where losses and thefts can be reported so that replacement checks can be issued. As a result, people may see little or no difference between American Express travelers' checks and those sold by First National City Bank.

Attitudes toward specific air carriers are also likely to be quite simple. People perceive very little difference between major competing airlines except, as discussed in Chapter 2, in terms of departure times, nonstop services, and other time conveniences. Attitudes toward air travel in general, however, are certainly more complex than toward individual air carriers. Attitudes about air travel — and other forms of transportation as well —involve speed, convenience, time savings, cost, status, prestige, inflight services, baggage handling, and more. Attitudes toward different types of lodging facilities can also be complex, involving rates, location, cleanliness, parking facilities, restaurants and lounges, room size, comfort, and swimming pools. Perhaps the most complex attitudes that a traveler might hold are those regarding foreign destination areas. These attitudes would involve beliefs, opinions, and feelings about unfamiliar hotels, unusual foods, foreign people, strange languages, different traditions, and guided tours — at the very least.

Complex attitudes are ordinarily more difficult to change than simple ones. If a traveler has a negative attitude toward travelers' checks simply because she does not think they are really necessary, it may be possible to change her attitude by demonstrating the terrible inconvenience of losing one's wallet when away from home. A person with a negative attitude toward foreign travel, however, will not quickly change her disposition. Even if she is persuaded that the cost of foreign travel is not unreasonable, she might still maintain her negative attitude on the basis of such factors as strange cultural surroundings, different food and traditions, or inexperience with guided tours. To change a negative attitude toward foreign travel would require that numerous negative elements of the overall attitude be changed.

The Salience of an Attribute.   Earlier in this chapter, the overall intensity or strength of an attitude was identified as one of its key characteristics. This characteristic is important because of the fact that it is normally much more difficult to change a strong attitude than a weaker one. Actually, any existing attitude toward an object is really composed of a number of attitudes toward each of the specific attributes of that object. For example, an overall attitude toward Sea Pines Plantation is a composite of attitudes toward the features one would expect to find there — scenic beauty, accommodations, food, recreational facilities, entertainment, and other amenities, as well as their price and perceived value. Each of these specific attributes, in turn, has what the psychologist would call its own **salience.** *This means that the relative importance of each attribute varies.* Climate, comfort, and golf courses could be very important to one visitor at Sea Pines. Yet another individual might consider tennis courts, beaches, and prices the most salient attributes. Thus, the salience of different attributes of a resort area will vary from one individual to another.

Salience also varies for the same individual depending on his or her needs and goals. Price, for example, may be a very salient attribute when one is deciding whether or not to fly the family to its vacation destination. In choosing a motel, however, price may not be an especially salient attribute. This is because airline tickets can represent a difference of hundreds of dollars relative to the cost of driving to some far-off destination. The price of a motel room, on the other hand, may not be as important if it represents only a few extra dollars a night over the course of a vacation.

The golf courses at Sea Pines would be more salient for golf enthusiasts than tennis buffs. Entertainment facilities might be important to people visiting a city like New Orleans, but not — in an extreme example — to a camper spending a week in the Great Smoky Mountains.

The salience of an attribute, as we will see shortly, usually plays a key role in the decision making of the individual traveler. Furthermore, the relative salience of each attribute involved in an overall attitude helps us to identify the primary benefits sought by a traveler when he makes a particular travel decision.

Benefits is a key word in our discussion of travel behavior and decision making. People do not go to Florida because of the sunshine *per se*. Rather, they go to Florida because of what the sunshine does for them — because it gives them a tan, it warms them, and it makes them feel good. People do not stay in luxury hotels because of king-size beds and atrium-like lobbies *per se*. Rather, they stay in luxury hotels because they sleep more comfortably in their beds and because the spacious, plant-filled lobbies somehow make them feel better.

Products and services are not purchased for their own sake, but for their ability to provide certain benefits. Therefore, those responsible for marketing and selling travel must understand buyer behavior in terms of the benefits sought by consumers. They should be able to identify the salient attributes associated with their service, along with the key benefits their service can offer in any given buying situation. This is no easy task, however, because of several factors.[12]

First, as indicated earlier, individuals differ in the relative importance they attach to each attribute. Second, there are times when what we would normally consider an important attribute will actually not be very salient. The safety record of a major air carrier serves as an example. Air travelers are naturally concerned with an air carrier's safety record, but presumably the safety records of all major carriers are more or less the same. Thus, safety would not be a salient attribute when one is choosing an airline to fly between two major cities. Similarly, when one chooses from among four or five major motels at a particular location, cleanliness would probably not be a salient attribute.

Identifying the salient attributes of a product can be difficult when people *do not know* why they prefer one product over another. And, even when they do, people will not always "truthfully" indicate the salient benefits to someone else. Instead, some people will recite the socially acceptable or expected reasons for their selections. These factors can make the marketing and selling of travel-related products especially difficult.

Seeking Benefits in the Travel Environment   The problem of determining salient attributes has led marketing researchers to develop reliable methods of identifying, from among all possible benefits, the most outstanding attributes that any given service provides.

One recent study, for example, examined the travel attitudes of a large sample of American Express customers from the Northeast, all of them frequent travelers outside of the United States. Each participant was presented with ten vacation travel benefits[13] and asked to consider the prospect of vacationing in nine different destination areas. The destinations included Florida, California, Mexico, Hawaii, the Bahamas, Jamaica, Puerto Rico, the Virgin Islands, and Barbados. All participants had, at one time or another, visited these destinations, and all preferred warm, sunny climates. These people were asked to indicate the relative importance of the ten vacation travel benefits in terms of their influence on the choice of a vacation destination. In this way, the most salient features of a particular destination type were identified.

The results of this study are presented in Figure 6-4. It shows that scenic beauty, the attitudes of local inhabitants, and suitable accommodations are the benefits most highly valued by travelers when they consider a vacation to one of the nine destinations in question. Rest and relaxation, cultural interests, cuisine, and the availability of facilities for water sports were found to be the second most valued cluster of benefits sought. The third and least valued cluster of benefits included the availability of entertainment (specifically night life), shopping, and golf and tennis facilities.

The reader should be cautious when interpreting the findings shown in Figure 6-4, because they reflect the attitudes of only one particular group. The people involved tended to be middle-aged, well-educated, and middle-to-high income earners. One would logically expect that saliency would vary according to demographic characteristics, wants, and needs. In a recent study of the vacation travel attitudes of young singles, for example, night life was given much more consideration in the choice of vacation destinations.[14] And in a study of the lodging decisions of automobile vacationers, it was found that the most salient benefits were moderate prices, proximity to the tourist's main route, and parking convenience.[15] Those traveling by automobile for business purposes, however, did not attach as much importance to moderate prices.[16]

Clearly, the saliency of an attribute will vary with individual needs and goals, and from one group of people to another. This does not lessen the need for those who market and sell travel services to make judgments about what the most salient benefits sought in any given situation may be. This, in fact, is the essence of good marketing and effective salesmanship.

The Development of Travel Preferences

The traveler's perception of salient benefits leads to the development of travel preferences. These, in turn, lead to intentions that directly influence the traveler's decision-making process. We have seen how each attribute

FIGURE 6-4   Relative importance of ten travel benefits.

RELATIVE IMPORTANCE OF TEN
TRAVEL BENEFITS (ATTRIBUTES)

OF GREAT
IMPORTANCE

   1.7 Scenic Beauty
   1.9 Pleasant Attitudes of "Natives"
   2.0 Suitable Accommodations

   2.6 Rest and Relaxation
   2.7 Cultural Interest
   2.8 Cuisine
   3.1 Water Sports

   4.1 Shopping Facilities
   4.4 Entertainment

OF LITTLE
IMPORTANCE

   5.1 Golfing and Tennis

Source: Jonathan N. Goodrich, "Benefit Bundle Analysis: An Empirical Analysis of International Travelers," *Journal of Travel Research*, Vol. 16 (Fall, 1977), pp. 6-9.

Note: Values are based on responses to a seven-point rating scale where 1 equals great importance and where 7 equals little importance. Thus, lower values indicate greater importance.

or potential benefit associated with a particular set of objects (e.g., desti-nation areas) is of varying importance (i.e., salience) to the traveler. As the individual considers alternative destination areas, he estimates *how much of each benefit* a particular destination would deliver if he were to travel there. This process is illustrated in Figure 6-5.

According to the study upon which Figure 6-5 is based, the typical American Express customer discussed earlier felt that Florida and Hawaii promised the most in benefits associated with water sports. Figure 6-5 also indicates that Florida, California, and Hawaii were judged more likely to deliver the benefits desired by golf and tennis enthusiasts. In terms of historical and cultural benefits, Mexico was perceived to have the greatest promise. The reader should examine Figure 6-5 to see how the typical American Express customer evaluated each of the nine destination areas in terms of its ability to deliver all ten benefits.

These evaluations, together with the salience of each benefit, enables the traveler to determine which destination would best satisfy his needs and goals. There are a number of ways in which this process is believed to work. One of the most popular is illustrated in Figure 6-6.

Figure 6-6 is a conceptual diagram of the process by which preferences are developed. Figures 6-7A and 6-7B provide numerical estimates that allow us to compare the relative preference of our typical American Express customer for visiting California and Florida.

These numerical estimates are computed by multiplying each item in Column 1 (relative importance of benefit) by each item in Column 2 (per-ceived potential to deliver the benefit). The results (see Column 3) are then added (see Total) to achieve a number that represents the customer's rel-ative preference for California and Florida.

Remember that the values assigned to the relative importance of a benefit and to the perceived potential of a destination to deliver that benefit are values assigned by the individual traveler. Also note that, in both figures, the attributes under consideration are the same. What differs are the travelers' perceptions of these two destination areas as to their ability to provide each benefit.

As Figures 6-7A and 6-7B indicate, the relative preference for California as a destination area is represented by the number 61.66, while the relative preference for Florida is represented by the number 68.01. In this study where a lower number means a greater preference, the typical American Express customer from the Northeast indicates a preference for vacationing in California over Florida. All other things being equal, the individual would be more likely to visit California on a future vacation journey.

Most people do not make travel decisions with the mathematical pre-cision that we have done here. If the individual's goal is to make a selection that will best satisfy his needs and provide him with desired benefits, then something like the process described will take place. Decisions might be

FIGURE 6-5 Perceived ability to deliver a specific travel benefit.

1. Florida	1.3	1.7	4.0	3.2	3.4	2.0	2.1	2.5	2.0	1.5
2. California	1.9	2.0	2.4	1.8	2.6	2.5	1.9	2.1	1.8	1.5
3. Mexico	2.7	4.0	1.9	2.1	3.4	2.6	3.0	3.9	3.3	2.7
4. Jamaica	1.8	3.0	3.7	2.2	3.6	2.2	4.0	3.5	3.1	2.5
5. The Virgin Islands	2.0	3.4	4.3	2.5	3.3	2.1	3.6	3.5	3.6	2.7
6. Puerto Rico	2.1	2.8	3.5	2.6	3.4	2.4	3.5	3.4	2.8	2.4
7. The Bahamas	1.6	2.7	4.3	2.6	3.5	2.1	3.6	3.2	2.7	2.1
8. Barbados	2.3	3.6	4.2	2.6	3.2	2.2	4.0	3.3	3.6	2.7
9. Hawaii	1.3	2.2	2.9	1.5	2.0	1.8	2.6	2.4	2.0	1.5

Note: Lower values indicate greater potential to deliver specific travel benefit.
Source: Jonathan N. Goodrich, "The Relationship between Preferences for and Perceptions of Vacation Destinations: Application of a Choice Model," *Journal of Travel Research*, Vol. 17 (Fall, 1978), pp. 8-13.

FIGURE 6-6 The development of preferences.

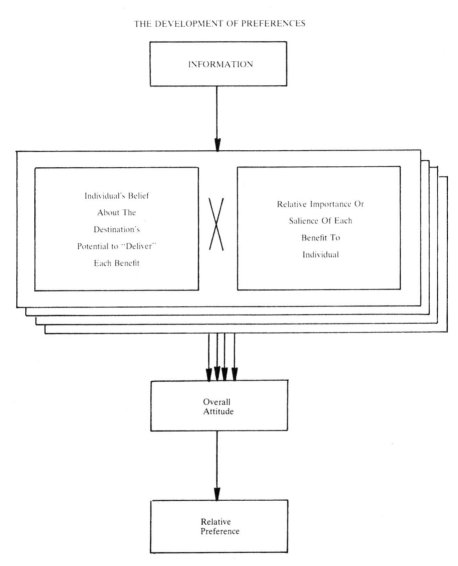

THE DEVELOPMENT OF PREFERENCES

INFORMATION

Individual's Belief About The Destination's Potential to "Deliver" Each Benefit

Relative Importance Or Salience Of Each Benefit To Individual

Overall Attitude

Relative Preference

made over an extended period of time or could be made in a matter of minutes, or even seconds. The evaluations and judgments that influence their decisions could be arrived at carefully and consciously, or subjectively and subconsciously. The important point is that travel decisions like the choice of destination — and many other choices as well —are made with the same factors in mind. We have computed these factors — the travel benefit, its relative importance, and the potential of a destination to deliver

FIGURE 6-7A   Computation of relative preference rating: California.

Attribute	(1) Relative Importance of Benefit	(2) Perceived Potential to Deliver the Benefit	(3) Column 1 X Column 2
Availability of water sports facilities	3.1	1.9	5.89
Golfing/tennis facilities	5.1	2.0	10.20
Historical and cultural attractions	2.7	2.4	6.48
Scenic beauty	1.7	1.8	3.06
Pleasant attitudes of natives	1.9	2.6	4.94
Opportunity to rest and relax	2.6	2.5	6.50
Shopping facilities	4.1	1.9	7.79
Cuisine	2.8	2.1	5.88
Entertainment	4.4	1.8	7.92
Suitable accommodations	2.0	1.5	3.00
		TOTAL	61.66

Note: *Values in columns (1) and (2) are averages based on American Express customers' attitude salience and perceptions of a destination's ability to deliver a particular benefit. Values are based on responses to a seven-point rating scale where 1 = great importance or great potential and where 7 = little importance or little potential. Thus, lower values indicate either greater salience or greater potential.

Source: Jonathan N. Goodrich, "The Relationship between Preferences for and Perceptions of Vacation Destinations: Application of a Choice Model," *Journal of Travel Research,* Vol. 17 (Fall, 1978), pp. 8-13.

it — mathematically. The majority of people weigh these factors psychologically to arrive at their travel decisions. The importance of the decision-making process described here is that it clearly identifies how those who market and sell travel services can influence potential travelers.

Influencing Travel Decisions

This last point can be illustrated by directing the reader's attention to Figure 6-8. Using the same group of American Express customers described

---

FIGURE 6-7B   Computation of relative preference rating: Florida.

Attribute	*(1)* *Relative Importance of Benefit*	*(2)* *Perceived Potential to Deliver the Benefit*	*(3)* *Column 1 X Column 2*
Availability of water sports facilities	3.1	1.3	4.03
Golfing/tennis facilities	5.1	1.7	8.67
Historical and cultural attractions	2.7	4.0	10.80
Scenic beauty	1.7	3.2	5.44
Pleasant attitudes of natives	1.9	3.4	6.46
Opportunity to rest and relax	2.6	2.0	5.20
Shopping facilities	4.1	2.1	8.61
Cuisine	2.8	2.5	7.00
Entertainment	4.4	2.0	8.80
Suitable accommodations	2.0	1.5	3.00
		TOTAL	68.01

Note: Values in columns (1) and (2) are averages based on American Express customers' attitude salience and perceptions of a destination's ability to deliver a particular benefit. Values are based on responses to a seven-point rating scale where 1 = great importance or great potential and where 7 = little importance or little potential. Thus, lower values indicate either greater salience or greater potential.

Source: Jonathan N. Goodrich, "The Relationship between Preferences for and Perceptions of Vacation Destinations: Application of a Choice Model," *Journal of Travel Research,* Vol. 17 (Fall, 1978), pp. 8-13.

earlier, the information in this figure shows the relative order of their preferences for the nine destination areas already discussed. The preference score for each destination listed was arrived at in the same way that was explained before, and the destinations are listed in the order in which they were preferred by the typical American Express customer.

The ranking of the destination areas in Figure 6-8 clearly shows that the top three areas — California, Hawaii, and Florida — are preferred more strongly than any of the other six destinations. Obviously, those responsible for marketing a destination such as The Bahamas would prefer to see their area ranked more highly than it is. Furthermore, travel agents and others who sell travel would stand to earn greater commissions by

---

FIGURE 6-8   Relative preferences for destination areas.

Rank	Destination Area	Preference Score
1	California	61.5
2	Hawaii	63.3
3	Florida	68.3
4	The Bahamas	86.9
5	Puerto Rico	88.4
6	Jamaica	89.2
7	Mexico	93.9
8	The Virgin Islands	97.0
9	Barbados	99.8

Source: Jonathan N. Goodrich, "The Relationship between Preferences for and Perceptions of Vacation Destinations: Application of a Choice Model," *Journal of Travel Research,* Vol. 17 (Fall, 1978), pp. 8-13.

FIGURE 6-9   Comparison of perceived ability to deliver benefits: Florida vs The Bahamas.

| Benefit | Greater Benefit | |
	Florida	The Bahamas
Scenery	X	X
Pleasant attitudes of natives	X	
Suitable accommodations	X	
Rest and relaxation	X	
Historical and cultural attrac- tions	X	
Cuisine	X	
Water sports	X	
Shopping	X	
Entertainment	X	
Golf/tennis	X	

Source: Jonathan N. Goodrich, "The Relationship between Preferences for and Perceptions of Vacation Destinations: Application of a Choice Model," *Journal of Travel Research,* Vol. 17 (Fall, 1978), pp. 8-13.

---

selling travel to some of the lower-ranked but more distant destinations. The decision-making process we have discussed identifies two ways in which these tasks — effectively marketing an area like The Bahamas, and selling travel to such a destination instead of, say, Florida — can be accomplished. Figure 6-9, which extracts information from Figure 6-8 for Florida and The Bahamas, will help to demonstrate these two approaches.

The information in Figure 6-9 shows that people perceive Florida as able to offer more of the benefits desired by the typical American Express customer described earlier. The Bahamas, in fact, are perceived to offer only better scenery. Despite the relative importance of this benefit, Florida is far and away the more attractive destination because it is perceived to offer more in terms of virtually all other benefits. To improve its competitive position relative to Florida, those responsible for marketing The Bahamas as a vacation destination would either have to (1) improve the image of The Bahamas (in terms of its perceived ability to deliver other benefits besides scenery) or (2) attempt to increase the relative importance to the traveler of those benefits where it is, in fact, competitive with or superior to Florida.

If an improved image is the goal, we must first know why Florida is perceived to offer more than The Bahamas in the way of certain benefits. We might consider suitable accommodations, for example. Florida certainly offers a larger number and presumably a greater diversity of lodging facilities to the prospective traveler. But does this really answer the question? Being both a foreign and also a smaller destination than Florida might have something to do with the image of accommodations in The Bahamas. But why, we should ask, would this affect the overall attractiveness of The Bahamas? Might it have something to do with the perceived absence of well-known American chain hotels in The Bahamas? If this is part of the problem, it can be corrected by publicizing the presence of hotel chains like Sheraton and Loews in The Bahamas. The problem can also be alleviated by using pictures in advertising and in promotional brochures to demonstrate the quality and comfort of both chain and independent hotels in The Bahamas.

The same types of questions must be asked about other benefits that are important to prospective travelers. Why is it, for example, that Florida is perceived to offer more in the way of opportunities for rest and relaxation, water sports activities, and entertainment? In those cases where it is judged that The Bahamas should be considered able to deliver as much or more in the way of specific benefits, advertising and other forms of promotion can be used to establish a clearer perception of the destination.

The Bahama's most recent advertising has been built around the theme, "It's better in the Bahamas," and stresses sandy beaches, privacy, and solitude (see Figure 6-10). This advertising may effectively communicate benefits that are of importance to some segments of the market, but to the American Express customer residing in the Northeast, such information is unlikely to alter current attitudes toward this destination. This is because the ad does not stress the attractiveness of The Bahamas in terms of the benefits that are most valued by these individuals — benefits for which The Bahamas are seen as inferior to some other destination areas. For this segment, advertising might stress the unspoiled beauty of The Bahamas, the British Colonial friendliness of the islanders, outstanding

FIGURE 6-10

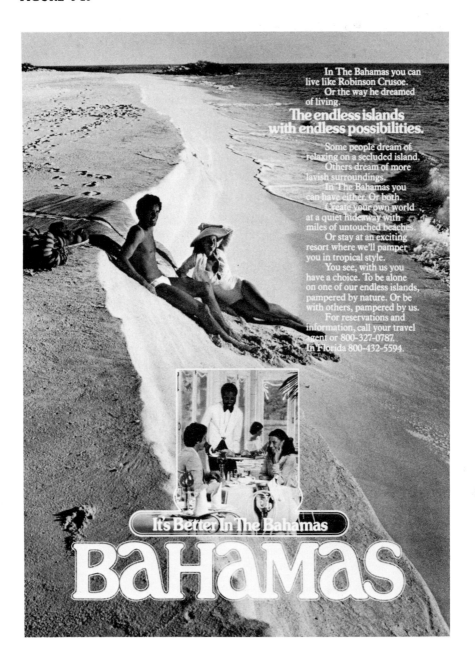

Copyright © Bahamas Ministry of Tourism, Nassau, NP, Bahamas. Reprinted by permission.

water sports opportunities, the facilities for tennis and golf, and — perhaps most important — the islands' casinos.

A second approach that the decision-making process suggests as a way of influencing travel decisions is to increase the relative importance of selected benefits. Instead of — or in addition to — attempting to improve the image of a destination in terms of its ability to deliver a specific benefit, the relative importance of a specific benefit can sometimes be changed. As Figure 6-11 suggests, Florida is at a competitive disadvantage to California in terms of scenic beauty. One approach to increasing the preference for Florida compared to California is to alter travelers' perceptions of Florida's scenic attractiveness, perhaps by acquainting them with scenery they were previously unfamiliar with. Alternatively, however, an attempt can be made to encourage travelers to consider the opportunity for rest and relaxation much more important than they presently do. This is one benefit where Florida is perceived to have a competitive advantage. If the relative importance of this benefit can be raised, then the overall attractiveness of Florida compared to California will increase.

Let us summarize to this point. The overall attractiveness to the traveler of a destination area has a great deal to do with the specific benefits that are desired by travelers and with the capability of the destination to deliver them. Figure 6-6 indicates that the attractiveness of a destination

$$\text{ATTRACTIVENESS} = \left(\begin{array}{c} \text{Relative Importance of} \\ \text{Individual Benefit} \end{array} \right) \times \left(\begin{array}{c} \text{Perceived Ability of Destination} \\ \text{to Deliver Individual Benefit} \end{array} \right)$$

FIGURE 6-11   Comparison of perceived ability to deliver benefits: California vs Florida.

| | Greater Benefit | |
Benefit	California	Florida
Scenery	X	
Pleasant attitudes of natives	X	
Suitable accommodations	-	-
Rest and relaxation		X
Historical and cultural attractions	X	
Cuisine	X	
Water sports		X
Shopping	X	
Entertainment	X	
Golf/tennis		X

Source: Jonathan N. Goodrich, "The Relationship between Preferences for and Perceptions of Vacation Destinations: Application of a Choice Model," *Journal of Travel Research,* Vol. 17 (Fall, 1978), pp. 8-13.

Overall attractiveness of the destination is a composite of this calculation for all relevant benefits.

Thus, to improve a destination's attractiveness, efforts must be made (1) to improve the perceived image of the destination in terms of its ability to deliver a specific benefit and/or (2) to change the relative importance of specific benefits. A third type of effort that can be made to improve the relative preference for a particular destination is to discount a competitive destination's ability to deliver a specific benefit; this, of course, is a variation of the first option.

Figure 6-12 reproduces an advertisement promoting travel to Brazil, and it demonstrates how each of the three approaches to attitude change identified above can be used. The advertisement attempts to create an image of Brazil as a place where the traveler can get real value for his dollars, and where he is treated as more than "just another tourist." It also attempts to increase the *importance* of greater dollar values and a warm, friendly atmosphere. Finally, the advertisement tries to show that the most popular foreign destination — Europe — does not deliver these benefits to today's pleasure traveler. These same approaches could be used just as effectively in a one-to-one personal sales situation where the sales person attempts to interest a client in a vacation journey to a far-off destination.

Although most of the discussion here focuses on destination-choice decisions, it should be emphasized that the travel decision-making process described applies as well to decisions concerning modes of transportation, airlines, car rental firms, hotels and motels, travel agencies, restaurants, vacation activities, and tourist attractions. In each of these instances, alternatives are evaluated on the basis of their ability to deliver benefits of importance to the traveler.

Becoming a Viable Alternative

We have seen that the travel decision maker chooses among alternatives in terms of the benefits he seeks, and by evaluating each alternative in terms of its potential to deliver the most salient of these benefits. So far, however, our discussion has assumed a given set of alternatives for the traveler to evaluate. We have not yet explained how a given alternative becomes just that; e.g., how Mexico, and not Canada, becomes a possible destination choice; how Holiday Inn comes to be considered an alternative, while Chalet Suisse does not; or how TWA, instead of Iberia, comes to be included among the alternatives for travel to Madrid.

Figure 6-13 will help us understand the process by which a travel alternative comes to be considered among those which are more carefully evaluated as a possible solution to a specific travel problem. Again, we can think in terms of travel problems such as these: Which airline is most likely

FIGURE 6-12

The dollar is shrinking fast. So your clients are beginning to look around for new vacation destinations. That's why so many of them are asking you about Brazil. Exciting, exotic Brazil. It's a place where their money still means something. A place that really makes your clients feel warm and welcome. That's our Brazil. And we want every one of your clients to feel like they belong here.

We want them to dance the samba with us. Feel the warmth of our sun, our people, our culture. We want them to do more than see our country. We want them to feel it. Varig's Brazil. An unusual vacation experience. And that's exactly why so many of your clients want to come here.

✹VARIG
Brazilian Airlines
Largest privately owned airline outside the United States.

WHY A LOT OF PEOPLE ARE NOW TAKING THEIR VACATIONS IN BRAZIL.

Copyright © Jonas Berger Associates, New York, NY. Reprinted by permission.

FIGURE 6-13   Categorizing alternative solutions.

CATEGORIZING ALTERNATIVE
SOLUTIONS

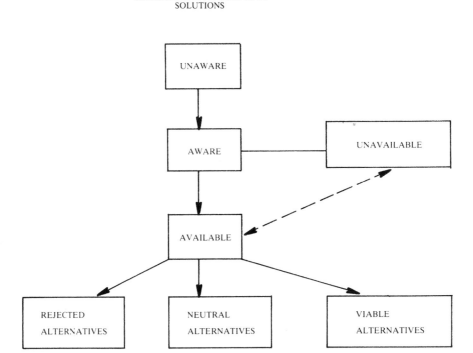

to get me to my destination at the time I want to get there? At which vacation destination will I have the best time? From which car rental firm should I rent an automobile? What should I do when I get to my destination? Where should I eat when I am away from home? At what motels should I stay along the way? Should I fly or drive to my destination, or perhaps use some other mode of transportation? What cruise line should I seek passage from? Should I use a travel agent? And which travel agent should I use?

Figure 6-13 shows that there are at least three stages through which an alternative must pass before it becomes viable.

1–Awareness.   No alternative can be seriously considered until the decision maker becomes aware of it as a potential choice. For example, before Puerto Vallarta can be evaluated as a Mexican vacation destination, the traveler must be aware that it exists and that it welcomes and can accommodate tourists. Before Amtrak can be seriously considered as a way of getting from Chicago to San Francisco, the traveler must be aware that Amtrak can transport a person between these two cities.

2–Availability. Having become aware of a particular alternative, the travel decision maker must judge whether it is actually available to him. This might be thought of in terms of the traveler's ability to afford the alternative. Can he afford, for example, the time and money for a trip to the South Seas? Or the time and money to take Amtrak to San Francisco? Can he afford to fly the Concorde to Paris? Other factors too, can influence whether a particular travel decision alternative is available to a traveler. Can he obtain a visa to travel to the People's Republic of China? Or reservations on Amtrak during the height of the summer travel season? Will passage on a popular cruise ship be available during the winter holiday season? Can he obtain tickets to the Super Bowl?

As Figure 6-13 illustrates, what are perceived as unavailable alternatives can, over time, become available. And the reverse is also true. Guadaloupe only became available as a tourist destination after hotel facilities were built and air routes established in the 1960s. Europe became available to a larger segment of the mass travel market in the United States when trans-Atlantic air fares were lowered in the mid-1970s. Political considerations have often played a role in whether a destination country could be considered available to American tourists. The People's Republic of China became available as a destination following the opening of diplomatic relations between China and the United States. Travel to Cuba, on the other hand, remained largely unavailable for many years following Castro's rise to power and the breaking of diplomatic relations with the United States.

3–Preliminary Screening. After becoming aware of a particular alternative, and judging whether the alternative is available, the travel decision maker makes a preliminary determination as to whether the alternative should be evaluated more carefully, according to the development-of-preference process we described earlier. This third step can be thought of as a preliminary screening.

Some alternatives may be immediately rejected in the early screening process. Upon reflection, the traveler quickly develops a negative attitude toward these alternatives for the travel purpose in mind. Other alternatives will not be immediately rejected, nor will they be immediately accepted: a neutral attitude — neither positive nor negative — will be formed. Still other possible choices will be placed into a mental category that we can label **viable alternatives.** This means that there is some chance that the decision maker, after further evaluation, will decide in favor of one of these alternatives.

Rejected destinations: those destinations which the travel decision maker immediately rejects are quickly perceived to have no potential to satisfy his goals and objectives. Someone who dislikes guns and the killing of wild game would immediately reject a hunting expedition to Alaska as a way to spend a vacation. Someone who detests snow and cold weather would immediately reject a winter trip to Canada. And someone who has a deep fear of flying would immediately reject an airplane trip anywhere.

Neutral Alternatives: those alternatives for which the traveler forms no immediate attitudes can be thought of as neutral, pending the gathering of more information about them or inputs from other family members. A young traveler might consider Amtrak an available transportation alternative but form no immediate positive or negative attitude about it until several important questions are answered. How long would a journey from Chicago to San Francisco take? What kind of sleeping accommodations are available? And how much extra do they cost? These are not unusual concerns for travelers who have no personal experience with rail travel.

Viable Alternatives: those alternatives in the viable alternatives category will be subjected to a more detailed evaluation. The traveler's preliminary judgment about these alternatives is that they appear to have some potential to satisfy his personal travel objectives. The goal of those responsible for marketing and selling various travel products and services is to have their products and services included in this mental category. It is from the alternatives in this mental category that the decision maker will make his selection, after evaluating each according to the decision-making process described earlier.

How Alternatives Become Viable.   How an alternative comes into the viable alternatives category is of particular interest to us here, because those who market and sell travel can influence this process.

Consumer behavior theorists generally agree that the number of viable alternatives is normally just a fraction of the total that one is aware of and that one considers available. Research in psychology and consumer behavior suggests that the number of alternatives that are placed in the viable category is purposely limited.[17] This kind of limitation helps the decision maker to transform a very complex decision involving a large number of alternatives into a more manageable decision involving a smaller number. In other words, the decision maker simplifies decision making by reducing the number of alternatives to be carefully evaluated.[18]

In the area of travel decision making, it has been estimated that a large majority of travelers carefully consider no more than seven alternatives when selecting a destination for one vacation journey.[19] Of course, the actual number of viable alternatives will vary from one individual to another. For example, people who have had recent overseas travel experiences will, for subsequent vacation travel, consider a larger number of viable alternative destinations than those who have not previously traveled overseas. One research study also found that Americans generally consider a larger number of viable alternative destinations than travelers in Finland[20] — suggesting, perhaps, that destination planning is strongly influenced by national borders and also by real income levels. In studies of the destination-choice decisions of automobile vacationers in two southeastern states, it has been found that the typical traveler gives serious consideration to traveling in just three different destination states.[21]

It is important to note that an individual's choice of viable alternatives is not necessarily permanent. A list of available and viable options will normally change over time, and from one situation to another. Staying in a Hyatt Regency hotel may not be a viable alternative when an individual is spending his own money for overnight accommodations, but it may very well be when someone else is footing the bill. After visiting Aruba, an individual may not give serious consideration to returning there on a future vacation — even though he had an enjoyable time when he was there. Viable alternatives can be added to, narrowed, or changed. And, as we will see, the travel marketer can play an important role in these modifications.

We should also keep in mind that the decision maker's search for solutions to various travel problems does not always occur after these problems have been recognized and identified. Our discussion may seem to imply that an individual arrives at his travel decisions in a neat, sequential sort of way; this, however, is not always the case.

Some travel decisions are made on the basis of information that has been gathered in the past and remembered with no particular travel problem in mind. When an individual decides, for example, on a travel destination, he may choose from among destinations that have already been placed in the viable category. In fact, the decision to take a trip and the decision about where to go may very well be made simultaneously; that is, the two decisions may actually be the same one. Recognizing that some travel decisions are made in this way, travel marketers can attempt to position their products in the category of viable alternatives even before a particular travel problem is consciously recognized by the traveler. Some travel advertisers, for example, place great importance on advertising that reaches potential travelers immediately prior to heavy travel seasons. Off-season advertising, meanwhile, is aimed at stimulating off-season business. In fact, however, off-season advertising may have as great an impact in July as it has in the off-season months of winter.

Finally, there is reason to speculate that the number of viable travel alternatives seriously evaluated by a traveler will vary depending on the specific travel decision itself. Consumer behavior theory holds that as the importance of a decision — and the risk of making a "bad" decision — increases, the number of viable alternatives seriously considered by an individual will decrease.[22] Let us consider some examples.

Suppose that an individual intends to select a new travel agency. Until he has had some experience with at least one agency, the person is not likely to perceive much difference among those that operate in his area. Thus, we would expect that the number of viable alternatives would be relatively large, while the actual selection in this particular case might be made solely on the basis of one salient factor: locational convenience.

In a second example, where the choice of destination is involved, the number of viable alternatives seems likely to be relatively small. The research findings cited earlier would support this. One reason why viable alternative destinations would be fewer in number is that, unlike travel agencies, most vacation destinations can be very unique. No two are exactly alike, and most differ somewhat even from their closest competitors.

Our discussion of travel alternatives is of no small consequence to the travel industry, because the number of viable alternatives customarily evaluated by the typical traveler defines the type of competitive environment in which travel marketers operate. In the airline business, for example, scheduling conveniences and on-time performance would have to be considered key determinants of success in the marketplace. In the retail travel agency field, locational convenience would have to be considered a key factor in capturing new business. Vacation destination marketing, on the other hand, faces a very different problem. Because multiple salient factors influence the success of a destination area in attracting pleasure travelers, the marketing and selling effort must be budgeted to give appropriate weight to each factor.

Finally, the reader is once more reminded that a major task facing those who market and sell travel is to make travelers aware of their particular services, to encourage travelers to perceive these services as being available, and to encourage the development of favorable attitudes toward these services so that travelers will view them as viable alternative solutions to travel problems. We are now ready to consider how the travel marketer can stimulate this kind of mental activity on the part of the consumer-traveler.

INFLUENCING TRAVEL BEHAVIOR THROUGH ATTITUDE CHANGE

With a deeper understanding of attitudes and the decision-making process, it is now possible to identify strategies that can effectively influence potential travelers. These strategies can be grouped into five different categories.

Change The Product

Often, the easiest way to get people to change their attitudes toward a particular product is to change the product itself — and then make sure that, in one way or another, consumers find out about the change. As one authority suggests, even a slight change in the product may quite literally be ten times more effective than all other advertising and promotion efforts. Physical changes in the product are readily observable to people, and sellers do not have to rely on persuasive promotional devices to convince consumers that a difference exists.[23] From time to time, for example, an automobile manufacturer dramatically changes the styling of the cars it produces so that a greater number of people will come to think positively about the manufacturer's product.

There are many things a seller can change besides the physical product. This is fortunate for those who sell travel products because, unlike the automobile, the travel product is essentially an invisible one, and any changes in the service are not readily observable to most people.

Before considering these options, however, it is important that the seller consider all dimensions of his product or service in terms of what they mean to the consumer. To the car rental customer, for example, the service offered entails more than just a car in working order available at a particular price. To the consumer, this service has a far broader meaning: cleanliness and state of repair of the vehicle, backup service in case of trouble encountered on the road, convenience of making reservations, and a multitude of other factors. The seller of this and other travel-related products must understand the relevant dimensions that the consumer uses to define the service. The seller's perspective alone is insufficient, because it may incorporate more, fewer, or different factors than the traveler does when considering alternative services.

A travel service can not be physically modified or improved in the way that an automobile, a refrigerator, or a TV dinner can. The travel marketer can, however, stimulate changes in attitudes toward the service he produces by changing, for example, the attitudes of his salespeople, the uniforms they wear, the price of the service, and how the service can be purchased.

- In the early 1970s more than 23,000 American Airlines employees (primarily stewardesses, reservation agents, and other customer-contact personnel) were given training in Transactional Analysis, a technique for improving interpersonal communications skills.
- Many travel service firms outfit their employees in uniforms to project an image that stimulates the development of a specific attitude toward the firm.
- Nearly all major air carriers in the last few years have offered discount fares, a strategy that encourages more people to think of air travel in terms of a "good value." The same strategy has been employed by lodging chains ("Kids Under 18 Free") and car rental firms ("Unlimited Free Mileage").
- Toll-free reservation numbers, mail-order ticketing, and computerized

reservations and ticketing are just some of the ways in which carriers, lodging organizations, car rental firms, and others have made it easier to purchase services, thereby stimulating more positive attitudes toward the service and the firm.

Location is a key factor in the success of many business firms. This is especially so for the firm that sells an intangible service. Since a service is both produced and consumed at the same time, it is therefore necessary that the consumer go to where the producer is located — or vice versa. Services like air transportation or overnight accommodations can not be stockpiled and delivered at some later date. Consequently, it is imperative that the service producer be located as near as possible to the people he will serve.

Changing or increasing the number of locations at which the service can be performed is one of the best ways for a travel service firm to stimulate positive attitudes toward it. Lodging organizations, therefore, compete for the best locations. Air carriers seek to serve as many profitable markets as possible. And travel agencies in large metropolitan areas open multiple branches.

In addition to convenient locations, travel service firms can offer time conveniences. Airlines and intercity bus firms attempt to offer, within the constraints imposed by a limited number of vehicles, convenient departure schedules that encourage favorable attitudes toward the services they provide. The Broadway Limited train departs from New York at a mid-afternoon hour and arrives in Chicago at a convenient, morning hour. Hotels establish convenient check-out hours, and some car rental agencies remain open around-the-clock.

Although the actual travel product may be intangible, most travel firms utilize tangible goods and equipment to produce their services. Car rental firms rent automobiles. Theme parks use roller coasters and ferris wheels. Hotels and motels house overnight lodgers in furnished buildings. Cruise lines provide dining, sleeping, and entertainment facilities on board large ships. All of this physical equipment has an impact on the attitudes people form about these various travel service firms, and it can be changed in ways that stimulate the formation of more positive attitudes.

Perhaps one of the classic examples of product change is the multicolored fleet of airplanes flown by Braniff International — the inspiration of an advertising executive who wanted to improve attitudes toward Braniff by changing its stodgy, conservative, just-another-airline image. Other air carriers have copied this attitude-changing strategy, and so has Amtrak. By investing in wide-body aircraft, the air carriers improved their operating performance, created an image of more comfortable air transportation, and encouraged the favorable attitudes associated with these attributes. Lodging chains seek to stimulate positive attitudes by developing unique architectural schemes and investing heavily in comfortable interior decor.

The retail travel agency tries to influence attitudes with an atmosphere that communicates warmth and organization, and by investing in computerized equipment that makes it more efficient in performance and appearance.

There are cases, however, in which tangible goods and equipment play only a very minor supporting role. Most of what happens in a retail travel agency, for example, can be described as interpersonal dealings between travel agent and traveler — a fact that makes the formation of attitudes less controllable by the agency owner. The travel agency faces the problem of creating attitudes about a truly intangible, invisible service — professional travel counseling — and this is a particularly difficult task. Although it is also selling an intangible service — overnight rest — the hotel chain, on the other hand, can more easily influence attitudes toward its product by advertising pictures of spacious rooms, comfortable furniture, king-size beds, and plant-filled lobbies.

Nevertheless, changes in the intangible service and in the tangible goods and equipment used to produce the service should normally be among the first things considered when a travel service firm desires improved attitudes toward itself. Where there is little in the way of supporting goods and services, careful consideration should be given to what does exist. The travel agency, for example, should give special attention to the image created by its overall appearance and surroundings, to the name of the agency, to its logo and letterhead, and to the behavior and appearance of its employees.

Perceptual Change

Attitude change can also be stimulated by new perceptions, even when the basic product remains the same. The Avis organization provides a classic example of the effective use of this type of attitude-change strategy.

Prior to Avis' "We're #2, We Try Harder" campaign, consumers perceived the auto rental market as consisting of Hertz — the leader — along with a number of relatively unknown, faceless competitors. The Avis campaign changed consumer perceptions in two important ways that resulted in attitude shifts favorable to the firm. First, by admitting to and playing up their second-place rank, consumers could now perceive Avis as closer to Hertz than they previously did when they envisioned this market to consist of one leader plus numerous also-rans. Then, the "We Try Harder" message promised that the underdog in the race would do more for the customer in order to catch up with the leader. Although the basic service offered by Avis may not have improved significantly, attitudes toward the company certainly did.

Wherever there is no real change in the service itself, advertising naturally plays a vital role in communicating an image that strengthens an existing attitude or encourages a changed attitude toward the service. American Airlines, for example, has long emphasized that it is the business man's airline, while its major competitors have stressed friendly skies, on-time performance, and "The Wings of Man." Cruise lines refer to Italian festivals. Car rental companies claim that they try harder or rely on superstar status. Mexico refers to itself as "The Amigo Country," while "Virginia is for lovers." Costa Rica calls itself "The Carefree Alternative;" Portugal, "The Portugese Alternative." Lodging organizations describe themselves as showplaces, "people pleasin' ", and "collections . . . rather than chains."

Sometimes a travel service firm changes its name to encourage people to change their perceptions of the firm and the service it offers. Allegheny Airlines has renamed itself USAir, a move intended to change people's perception of the airline as a strictly regional carrier operating in the eastern United States. The merger of North Central and Southern Airlines also produced a new name, Republic Airlines, with the same intention: to communicate the fact that the new carrier is also no second-rate regional carrier but one that serves more cities in the United States than any other airline.

The name chosen for a travel service firm can do much to help form an image of the firm in the minds of travelers. Consider, for example, such names as Holiday Inn, TraveLodge, Red Carpet Inns, and Princess Hotels — and contrast them with names like Hilton, Howard Johnson, Marriott, and Pick — names that glorify the founders of these lodging firms, but that do little to help the younger consumer-traveler form images in her mind. Travel agencies provide an endless list of imaginative names that no doubt help to form images in the minds of consumers — names like Travelon, Welcome Aboard, Love Travel, Travelmore, Travel Bug, Masters of Travel, and Anytime, Anywhere Travel.

The objective of the image-building strategies discussed here is to expose the consumer to perceptual messages that communicate the travel firm's capacity to provide specific benefits. Without the benefits themselves, however, it is doubtful that a firm's name or the advertising claims that it makes would successfully stimulate the development of sustained, favorable attitudes. If Avis claims that, "we try harder," its employees must also be perceived to try harder. A travel agency that goes by the name "Love Travel" cannot be staffed with people who hate travel. And an agency called "Masters of Travel" must be staffed with people who are professional travel counselors in every sense. The kinds of perceptual changes discussed here will only occur when the service itself meets the expectations created for it through advertising and other forms of communication.

Changing perceptions for the purpose of encouraging the development of favorable attitudes toward the travel service firm is by no means an easy undertaking. As indicated earlier in this chapter, attitudes resist change because consumers tend to avoid information that is inconsistent with their current attitude structure. One effective way of lowering the consumer's perceptual defenses is to assign a new **label** to the firm's service.[24] A new label — calling itself something other than what it has been called in the past — actually prompts the consumer to view this service as something different or new. As a result, the individual is more likely to absorb new information that alters her perceptions of the service and the firm that produces it. New labels led to perceptual changes in the following cases:

- Disney brought new life to the amusement park by first dramatically improving the product itself, and second, by providing an important new label: the **theme park.** Almost overnight, Disneyland turned amusement parks into a new business that offered wholesome entertainment for the entire family.
- Eastern Airlines labeled its fleet **Whisper Jets,** hoping to set their fleet apart from those of other air carriers in the minds of travelers.
- Over time, the image of Las Vegas and attitudes toward it changed and improved when it came to be referred to as an **entertainment center** instead of a gambling oasis.
- Holiday Inn called itself a motel chain until it saw the need to expand into downtown locations and major resort areas. Then the firm began referring to itself as a **hotel chain** ("We Welcome You to the #1 People Pleasin' Hotels in the World").

The reader can think of other examples. One mentioned earlier was Day's Inns, which has tried to label itself a full-service lodging chain instead of a chain of economy or budget motels. Travel agents who fulfill the educational and experience requirements of the Institute of Certified Travel Agents are designated as Certified Travel Counselors — a "label" which fosters a more positive attitude toward them by clients and prospective clients.

Prompt a Behavioral Change

Earlier we mentioned that weak attitudes are more susceptible to change than stronger or extreme ones. A strong attitude requires more time and patience to change because it must be chipped away, so to speak, a little at a time. An individual with strong attitudes must be exposed to new information repeatedly until, gradually, his defense mechanisms weaken.

One authority suggests that *repetition* is one of the keys for changing strong attitudes.[25] Sound reasons for the attitude change must be given to the person who holds the attitude. People who hold strong negative attitudes about flying, camping, foreign travel, or staying in high-priced luxury hotels do not change their attitudes overnight. Repeating the sound reasons to change such attitudes without antagonizing the individual is certainly one of the most difficult tasks of effective salesmanship and marketing.

Perhaps one of the most useful tools in accomplishing this is the use of *humor*. Humor can be particularly effective in that it does not directly or offensively confront the strongly held attitudes that one is trying to change. British Airways' use of the charm and wit of Robert Morley, illustrated in the advertisement in Figure 6-14, is probably one of the best examples of the use of humor and repetition to change what appeared to be, in the early and mid-1970s, rather strong negative attitudes toward travel to Great Britain.

The use of repetition and humor would also be useful in direct personal selling situations involving travelers with strong attitudes. Each time that an argument encouraging attitude change is repeated, the strength of the existing attitude lessens. It would be unrealistic, however, to assume that someone would do a complete about-face, changing a strong negative attitude to a strong positive one all at once.

Sometimes the unique experience of travel itself can create a state of mind that lowers the mental barriers to resist attitude change. Away from home, away from work, and away from the demands of the clock and everyday responsibilities, the individual traveler is generally receptive to new experiences, to meeting new people, and to absorbing the kind of new information that weakens existing attitudes and leads to attitude change. For many, travel is clearly linked to changes in attitudes toward foreign cultures and strange people, the foods they eat, and the languages they speak. An opportune time for changing people's attitudes toward various travel services, therefore, may be when they are traveling away from home.

Early in this chapter, we examined attitudes in terms of knowledge, feeling, and behavioral components. By breaking down attitudes, it is easier to see how they can be developed or altered to encourage a desired behavioral change. For example, a travel advertiser could communicate factual information that would alter beliefs about his product or service — beliefs that could lead to attitude change. The car rental advertisement in Figure 6-15, for instance, primarily stresses data about daily rates. In fact, most car rental advertising seems to stress daily rate information.

Advertising can also aim at altering the feeling component of an attitude. Because people try to harmonize their feelings and their beliefs, effective mood and image advertising can influence feelings, beliefs, and opinions simultaneously. The Los Angeles Bonaventure advertisement in

FIGURE 6-14

Figure 6-16 tries to emphasize a mood and an image, equating the Bon-aventure with the finest of wines through a powerful picture and words like luxurious, sparkling, warm, exciting, savor, and spirit.

Finally, if a consumer can be induced, perhaps impulsively, to change his behavior — through the distribution of free samples, for example, or other incentives — the development of or a change in attitude may follow. The Harolds Club eleven-dollar "jet set pass" advertisement in

FIGURE 6-15

FIGURE 6-16

Copyright © Los Angeles Bonaventure Hotel, Los Angeles, CA. Reprinted by permission.

FIGURE 6-17

Copyright © Harolds Club, Reno, NV. Reprinted by permission.

Figure 6-17, would ideally motivate a visitor to Reno to patronize Harolds Club first rather than having to collect information, evaluate that information, and then develop an attitude before visiting.

Because many people are predisposed to make impulse travel decisions enroute to their destinations, efforts aimed at capitalizing on this tendency hold considerable promise. If a traveler can be persuaded to decide on the spur of the moment to stay at a Quality Inn, to take a detour through the state of Tennessee, or to climb aboard the Delta Queen, his attitude may change as a result of such an experience. A key to this approach to attitude change is an understanding of how to reach the enroute traveler and how to motivate him to make the appropriate impulsive decision.

When communicating motivational information, one must remember that the traveler is often, in effect, a moving target. The media that can be used to communicate with him are, therefore, limited. They include inflight magazines, airline ticket jackets, and airport terminal advertising. They also include Yellow Page advertising, visitor magazines like *Where* and *Key*, and the various brochures that are distributed through hotels, restaurants, and highway information centers. Finally, there is outdoor advertising (billboards), which communicates with people traveling in automobiles.

There are no simple guidelines motivating spur-of-the-moment travel decisions. Certain possibilities suggest themselves, however, when we understand why people make impulse decisions.

It has been found that people who act impulsively tend to be restless and easily bored, and they fight boredom and routine by indulging in exciting, adventurous, or novel activities.[26] Thus, an appeal to do something for the "sake of variety" could be very effective.

Among the most potent catalysts known for changing the behavior of impulsive individuals are threats of one sort or another, sexual appeals, and appeals that emphasize monetary rewards.[27] A billboard that reads, "Stop Now — Next Service 48 Miles" threatens an auto traveler. Inflight magazine ads for Las Vegas hotels often incorporate not-so-subtle sexual appeals. And advertising that emphasizes low daily and mileage rates for car rental companies promises a monetary reward, as do dollars-off coupons and similar promotional devices.

The effect of any effort to persuade travelers to make spur-of-the-moment decisions is actually to increase the perceived importance of the product in question. The billboard which reminds the traveler that the next services are forty-eight miles down the road is attempting to increase the perceived importance of the service stations, restaurants, and motels located at the very next exit off the Interstate. Advertising which emphasizes low daily and mileage car rental rates is attempting to increase the perceived importance of renting a car from one car rental company rather than another.

Activate a Latent Motivation

One other way of increasing the perceived importance of a given travel service is to address latent motivations — that is, motivations that may be relevant to a particular situation but that may not have influenced the travel decision maker. An example mentioned earlier focused on the individual with a negative attitude toward Disney World. When reminded of his obligation to his children, however, his attitude toward parental duty surfaced and prompted him to change his mind about visiting Orlando. Initially, this person's motivation to satisfy the needs of his children was latent — concealed, so to speak, from the decision-making process. Identifying and activating such latent motivations can be a powerful force in intensifying attitudes and stimulating specific types of travel behavior.

Changing the Store of Knowledge

Nearly all of the strategies we discuss in this chapter require, in one way or another, the communication of new and additional information — information about a particular travel product or service and how it can benefit the individual traveler. People who have a limited amount of information about a service or the firm that produces it are generally more susceptible to a change in attitude than those people with a greater store of knowledge. Where information is limited, contradictory information is more likely to bring about an attitude change.[28] For example, when people know very little about the function of travel agents, a presentation of information that describes their services is likely to bring about positive changes in attitude toward travel agents. On the other hand, a person whose travel experience was marred by a travel agent's mistake may generalize this experience and be unconvinced by the presentation of new information. His negative attitude is more likely to remain negative.

It is also important to note that, as a general rule, the attitudes of children and poorly educated adults tend to be easier to change than the attitudes of the more highly educated. The reason for this is quite simple: highly educated people generally possess more information about a large number of topics.[29] This general tendency holds an important implication for the travel industry because the pleasure travel market, on average, consists of people with higher educations. Consequently, changing attitudes in the travel market as a whole will be no easy task, because the pleasure traveler is a relatively sophisticated consumer who is more likely to respond to appeals based on services that help solve genuine travel needs, rather than appeals based largely on superficial perceptual manipulations and imagery.

SUMMARY

As indicated in the first part of this chapter, attitude formation is a key psychological concept in the understanding of travel decision making. An attitude — whether it be toward travel in general or toward a specific destination, a mode of transportation, an airline, hotel chain, cruise line, car-rental firm, or travel agent who sells the services of such firms — leads to a predisposition to purchase any of these services. In a very important sense, those who market and sell various travel services are concerned primarily with helping to create favorable attitudes toward their services.

Once the traveler has formed a favorable attitude toward a specific travel service, there is an improved chance that he will actually purchase the service if it is available when and where he needs it. One group of major factors that can interfere with the actual purchase has been referred to as *social influences*. These influences are most often exerted through other people, and this is the subject of the last chapter of this book.

REFERENCES

[1] C. Glenn Walters, *Consumer Behavior* (Homewood, Illinois: Richard D. Irwin, Inc., 1974), p. 161.

[2] Lance P. Jarvis and Edward J. Mayo, "Chain Loyalty in the Lodging Market," *Hotel and Motel Management* (August, 1978), pp. 26-29.

[3] George S. Day, "Theories of Attitude Structure and Change," in *Consumer Behavior: Theoretical Sources*, Scott Ward and Thomas S. Robertson, eds. (Englewood Cliffs, New Jersey: Prentice-Hall, Inc., 1973), pp. 303-53 at p. 331.

[4] Walters, *Consumer Behavior*, pp. 169-70.

[5] E.R. Carlson, "Attitude Change Through Modification of Attitude Structure," *Journal of Abnormal and Social Psychology*, Vol. 52 (1956), pp. 256-61.

[6] James Zavertnik et al, "Congruence of Air Traveler Self-Images and Air Carrier Images," working paper (Notre Dame, Indiana: Hayes-Healy Travel Management Program, University of Notre Dame, 1979), pp. 22. Also: John Levy and Dewey Ratliff, "Transactional Analysis and the Airline Ticket Counter," *The 80s: Its Impact on Travel and Tourism Marketing*, Proceedings of the Eighth Annual Conference (Salt Lake City: Travel Research Association, 1977), pp. 163-65.

[7] Edward J. Mayo, *Regional Travel Characteristics of the United States* (Bedford Park, Illinois: 3M National Advertising Company, 1973), pp. 16-19.

[8] Behavior Science Corporation, *Developing the Family Travel Market* (Des Moines, Iowa: Better Homes and Gardens, 1972), p. 4. Also: Rena Bartos, "Social Change and the Travel Marketer," *Marketing Travel and Tourism*, Seventh Annual Conference Proceedings (Salt Lake City: Travel Research Association, 1976), pp. 191-97 at p. 194.

[9] Bartos, "Social Change and the Travel Marketer," p. 195.

[10] John J. Casson, "Do Consumer Attitudes Really Matter?" *Using Travel Research for Planning and Profits*, Ninth Annual Conference Proceedings (Salt Lake City: Travel Research Association, 1978), pp. 21-24 at p. 22.

[11] Newspaper Advertising Bureau, *Young Singles and Vacation Travel* (New York: 1979).

[12] Day, "Theories of Attitude Structure and Change," pp. 310-11.

[13] Jonathan N. Goodrich, "Benefit Bundle Analysis: An Empirical Study of International Travelers," *Journal of Travel Research*, Vol. 16 (Fall, 1977), pp. 6-9.

[14] Newspaper Advertising Bureau, *Young Singles and Vacation Travel*, p. 34.

[15] Edward J. Mayo, *The Psychology of Choice in the Lodging Market* (Bedford Park, Illinois: 3M National Advertising Company, 1974), p. 31.

[16] Based on the results of a proprietary study conducted by the authors for Best Western International.

[17] Arch G. Woodside, Ilkka Ronkainen, and David M. Reid, "Measurement and Utilization of the Evoked Set as a Travel Marketing Variable," *The 80s: Its Impact on Travel and Tourism Marketing*, Proceedings of the Eighth Annual Conference (Salt Lake City: Travel Research Association, 1977), pp. 123-30.

[18] John A. Howard and Jagdish N. Sheth, *The Theory of Buyer Behavior* (New York: John Wiley & Sons, Inc., 1969), p. 26.

[19] Woodside, et al, "Measurement and Utilization . . . ," p. 123.

[20] Ibid., p. 125.

[21] John R. Thompson and Philip D. Cooper, "Additional Evidence on the Limited Size of Evoked and Inept Sets of Travel Destinations," *Journal of Travel Research*, Vol. 17 (Winter, 1979), pp. 23-25.

[22] Howard and Sheth, *The Theory of Buyer Behavior*, p. 322.

[23] Walters, *Consumer Behavior*, p. 173.

[24] Edgar Crane, *Marketing Communications*, second edition (New York: John Wiley & Sons, Inc., 1972), pp. 65-66.

[25] Walters, *Consumer Behavior*, pp. 169-70.

[26] David Kipnis, *Character Structure and Impulsiveness* (New York: Academic Press, 1971), p. 34.

[27] Ibid., p. 58.

[28] Walters, *Consumer Behavior*, p. 174.

[29] Ibid., pp. 174-75.

QUESTIONS FOR DISCUSSION

1. What is an attitude? What is meant when we say that those who market and sell travel services are concerned primarily with creating favorable attitudes?
2. What are the differences between beliefs, opinions, and feelings?
3. When you are traveling, it is likely that you often make decisions that are inconsistent with your attitudes. Explain why this happens. Give examples.
4. This chapter identifies six different factors that contribute either to the stability or the instability of attitudes. Imagine that you are trying to convince someone to take a cruise of the Mediterranean. What attitudes might they have that would lead them to resist your sales effort? How could you overcome their resistance?
5. Under what conditions might a person's strong positive attitude toward leisure travel change and become a strong negative attitude? Do you know anyone who has experienced this type of attitudinal change? Was it a long-lasting change in attitude?
6. In what ways would you expect travel behavior to change during a downturn in the economy? Do you expect that attitudes toward travel would change if and when the price of gasoline and jet fuel once again doubled? Why?
7. Pick out any one of the travel advertisements reproduced in this book. In your

opinion, does the advertisement do a good job of clearly identifying the benefits that a person could expect if he were to purchase the advertised product or service? How could the advertisement be improved to better stress a key benefit?

8. What is meant by a salient attribute of a product or service? Is cleanliness a salient attribute when someone selects a motel at which to spend a night?

9. Out of all the hundreds of possible vacation destinations that a leisure traveler might visit, he normally gives serious consideration to a small handful of them. Why? What does this suggest to those responsible for marketing vacation destinations?

10. There are three basic approaches to changing someone else's attitudes. What are they? Choose a vacation destination and discuss how you would go about changing the attitude of someone who did not think highly of it.

11. Improved attitudes can be stimulated by new perceptions even though the basic product or service remains the same. One way of doing this is by attaching a new label to the product or service. Can you think of a new label — a new name — that could possibly improve attitudes toward Amtrak?

12. What are some of the key personality characteristics of impulsive decision makers? How would a knowledge of these distinguishing personality characteristics help an airline market its services? How might it help a travel agency?

7

GROUP INFLUENCES ON TRAVEL BEHAVIOR

Up to this point we have been concerned with several psychological factors — perception, learning, personality, motivation, and attitudes — as they affect the individual traveler and his decisions. The consumer-traveler, however, does not function independently of those around him. He has contact with any number of other people — with members of his family, fellow workers, neighbors, sales clerks, cab drivers, and complete strangers — and any one of these people can have a substantial influence on his travel and leisure-time decisions. A casual comment — "Are you *really* thinking about going to South America next winter?!" — may do more to influence the decision in question than any other factor.

Often, the people around us influence our behavior because we are members of the same groups. American leisure is what it is partly because of what American groups are.[1] A noted French statesman and author, de Tocqueville, observed over a hundred years ago that Americans seemed to be the greatest joiners in the world. The United States is famous for its clubs, lodges, leagues, fraternities, sororities, associations, societies, and other voluntary organizations. In addition, there are groups to which a person belongs whether he wants to or not. These include the family, the military, unions, and schools, as well as various informal groups made up of neighbors, fellow workers, and members of one's religious congregation. Moreover, people are bonded by social class. They share cultural and subcultural affiliations. All of these groups have a role in determining how one spends his or her leisure time.

A study of the psychology of travel would be incomplete if we did not examine how individual travel behavior is influenced by other people. This is the purpose of our final chapter. The first section identifies those groups that can influence individual travel behavior and discusses the functions that each group performs for its individual members. We also explain how people come to conform to the norms of behavior established by a group, and how this conformity is reflected in leisure-time and travel behavior.

The concept of social class has been found useful in explaining many different types of social behavior. The second section of this chapter explains what is meant by social class, describes how it affects the individual through group pressures to conform, and then discusses how it influences the behavior of individual travelers.

The third section of the chapter focuses on the family unit, considered to be the single most important leisure group in Western societies.[2] While family vacation travel and decision making were discussed earlier (see Chapter 3), this chapter develops other, equally important issues related to the family and leisure travel.

Finally, the impact of cultural norms and traditions on individual leisure and travel behavior is discussed. A special section is devoted to the increasing importance of sports in motivating leisure travel. Gift giving — a cultural phenomenon that plays a largely untapped role in the travel market — is also discussed.

CONFORMITY TO THE GROUP

A person joins groups because they satisfy certain needs. They protect, they help solve problems, they allow him to meet and associate with certain types of people, they provide models of behavior, they enhance his self-image, and they provide him with numerous yardsticks for evaluating his own behavior. Someone who joins an exclusive country club may do so because it gives him status and allows him to meet with successful people in his community. A business person who travels frequently joins the Airlines Passengers Association to keep abreast of matters concerning airline safety, convenience, and fares, in addition to enjoying such benefits as hotel and car rental discounts.

A group survives over an extended period of time only because it serves important, even vital, functions for its individual members. A travel agent becomes associated with the Institute of Certified Travel Agents to upgrade her professional skills. In addition, completion of the ICTA program bestows increased professional status on her through the organization's recognition of her as a Certified Travel Counselor. Thus, ICTA serves multiple functions for her.

We might also consider the multiple functions served by the guided tour group. A guided tour group provides at least five fundamental benefits for its members. These are physical, psychological, economic, and social in nature.[3]

1. Planned tours solve the problem of what to see within a limited amount of time. The itinerary condenses a large geographic area into a selective smorgasbord of highlights of tourist attractions. As discussed elsewhere, this makes the guided tour particularly attractive to inexperienced travelers and first-time visitors to a particular area.
2. The planned itinerary provides psychological security to group members, who know beforehand where they will be going and in what hotels they will stay.
3. The planned tour also provides economic simplification and security. Group members know ahead of time the cost of the entire trip. In their promotional literature, tour companies try to give the impression that there are no hidden extras.
4. The guided tour minimizes external social problems for group members. Tour coordinators, hosts and hostesses, and tour guides act as buffers between group members and the foreign social environment by arranging for transportation, interpreting, and handling various problems that arise.
5. The guided tour serves other functions that are not acknowledged in promotional literature. The tour minimizes potential friction between group members and sets the scene for in-group solidarity. People traveling together may have difficulty reaching a consensus on what to see, and may therefore find that the guided tour solves this problem for them. Even those who are able to reach a consensus may find security and social support in group travel. The group tour provides opportunities for sharing experiences and confronting the unfamiliar in a collective way. Finally, among some types of tours, the group itself is the main attraction (e.g., singles' tours).

A group may fulfill different needs for each individual. One person, for example, may be attracted to a tour group because he thinks he will spend less money than if he were to travel alone to the same destination. Another person may join the same group primarily because he is apprehensive about traveling alone to a strange foreign country. A third person may join the tour group because several of his friends have already done so.

The Importance of Groups

For each formal and informal group to which a person belongs, he has an assigned role. A 35-year-old man, for example, might play each of the following roles: father, husband, business executive, little league coach, church member, chairman of the finance committee for the United Way, vice president of a rod and gun club, and committee member of his college alumni organization. In addition, he may share many household responsibilities with his wife, serve as a part-time chauffeur for his children, attend periodically to the needs of his aging parents, and be active with a group of neighbors who fish regularly in the summer and who play poker in the winter. To fully understand how this individual's behavior is affected by each of these various groups, it is necessary to discuss the psychological concept of **role playing.**

Role Playing and the Group. Everyone is familiar with the term *role* as it is used in the theater or movies. An actor will put something of himself into the role he is playing, but at the same time he will play the part as it was conceived by the playwright or screenwriter. If he deviates too much from that role, he will have done a poor job of acting.

Role, as defined by the social psychologist, is really not much different from its meaning in a theatrical context. Our day-to-day activities thrust us into a variety of roles that require us to perform in certain ways, to say certain things in a certain special tone of voice, and to maintain a certain set of attitudes. In other words, an individual in a given role is expected to behave in a prescribed way.

The number and variety of roles that any one person plays, willingly or otherwise, can be appreciated by considering several different categories of roles. These types of roles include — [4]

Biological roles: for example, age and sex roles
Semibiological roles: for example, kinship and social class roles
Institutional roles: for example, occupational, religious, political, and recreational roles
Transitional roles: for example, the role of guest
Character roles: for example, hero, villain, and fool roles

These role categories suggest the many roles one person plays throughout his lifetime. Very often, detailed instructions are transmitted to help a person learn a given role. Youngsters are told, "Act your age," and given instructions on how to do so. Little girls are told, "Act like a lady," and taught that they shouldn't throw rocks, spit, swear, or be dirty. Little boys are told, "Act like a man," and taught not to hit girls, to stick up for their rights with force if necessary, and that it is all right to be dirty once in awhile. By the time he is a young adult, the typical American male will have learned that to be a man is to be aggressive, fearless, hardy, and independent, and that it is all right to be rough in manners, language, and sentiment as long as he holds doors open for ladies. By the time she is a young adult, the typical American female will have learned to be compassionate, sympathetic, fastidious, sensitive, and polite, and that it is acceptable to be emotional and dependent.

Much of this role programming takes place in the family — with a great deal of assistance, of course, from teachers (the school group), peers (friendship groups), and others. Later on, the role programming takes place in other group settings — in work groups, church groups, neighborhood groups, and so forth. In addition, much of the teaching is reinforced by television, magazines, and media advertising.

Because the family and other groups are so important to people, most are more than willing to learn their roles and act them out as best they can. For the same reasons and in much the same way, one learns how to be a good Christian or Jew, a good Democrat or Republican, a good parent, a good doctor or lawyer, a good citizen, and a good guest.

Because of the assortment of roles that he undertakes and his willingness to act them out, an individual's behavior is affected in many different ways. The groups to which he belongs and the roles he plays influence what he does, with whom he does it, and where and when he does it. Moreover, the roles he plays affect the goods and services he buys and consumes. Like the actor in a movie, someone playing a role in real life must not only learn his lines, so to speak, but also surround himself with the right props, dress in the right costume, and so forth. A person playing the role of expert skier, for instance, needs to be able to talk comfortably and authoritatively in terms of such things as moguls, flat light, and corn snow; should dress in the right clothing; and should own the right equipment.

As we will see, group memberships have an important impact on how people spend their leisure time, the attitudes they have about travel, and how they spend their time and money on travel activities. Group and role influences are probably greatest in situations where there is ego involvement and significant potential for expressing one's self and personality.[5] For many people, leisure time and travel provide such an occasion.

Leisure and Travel Roles

Even when a person travels alone, his behavior is still influenced by other people and groups of one kind or another. A traveler continues to play roles when he is away from home, and there are a variety of leisure and travel roles to be played. When selecting a particular type of journey, a person chooses either to be a vacationer or a tourist. As a vacationer, he will travel to one destination (such as a resort) and spend most of his vacation time there. As a tourist, he will visit several destinations and attractions during the course of a vacation.[6] Each of these roles fosters a different type of behavior.

When selecting a mode of transportation for his journey, a person is again choosing to play a role and behave according to the norms of behavior for that role. Someone who decides to take his family on a vacation in the family car, for example, chooses to play the role of chauffeur. He may also choose to play the roles of tour guide, navigator, financial planner, decision maker, and auto mechanic. If, on the other hand, he decides to fly his family to a destination, he will have rejected several of these roles in favor of playing roles such as travel agent and companion. If the family visits a ski resort, each member may have to choose between playing the role of novice or expert. Those who carry cameras with them choose to play the role of photographer — either amateur or expert photographer. Many who travel to Las Vegas or Reno choose the role of gambler. Those who travel to see the Super Bowl choose the role of spectator. The list is infinite, but important because each role carries with it a unique set of behavioral expectations. Tourists behave differently than natives. Experts behave differently than novices or amateurs. Guests behave differently than "hosts," and "hosts" behave differently than "hostesses." First-class passengers behave differently than those who sit in the rear of an airplane — and, in fact, they are treated differently as well.

A traveler's behavior is likely to be quite different from what it is at home — not only because different roles are played, but simply because he is away from home as well. When he leaves home, the pleasure traveler can be said to enter a fantasy world — or, as one authority puts it, a "play world." The play world of travel is unique in ways which clearly demarcate it from everyday life.[7] As a player, the traveler leaves behind everyday commitments and responsibilities that tend to constrain his behavior. On the job, at school, in church, and in other group settings near his home, the individual's behavior is often programmed by a well-established system of norms.

Leisure and travel settings allow the individual greater flexibility in acting out roles. Human interaction may gain in intensity, especially when people find themselves in unique settings far removed from home. One can experience intense social relationships with a small number of intimate friends, extensive social relationships with a large number of strangers[8] — or go off and be entirely by oneself. The first of these alternatives might be illustrated by the group of four or five men who join in a ten-day fishing expedition to a remote Canadian site. There they fish a little, drink a lot, tell the same old stories, and are apt to reveal themselves — bare their souls, if you will — in ways that they might find impossible at home. Time, distance, and a unique setting encourage their kind of behavior. Away from home, people may also experience extensive social interaction with a large number of relative strangers. This might occur on a cruise ship, an extended group tour, or during a stay of a week or more at a resort.

It has often been said that those who market and sell travel deal in dreams and fantasies, and our discussion should suggest some of the important implications of this concept. When acting on dreams and fantasies, a consumer is likely to behave quite differently than he does under more normal conditions. Earlier, for example, we noted that many people behave more impulsively in a travel environment. It was also suggested, when we discussed perception in Chapter 2, that the pleasure traveler lowers his perceptual barriers and notices things that he would not otherwise notice. This, in turn, can lead to behavior in no way ordinary to the individual.

Previous travel experiences often remain lifelong memories because they are unique, because people remember being closer for a time to another, or because they remember meeting many new people and sharing good times and new experiences with them. Although roles are still played in a travel environment, it seems reasonable to conclude that travelers remember putting more of themselves into those roles and learning more about themselves in the process. Those who market and sell travel can do so more effectively by keeping this perspective of the travel experience in mind.

In leisure, one has an option to either accept or reject a set of behavioral norms. Leisure provides the flexibility to accept or reject a given form of play such as a specific activity and the roles that go along with it. If someone is uncomfortable in the role of guest, he can avoid staying with friends or relatives when away from home. If he is uncomfortable with the role of chauffeur, he can travel by some mode of transportation other than the automobile. The same level of freedom does not exist either at home or at work.

Travel experiences are often memorable and unique because they take place in what we call a play world. The flexibility we enjoy in selecting leisure and travel roles exists because these roles are, in a sense, play roles. The significance of this can be illustrated by examining camping as a leisure experience which offers a variety of roles. This discussion can aid us in analyzing and identifying roles that exist in other types of travel settings as well.

Role Playing and Outdoor Recreation.   Although isolated from the commitments of everyday life, many of life's daily routines are present in the typical camping environment.[9] The same is true of other travel experiences as well. The camping party — usually the family — is a relatively self-sufficient unit that does not have to rely *directly* on others. The group prepares its own food, builds the fire over which it is cooked, and chops the wood for this fire. The campers interact with one another on a social level, they entertain each other, play games, and so forth. In other words, within the camping environment several different types of activities occur. Because of the unique environment in which camping takes place, however, many camping activities take on special meanings and thereby have a special impact on individual behavior. To one extent or another, the same can be said about most types of pleasure travel.

One group of camping activities can be referred to as **subsistence activities.** These include meeting ordinary demands for food, shelter, and protection. The unique conditions under which these needs are met, however, often make these activities seem extraordinary. Normally, food preparation and home care are work activities. In the camping environment, however, these activities become a special form of play.

Several other groups of camping activities can be identified:

> **symbolic labor:** hunting, fishing, rock collecting, and other activities characterized by the quest for trophies and other tangibles which signify that the labor was productive, that the search was not in vain
> **unstructured play:** rock throwing, squirrel chasing, and other activities in which an individual experiments with the environment and with himself
> **structured play:** horseshoes, badminton, card games, hide-and-seek, and other games and contests where there are clearly defined goals and traditionalized roles
> **sociability:** fireside chats, storytelling, singing, drinking, and other activities where the main focus is the interaction among people who are more or less equal
> **expressive play:** dancing, water skiing, sailing, tree climbing, and other activities where an individual can put a great deal of himself into the activity

These and other categories of leisure activities can provide insight into leisure and travel behavior. At some camps, the predominant activities are expressive, while at others most activities fall under the heading of symbolic labor. We can classify other types of travel destinations in a similar way. Hilton Head, for instance, is a destination where structured play is a primary activity (golf and tennis). Vail, on the other hand, is a destination where expressive play predominates (skiing).

Other categories of leisure activities can be constructed in addition to these. But the most important point is that for each group of leisure activities there exists a set of roles that regulate individual behavior. We can see this clearly in the relationship between men and women in the camping environment — and then apply the same type of analysis to other leisure and travel settings.

With only a few exceptions, it appears that women's activities in the camping environment tend to be prosaic and practical, including such things as food preparation (subsistence play) and relaxing, drawing, reading, and sunbathing (unstructured play).* The female in the camping environment tends to get involved in other forms of play only when an activity is experienced simultaneously with a male — such as water skiing and swimming (expressive play); card games (structured play); and conversation, singing, and walking (sociability).

Male roles in the camping environment tend to be more dramatic. Men tend to become involved in a greater variety of activities, many of them physically rough and sometimes "dirty." Their activities usually involve all except unstructured forms of play (relaxing, drawing, sunbathing, reading). In addition to the activities they share with women, men generally get involved by themselves, alone, or with other men, in activities of symbolic labor, certain types of expressive play, structured play, subsistence play, and certain forms of sociability.

In short, certain leisure activities involve roles that are exclusive to either sex. The observations noted here, drawn from studies of leisure behavior in the outdoor recreation area, can be usefully applied to other leisure and travel settings. The fact that men tend to avoid various types of unstructured play may be important to tour operators, cruise lines, and resort operators. Similarly, those who market and sell travel can benefit from knowing that women tend to get involved in activities besides subsistence and unstructured play only when they participate jointly with their husbands or other men. These observations do not purposely overlook changes in role patterns that have occurred in recent years. There is no doubt that the woman of the 1980s has much greater freedom to choose certain roles than did her counterpart of ten or twenty years ago. With just a few exceptions, however, it is not altogether clear that women in large numbers have chosen to expand the number and variety of roles they play in the leisure area.

SOCIAL CLASS AND TRAVEL BEHAVIOR

One of the fundamental thoughts underlying this book is that there is ample reason to be disenchanted with purely economic explanations of travel behavior. Income and price, though important, do not explain very much about individual leisure and travel decisions. Real incomes today are higher than they were a generation or two ago. People have more alternatives on which to spend their money, since a greater proportion of

---

*Obviously, there are exceptions to these research-based generalizations, just as some women are bus drivers and surgeons in the world of work. In general, however, most western societies assign these roles to males.

their incomes can be used for nonessentials — including travel. In addition, there has emerged a large middle income group of Americans — families earning essentially similar amounts of money. Because they spend their money in a greater variety of ways, their income level does not go very far toward helping us to understand how they will spend their discretionary dollars.[10] Thus, we have turned to psychological factors and, in this final chapter, to sociological factors to help explain travel behavior. One of these sociological factors is called **social class**, a concept that has been found useful in explaining many kinds of social behavior. Fortunately, there is a rich history of research in the area of social class, research that can suggest possible answers to many important questions about leisure and travel.

What is a Social Class?

All human societies can be broken down into groups on the basis of status and prestige. The reason is quite simple. Every society has functions that must be performed, and every individual assumes one role or another in performing them. This is true of even the most primitive societies. Someone becomes the chief and someone else the medicine man, while others become hunters or warriors. In a more advanced and complex society, the number and variety of such roles multiply. In both primitive and modern societies, each role is *valued* differently by the members of society. The functions performed by a laborer may be just as important as those performed by a doctor, but normally the doctor's contribution to the society will be valued more highly than the laborer's.[11]

Even where there is a deliberate effort to avoid social stratification, as in the Soviet Union, some roles are valued differently than others. All of the members of a society are not equal. All do not have the same power, the same possessions, or the same value systems. All occupations are not equally prestigious. And almost everyone is at least somewhat conscious of class differences. There is an understanding that some individuals rank higher and others lower on a social scale.

A social class consists of a large number of individuals who are approximately equal to each other in terms of social status. One popular social class theory holds that a western society like the United States can be broken up into six different social classes, ranging from what is called the upper-upper class to the lower-lower class.[12] These six social classes are listed in Figure 7-1, which gives an estimate of the percentage of people in the U.S. society who might fall into each of the classes.

The social class to which any given individual or family belongs can depend on several factors, but it is widely agreed that two of the most important are education and occupation.[13] Wealth and income sometimes

FIGURE 7-1   A social class system.

Social Class	Membership	Population Percentage
Upper-upper	Locally prominent families, third or fourth generation wealth. The aristocracy. Merchants, financiers, or higher professionals. Wealth is inherited.	1.5
Lower-upper	Newly arrived in upper class. *Nouveau riche.* Not accepted by upper-upper class. Executive elite, founders of large businesses, doctors, and lawyers.	1.5
Upper-middle	Moderately successful professionals, owners of medium-sized businesses, and middle management. Status conscious. Child and home centered.	10.0
Lower-middle	Top of the average-man world. Non-managerial office workers, small business owners, and blue-collar families. Described as striving and respectable. Conservative.	33.0
Upper-lower	Ordinary working class. Semiskilled workers. Income often as high as next two classes above. Enjoy life. Live from day to day.	38.0
Lower-lower	Unskilled, unemployed, and unassimilated ethnic groups. Fatalistic. Apathetic.	16.0
	TOTAL	100.0

Source: C.G. Walters and G. W. Paul, *Consumer Behavior* (Homewood, Illinois: Richard D. Irwin, Inc., 1970), p. 399.

have very little to do with a person's social class position, except at the upper class and lower-lower class levels. This is so because equal incomes do not necessarily lead to similar behavior patterns. This is the essential message of social class theory. Each social class displays a distinctive life style which is reflected in values, interpersonal attitudes, and self-perceptions that differ from those held by any other class. These differences lead to behavioral patterns that are similar among the members of the same social class but different, and sometimes dramatically so, from one class to another. The minister, with perhaps a very low income, will nevertheless have values and attitudes in common with a well-paid lawyer, and both may be members of the upper-middle social class. The financially secure bookie, however, would surely be part of a lower social class.

Social Class Values and Attitudes

People who belong to the same social class very often show remarkable similarity in how they behave. When we examine social class behavior, we see that similarities among members of the same class begin with many commonly held attitudes and values. It is useful here to identify some of the key attitudes and values that account for the distinctive behavior of social classes. We will be concerned primarily with drawing contrasts between the middle and the upper-lower or so-called working class, because together these groups account for an estimated 75 to 80 percent of the U.S. population.

The lower-lower class is of little interest to us here because income levels in this class generally preclude substantial involvement with pleasure travel. The aristocracy and the *nouveau riche* — the upper-class groups — represent perhaps no more than five percent of the population, although they probably account for a considerably larger proportion of leisure travel. With regard to the upper classes, it should at least be mentioned that individual and family behavior within these groups sometimes serves as a model for members of the upper-middle class. Those in the upper-middle class who aspire to rise into the upper class will emulate the behavior of its members. Upper-class people tend to emphasize gracious living and the proper spending of wealth — on art, antiques, travel, exclusive clubs, and Ivy League educations. Thus, the behavior of the upper classes can have a great impact on the behavior of those in the upper-middle class.

Self-Perceptions.   In our discussion of perception (see Chapter 2), we noted that social class exerts a powerful effect on the perception of travel phenomena. We stated that middle-class people generally have a broader view of the world and their place in it than people from lower social classes. They feel personally connected to national events and the world at large. Moreover, the middle class tends to be much more self-confident, adventuresome, and willing to take risks than lower social classes. As a result, the middle class is likely to take greater interest in travel than a lower social class.

A person from a lower social class generally perceives the world in somewhat limited and threatening terms.[14] He may perceive a trip to Europe or some other far-off destination as unnecessary, frivolous, and therefore of no interest. His ideal vacation may be a trip to some domestic destination or, perhaps even better, three weeks each summer at a family cottage at a nearby lake. He is more likely to see his home as his castle and, if he can afford it, he loads it down with hardware — expensive appliances in the kitchen, a swimming pool, expensive television sets. These objects symbolize security. In contrast, the middle-class person is more likely to spend his money on intangibles such as Broadway plays, education, and travel.[15]

When we consider these differences in values and attitudes, it becomes easy to see why social class can be much more effective than income or wealth in explaining travel behavior. A working-class family may have an income equal to or greater than that of a comparable middle-class family. Research clearly shows, however, that the middle-class family is much more likely to travel. Income has little to do with it. What matters is the family's general view of the world and its attitude toward travel as a way of exploring it.

Parent-Child Relationships.   A study of the general values and attitudes of middle- and working-class women can also be helpful to us. Both are highly child-centered. Children are proof of each woman's self-worth, although children are likely to play a more central role in the life of the working-class woman. She is much more protective of her children since, for her, the world is a more threatening place.[16]

Social class clearly influences mothers' attitudes toward their children's education. As we shall see, this can have a tremendous impact on family travel. Working-class mothers do not attach as much importance to their children's education as middle-class mothers.[17] To the middle-class mother, education is seen as the ticket to better jobs, to better-paying and more rewarding careers, and to social mobility (potential membership in higher social classes). The working-class mother, too, recognizes the value of a good education for her children, but social mobility for her is generally a less important factor. For her children to eventually assume a respectable place in the working class is something that she and they can be proud of.

Parental attitudes toward the education of children offer another good explanation of why the middle-class family is more likely than the working-class family to travel, even when their incomes are identical. To the extent that travel is perceived as an educational experience, the middle-class family will respond by traveling more. The working-class family, on the other hand, is not as likely to respond in the same way because it does not attach the same importance to education. This underscores the value of positioning travel as an educational experience when selling vacations to middle-class family markets. It also suggests that to successfully market travel to the working class, it is either necessary to stress benefits other than education, or to convince working-class people that family educational experiences are important.

The latter approach may not be as difficult as it seems, because there are different types of educational experiences. The middle-class parent might seek a travel experience from which his or her child stands to learn something of importance, say, about history, government, or science. The working-class parent, on the other hand, might be moved by a travel experience that promises to teach his or her child something of importance, say, about hunting, fishing, or the great outdoors. Each social class will prefer different types of travel destinations and attractions. The middle-class family might very likely be attracted to destinations like Washington, D.C., Pennsylvania Dutch Country, the NASA Space Center, and Western Europe. The working-class family, on the other hand, might find fishing, hunting, or camping vacations more attractive. As we will see, there are additional social class values and attitudes that would support the notion that each group gravitates toward different types of travel destinations and vacation activities.

Husband-Wife Relationships.   Spouse relationships also tend to differ between the middle and working classes in ways that can clearly influence leisure and travel behavior. In a working-class marriage, the roles played by the husband and wife tend to be more clearly delineated than in a middle-class marriage. The working-class wife typically assumes most of the day-to-day responsibility for rearing the couple's children; she is expected to keep a clean house, be a good cook, and agree with her husband on most important family matters. The working-class wife tends to be submissive largely because she has learned to depend on her husband as someone who takes care of her and gives her a sense of identity.[18]

The working-class husband also acts out a traditional role. While his wife tends to matters inside the home, he cuts the lawn, paints the house, earns a living, disciplines the children when they challenge their mother, demands respect from each member of the family, and strives to maintain his position and image as the dominant member of the household. Compared to his middle-class counterpart, the working-class male has a more formal relationship with his children, and he also tends to be more concerned about his physical strength and masculinity.[19]

The separate and distinct male and female roles played by the typical working-class couple often carry over into their leisure-time pursuits. More so than his middle-class counterpart, the working-class husband is likely to enjoy regular "nights out with the boys," perhaps at a local bowling alley or tavern. He is more apt to leave his family behind periodically and take off with a small number of friends on a long fishing or hunting expedition — the kind of journey that allows him to affirm his masculinity.

The middle-class couple provides a marked contrast to this description. Middle-class husbands and wives are more likely to work together as a team, the husband attending to some household chores, while the wife helps paint the house or care for the yard. The wife, especially in upper-middle class families, is expected to help further her husband's career interests while the husband shares in the responsibility of raising their children. The middle-class couple, in other words, is likely to have less traditional ideas about interpersonal relationships and male-female roles.

The greater degree of togetherness in the middle-class marriage is reflected in the family's leisure-time activities. Although the middle-class husband, too, may go off occasionally on all-male hunting or fishing expeditions, his vacations nearly always include time spent with his family.[20]

When we consider that the middle class sees the world in much broader and less threatening terms than the working class, it is not surprising that the middle-class couple would relate socially to a greater number of people outside the home. The social relationships of working-class people tend to be restricted in large part to relatives.[21] These social class differences, too, should have an effect on how leisure time is spent. They may affect the destinations to which people travel, their preferred modes of transportation, and what they prefer to do when they are away from home. This again suggests that there is much about leisure and travel behavior that just cannot be explained by income levels, prices, age, and other economic and demographic factors.

Social Class and Consumption Behavior

Members of the same social class possess many of the same things that are valued by the group. In some cases, it is wealth. In others, it is power, prestige, wisdom, or position. Shared values, attitudes, and behavioral norms also translate into an attraction to many of the same types of goods and services. People in the same social class — particularly those who are members of the same groups which spring from these social classes — often spend time and money in the same ways. Shared values and attitudes, in other words, result in similar tastes, life styles, and preferences for many of the same kinds of goods and services.

The upper-class family budget, for example, often reflects a concern for such things as books, magazine subscriptions, country club memberships, travel, art, antiques, Ivy League educations, and certain sporting and recreational paraphernalia. At the other end of the social class scale, the budget of the lower-class family reflects a necessary preoccupation with food, clothing, and its own special set of luxuries. Between these two extremes, there is remarkable similarity within different social classes in terms of the goods and services for which they spend their money.

Members of the same social class also tend to behave similarly in terms of their attitudes toward and use of credit, the types of stores to which they are attracted, and how they react to advertising and promotion. Research on the marketplace behavior of different social classes will help us to formulate answers to a number of important travel-related questions.

Credit Card Usage. Research indicates that upper classes tend to use credit cards more as a convenience that frees them from carrying large sums of money and to facilitate accurate record keeping for tax and budget purposes. Lower classes tend to use credit cards more often for installment finance, and it is argued that this stems, in part, from the lower classes' inability to delay the gratification of their needs and wants.[22]

Middle and upper social class consumers are more likely to avoid using credit cards for installment financing purposes because, psychologically, people in these social classes are more willing to defer the gratification of their needs and wants. Again, something more than economics explains this. Middle- and upper-class persons tend to have wider time horizons and to plan over longer periods of time. Moreover, such people have a greater reason to plan ahead. They have more of an investment in career, reputation, and accumulated property to risk if they get into serious financial difficulty. A lower-class person, it is argued, has less to risk in terms of such long-run investments.[23] Thus, the lower social classes are more likely to follow their impulses, buy what they want, and use credit to do so if necessary.

Thus, when selling travel to middle and upper social classes, stressing the use of credit to finance a vacation may be a less successful strategy than one might first imagine. Middle- and upper-class people are often seriously committed to regular savings plans and must think long and hard before incurring additional debt. This is not to say that middle- and upper-class people do not go into debt, even for luxuries like travel. Rather, the decision to incur significant debt for these people — who make up the bulk of the travel market — is normally a serious matter, and using the appeal of credit to help sell travel is probably not as successful a strategy as it might seem. Perhaps travel savings club programs would make more sense than selling travel on credit.

Shopping Behavior. Some of the earliest studies of the impact of social class on consumer behavior dealt with its effect on shopping behavior. Obviously, the clientele of Saks Fifth Avenue differs from that of Montgomery Ward or Sears. Shoppers of all social classes are often attracted to retail outlets that reflect and cater to their particular class.[24] Lower-status people are as anxious to avoid the upper-class stores as the upper classes are to avoid the lower-status stores. Many businesses have a definite social class image, and their regular customers feel very much at home in them. They carry the quality of merchandise that the customer is interested in. People like themselves — from the same social class — shop in these stores.

Differences between retail outlets are, of course, relative. The middle-class shopper may be willing to buy products such as refrigerators or washing machines at discount stores. With such items, the brand name is the assurance of quality. Where style and taste are important, or where there is greater risk in trusting a little-known brand name — as with furniture or jewelry — the "right" store is apt to be very important to the shopper. While the working class generally tends to show a narrowness in store choice, middle-class shoppers are usually willing to shop in more places and to consider a wider range of possibilities.[25] In part, this reflects a difference in the capacity to experience adventure. This capacity can also explain the places travelers choose to eat when they are away from home, the hotels and motels they choose to patronize, the destinations they choose to visit, and so forth.

Like retail stores, many tourist destinations have a definite social class orientation that appeals to a specific social class group. Western ski resorts, for example, can probably be categorized on the basis of the social classes which they attract. So might resort communities along the New Jersey and Florida coastlines, as well as Carribean resorts. It also seems clear that different social class groups would be attracted to different modes of transportation, to different types of leisure activities, and so forth. There are, of course, some travel service businesses that appeal to the very large middle class. Holiday Inn, for example, undoubtedly appeals not only to the upper- and lower-middle classes, but to the working class as well. Florida attracts people from all social classes but, as we suggested earlier, the different social classes tend to segregate themselves once they arrive.

The issue of social class attraction to particular retail stores raises some interesting questions about retail travel agencies and the types of customers they serve. The better than 16,000 travel agencies in the U.S. handle more than $15 billion worth of travel business each year. Yet the industry considers this much less than its true potential. The major travel agency trade association, the American Society of Travel Agents (ASTA), has considered the use of advertising to create greater awareness of the services performed by travel agencies. Such a strategy, it seems, would be more productive if more were known about the typical travel agency client. Unfortunately, there seems to be little of this type of knowledge available. Does the majority of a typical travel agency's clients come primarily from one social class? How do they learn about travel agencies and what prompts them to rely on a travel agent for planning their travels away from home?

Response to Promotion. Consumer response to promotional efforts also differs on the basis of social class. Social class influences what is read, listened to, and watched. Thus, advertising is affected by social class considerations. Some of the most obvious differences between social classes are in terms of their exposure to various magazines. Some magazines, like the *New Yorker* and *Saturday Review*, are read almost exclusively by the upper and upper-middle classes. This is reflected not only in the editorial content of these magazines, but also in terms of the advertisers and the appeals they use the promotional content as well. In a typical issue of either magazine, there is a considerable amount of advertising by foreign destination areas, international carriers, and cruise lines. Moreover, the appeals in this advertising stress many of those things which would appeal primarily to the upper and upper-middle classes: visits to art festivals, operas, archeological sites, and so forth — as well as elegance, luxury, gourmet dining, and gracious living.

By contrast, the travel advertising normally found in magazines like *Time, Newsweek, Sports Illustrated, Better Homes and Gardens,* and other magazines aimed at the large mass market (the middle class market) mainly promotes the services of firms serving the domestic travel market. These firms include domestic air carriers, U.S. hotel and motel chains, car rental companies, and domestic vacation destinations. Occasionally, these mass market magazines will carry advertising that promotes travel to such destinations as Western Europe and Hawaii because, as noted in Chapter 4, such destinations now appeal to the large middle-class market. In addition, travel advertising in the mass market magazines very often stresses such things as economy, unlimited mileage fares, super saver fares, and specially-priced travel package programs.

Social classes also differ in the amount of television and kinds of programs they watch; in their exposure to radio and newspaper advertising; and in their reactions to different advertising formats. Middle-class families, for example, generally watch less television than working-class families, read more of the newspaper, and are more likely to listen to FM rather than AM radio stations. The type of humor that can be used effectively in advertising also varies from one social class audience to another. Humor that appeals to the middle class, for example, is generally more subtle and often not appreciated at lower social class levels.

THE FAMILY GROUP AND TRAVEL BEHAVIOR

One authority estimates that a minimum of 90 percent of the people living in a society like the United States spend their leisure hours on group-oriented activities. In fact, it is argued that specific leisure activities are sometimes secondary to the social interaction that takes place within the group. Some leisure activities, it is suggested, appear to be interchangeable. That is, for social groups whose members gather to enjoy a special activity, several other activities and a variety of leisure settings will suffice to achieve the group's primary objective: to spend time enjoying one another's company. Whether a family spends time camping in West Virginia, fishing in Wyoming, or water skiing in Wisconsin is said to be secondary to the fact that the family spends its vacation time together.[26]

This argument can be carried too far, however. It seems clear that activities and settings have some impact on the relative pleasure that group members derive from a particular leisure experience. It may be true, for instance, that children will enjoy nearly any kind of vacation experience, but it is also true that — beyond a certain age — they perceive certain travel destinations and leisure activities as preferable to others.[27]

The point of greatest interest to us here is the social nature of leisure and travel activities, which are most often experienced in some type of group setting. Moreover, we should not lose sight of the fact that the family unit is the single most important leisure group in western societies.[28] It has been estimated, for example, that better than two out of every three recreational activities in which Americans participate tend to be family oriented. Of those leisure activities that can be classified as cultural, nearly 40 percent are estimated to be family oriented.[29] Because of the importance of the family unit in leisure and travel, we return to it here in order to discuss other factors that influence leisure and travel behavior.

The Family Life Cycle

Perhaps the most important source of group influence comes from the families to which we belong. What is called the **family life cycle** can be a valuable tool for helping us to better understand how the family group influences individual travel and leisure behavior. The family life cycle is concerned with how the attitudes and behavior of the family and its members change over time. Attitude and behavior changes are often caused by changes in the roles played by family members. These role changes, in turn, are caused by changes in the size of the family, the maturity and experience of the family members, and by changes in their needs, values, perceptions, and interests.

Newly married couples are typically concerned with the purchase of household furnishings, small appliances, and accessories. Before any children are born, the couple is more likely to be oriented toward entertainment, recreation, and the advancement of their careers. They are more inclined to be on the go, so to speak, and thus concerned with style and fashion in clothes as well as in furnishings and other things.

The arrival of children alters this orientation. Now a major concern is with the nursery and more space — a house, perhaps, rather than an apartment. The need for savings and insurance arises. The wife, who may have been working, may now decide to stay home; hence, family income declines. Family needs change over time as the family moves from one stage of life to another, as people grow older, as income levels rise or fall. And, when we know the family life cycle stage in which a family belongs, we are better able to predict and understand how it will behave — how it is likely to spend its time and money, and the role that travel will play in its overall life-style.

It is generally acknowledged that most American households pass through an orderly progression of stages over time. Some authorities have identified four distinct family life stages:[30]

1. Married couples just starting their independent economic existence
2. Couples with one or more children
3. Couples with one or more adult, self-supporting children
4. Couples growing old

Other authorities have identified as many as 24 family life cycle stages.[31] A recently developed model of the family life cycle that takes into consideration rising divorce rates, an overall decline in the average family size, later marriages, and other factors is presented in Figure 7-2.[32]

It shows a life cycle consisting of three major stages, each of which we will discuss in more detail. The role that travel is likely to play in the life-style of a family in each stage is identified.

Young Stages. One traditional life cycle stage includes young, married people (under 35) without children. Traditionally, this "honeymoon" stage has been rather short, lasting less than two years before the first child was born. But today, because of birth control, changing attitudes toward parenthood, and more wives who work for financial or career reasons, this stage may be extended by several years. This allows the young married couple to establish a degree of financial security that young couples of earlier generations rarely enjoyed. This, of course, can have a significant influence on the present and future travel behavior of the family.

During the "honeymoon" stage of a family's life cycle, the couple typically spends heavily on new automobiles, refrigerators, stoves, furniture, and other durable products. Vacation travel may also play an important part in their lives. Realizing that their freedom may be severely restricted when they begin having children and that their discretionary income may decrease as well, the young couple may be very active in the travel market. This may last for several years if they decide to postpone having children.

FIGURE 7-2   A modernized family life cycle.

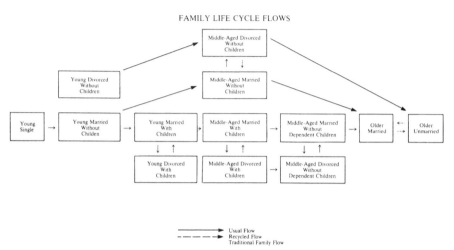

A MODERNIZED FAMILY LIFE CYCLE

FAMILY LIFE CYCLE FLOWS

Source: Patrick E. Murphy and William A. Staples, "A Modernized Family Life Cycle,"
Journal of Consumer Research, Vol. 6 (June, 1979), p. 17.

Beyond the "honeymoon" stage, people will move in one of three directions. In the traditional life cycle, young married couples have children. This young-married-with-children stage is customarily broken down into substages depending on the ages of children: infants, children four-to twelve-years-old, and adolescents. The presence of children usually alters the life-style and financial situation of the family. Often the family buys a home and begins to equip it with things such as washers, dryers, and new furniture, and it must begin spending more of its income on children's clothing, toys, baby foods, cough medicines, vitamins, and so forth. The family's interest in travel during this stage will, of course, be strongly influenced by the presence of its children. Often, the family travel budget will be spent on vacations designed for the entire family's enjoyment and might include trips specifically intended to add to the children's overall education. In the past, this has meant long summer family vacations that normally preclude separate vacations for the parents. The family's travel behavior will depend on its income, on its social class orientation, and on the number and ages of its children.

It is important to note that the length of this life cycle stage has become shorter in recent years because the average family is having fewer children, and they are not being spaced as far apart.This means that the traditional family will move more quickly into its next life cycle stage, a stage which is more conducive to vacation travel other than the two-week, family summer vacation in an automobile.

Some people move from young-married-without-children into what Figure 7-2 refers to as young-divorced-without-children. It is important to recognize this as a distinct life-cycle stage because, as recent statistics show, one of every three marriages in the U.S. ends in divorce. Divorce has become more prevalent in U.S. society, more accepted, and is occurring at earlier points in the marriage. Unless they are involved in well-paying careers, young divorced people sometimes have serious financial problems which, among other things, temporarily limit their ability to spend heavily on travel.

Yet another alternative stage in the early part of the modern family's life cycle includes young divorced people with children. In 1976, about 40 percent of the divorces in the U.S. involved mothers under the age of thirty. No matter what the number and ages of children, divorce results in significant life-style and financial changes. Typically, the wife retains custody of any children and often finds child support payments inadequate. She must seek employment, sometimes several years after having left the labor force. For the husband, the cost of divorce and of maintaining a separate household often leaves him without much discretionary income. In both cases, the implications for spending heavily on travel are obvious.

Middle-Aged Stages. The middle-aged stages of the modern family life-cycle contain six different possibilities. Those who head families in any of these stages can range in age from thirty-five to sixty-four. One stage involves the middle-aged married couple without children. Historically, this group has been relatively small, but it is likely to become larger in the future as more couples make the conscious decision not to have children. For a childless couple with good health and financial security, this life cycle stage can be characterized as carefree. Careers are apt to be well-established, and couples in this stage may spend heavily on travel.[33]

The most traditional middle-aged group consists of married people with young and adolescent children. An estimated one out of every three individuals in the U.S. is a part of this type of family group. The predominant life-style here revolves more or less around the children. Traveling together may be of considerable importance in this type of family and may consist of more than just two weeks in its automobile every summer. This will depend to a great extent on the actual number and ages of the children, their personalities, and the nature of the parents' career commitments. The financial position of this family is likely to be comfortable because the father's career may have advanced to a higher level, and because a larger percentage of wives will be working. During this life cycle stage, the family is much more likely to spend money on expensive luxury items like boats, recreational vehicles, vacation homes, foreign vacations, and so forth.

Two of the middle-aged family life cycle stages are sometimes referred to as *empty nest* stages. These stages are experienced by people, married and divorced, who no longer have dependent children to support. After children are gone, people have greater financial freedom and can begin to seriously consider new life-style options such as round-the-world trips, expensive cruises, and so forth. Of course, their choices will depend on their relative financial situations, their social class, and other factors. But for most, these options cannot even be seriously considered until after the children have grown and left home.

Due to smaller family sizes and less spacing between children, this stage is becoming longer — a fact of importance to us here because travel can take on great value during the empty nest stage of the family life cycle. People in this stage are in the market for travel for a longer period of time. It is a life cycle stage that can begin as early as the mid-forties and last until retirement years. Even if a family is not wealthy, the extended length of this stage may allow couples to save for their dream vacations to more distant destinations.

Older Stages.   These family life cycle stages begin when the head of the family retires. Retirement, of course, represents a major life-style and financial change for most. Older retired people have few time commitments, but may have to reduce their standard of living. Those with substantial savings or pensions and good health can enjoy an active retirement. For many, this means frequent traveling.

Life Cycle Stages and Travel Behavior

What Figure 7-2 shows us is a variety of life cycle combinations consisting of families with unique needs, financial situations, and patterns of behavior. Some of these groups — such as the young-married-without-children couples and the empty-nest families — represent attractive market segments for those who market and sell various travel products and services. The people in these kinds of families usually have the time, the freedom, and often the money to travel extensively.

Other modern life cycle groups, however, consist of families which do not have the time and the freedom to travel extensively, even if they have the money. This is not to say that such families do not represent attractive marketing opportunities. The fact that a family is headed by a single divorced parent or that it has several young children does not mean that the *need* or *desire* of family members to travel has disappeared. The challenge to those who market and sell travel is to develop and promote products and services that are viable within family role playing and financial constraints.

Many travel service firms have segmented their markets in terms of various family life cycle groups for which they design and promote specific services. Examples include the tour wholesalers who market tours specifically for singles and the resort hotels which market vacations for honeymooners. For many years, cruise lines offered their product primarily to the older life cycle groups. The industry began a long period of prosperity when it modified its product and began to appeal to younger life cycle groups as well. Theme parks likewise entered a period of sustained growth when they developed a product that appealed to families stretching across many life cycle stages — a product that appealed not only to young children and their older brothers and sisters but to their parents as well. The ski resort business was once patronized by a relatively small number of enthusiasts who braved cold weather and sometimes spartan facilities to ski. Skiing was the sole attraction, and après-ski activities were virtually nonexistent. In the late 1950s, the ski resort blossomed into a place for family outings when it started to meet demands for convenience, comfort, a variety of recreational facilities, and activities that continue after the sun disappears behind the mountain. Families now constitute better than 40 percent of the total ski market.[34]

These examples illustrate the value of analyzing marketing and selling opportunities not in terms of the ages of prospective buyers, but in terms of family situations and what they suggest about individual and group needs and interests. In addition, it might prove useful to know whether what can be called **travel strategies** vary systematically from one life cycle group to another.

Five different travel strategies can be identified:[35]

1. rapid movement to a specific place or region and participation in various vacation activities at the destination;
2. leisurely movement in the direction of a specific destination, with the attraction of both the trip itself and the destination assuming equal importance;
3. the fast-paced tour in which the object of the trip is to cover as much ground as possible and to visit a maximum number of attractions, no one of which is more important than any other;
4. the exploratory trip where a planned destination or activity may be nonexistent, and where the intrinsic pleasure of the trip lies in the journey itself; and
5. the multipurpose, multidestination trip in which the travel party imaginatively tosses friends, relatives, religious, economic, business, and professional reasons for travel into a hat with recreational interests, shakes well, and goes.

It seems likely that some of these travel strategies would be more popular with certain family life cycle groups than with others. Logical cases can be made for the popularity of strategy #1 with families whose children are young, because research has suggested that 5- to 10-year-olds are especially intolerant of leisurely travel toward a destination. Moreover, older children are more interested in actively participating in some leisure activity than in spending an inordinate amount of time passively sitting in an automobile. Strategy #2, it seems, would probably be especially popular with older life cycle groups. The reader can draw further conclusions about the travel strategies that would seem to be most popular with other life cycle groups.

THE IMPACT OF CULTURE ON TRAVEL BEHAVIOR

So far this chapter has focused on how various groups influence the leisure and travel behavior of individuals. We have seen how small groups (such as the family) and large groups (such as social classes) influence leisure and travel behavior. It is also important to recognize that the culture in which a person lives has a significant impact on his or her leisure and travel behavior.

The culture in which one lives can be viewed as a large, impersonal reference group. We can speak of Western culture, European culture, and Oriental culture, or we can speak of cultures in national terms, such as American and French culture. As we shall see, we can also speak of subcultures, such as the Mexican-American and French-Canadian subcultures.

Culture is learned behavior. Someone who lives in the U.S. society learns from its culture a unique set of beliefs, values, attitudes, habits, customs, traditions, and forms of behavior. Culture influences a person's aspirations in life, the roles he fills, how he relates to other people, the way he perceives things, the goods and services he feels he needs, and the way he behaves as a consumer.

Often, the influence of culture on individual behavior is overlooked. For example, we often think of men and women in terms of distinct personalities or patterns of behavior that are due in large part to basic physiological differences. Men are often assumed to be more dominant, aggressive, and task-oriented than women who, in turn, are assumed to be more passive and emotional. In the U.S., such descriptions may seem to be fairly accurate. Sex-role differences vary widely, however, from one culture to another, indicating that many of the differences between male and female behavior are in reality due to role differences learned from the cultural environment in which people live.[36] If many American women are not active participants in outdoor leisure activities such as hunting and fishing, it is not really due to any physical or emotional factor. Rather,

American culture has taught women that such activities are for men. The culture also teaches men and women appropriate travel roles: men do the driving, select the destination, and register at hotels, while women tend to the children, prepare any roadside meals, and so forth.

We also tend to expect different patterns of behavior according to age groups in our society. Children are expected to act differently from adolescents, young adults, or older adults and, for the most part, they do. Again, we tend to assume that these are natural differences — differences that are due to the unique biological characteristics of people at different age levels. Patterns of behavior that seem to be related to age, however, are not always due to biological factors. Rather, they are in large part cultural and social phenomena. In the U.S. culture, for example, children are pushed toward growing up. In other societies, however, the passage from childhood to adolescence and adulthood is deliberately prolonged.

Those who market and sell travel must take individual travel behavior that is dictated by cultural norms and traditions as given. There is nothing that a single travel service firm and little, if anything, that the travel industry as a whole can do to bring about changes in travel behavior that is governed by social and cultural traditions. If, for example, men generally make family vacation decisions while women are generally expected to play a more passive travel role, then those who market and sell travel must be aware of these factors and market their services accordingly. Male and female travel roles will change only to the extent that male and female roles in general change within the context of the larger cultural setting.

Cultures within A Culture

Normally within any given society we find any number of subcultures. Some of these groups are based on nationality, such as the Italian-American and Mexican-American subcultures. Religion is often the basis for subcultures: the Amish in the United States are one example. Subcultures might be based on race, language, age, social class, and other factors. The important point here is that members of a subculture typically conform to many of the norms of the dominant culture, but deviate from other norms which are not compatible with those of their subculture. In the U.S., for example, teenagers form a distinct subcultural group. They embrace most of the values of the overall culture in which they live, but adhere to their own unique set of values as well. One such value relates to the importance of relationships with peers.

The values and traditions that are unique to a particular subculture affect the behavior of its members in various ways. To illustrate this point it will be useful to summarize the findings of a research study that examined the leisure and travel attitudes and behavior of a group of Mexican-Americans in the southwestern United States.

Leisure and Travel in the Mexican-American Subculture.   When we talk about cultures and subcultures and about their different value and belief systems, we could be referring to any number of value orientations, including the following:[37]

- man's basic nature (good vs. evil)
- man's orientation toward time (toward the past, the present, the future)
- man's relationship to nature (subordinate to it, an integral part of it, or master of it)
- man's primary purpose in life (being, self-actualizing, or achieving)
- man's primary relationship to his fellow man (individualistic, family-oriented, or peer-oriented)

Some authorities believe that the middle class in the United States represents the dominant cultural group and that its values are the dominant ones in American society. These dominant values include (1) an orientation toward the future, (2) a relationship of mastery over nature, (3) an achievement orientation, and (4) an individualistic orientation.[38]

There is considerable evidence that Mexican-Americans as an ethnic subculture subscribe to a somewhat different set of values.[39] These values include (1) an orientation toward the present rather than the future, (2) a subordinate role with respect to nature, (3) a "being" rather than an achievement orientation, and (4) a family rather than an individualistic orientation. It should not be surprising to learn that research indicates that these different subcultural values affect the attitudes that members of the Mexican-American subculture hold toward leisure.

Whereas the middle class Anglo-American culture attaches significant importance to the role of work as a central life interest and as a source of primary social relationships, the Mexican-American subculture holds that a person knows himself primarily through his leisure or nonwork activities. The Mexican-American is less likely to view his work as a central life interest, and his primary social relationships are more likely to be rooted in his leisure. Within the middle-class Anglo-American culture, where the Protestant Work Ethic still prevails, guilt sometimes accompanies leisure that is not productive. Mexican-Americans, however, are far less likely to feel any guilt about enjoying leisure for its own sake.

What are the implications of these cultural differences? For one thing, leisure is likelier to be task-oriented for those who embrace the Protestant Work Ethic and who consider work to be virtuous. Such people might be found spending their leisure time working in backyard gardens, painting their homes, finishing off attics, or building their own lake cottages. When they travel, it seems less likely that they would be interested either in leisurely movement in the direction of a specific destination or the exploratory type of trip where a planned destination or activity may be nonexistent. Instead, these people would have a greater interest in trips with specific objectives: multipurpose and multidestination trips; trips involving rapid movement to a specific destination and participation in various vacation activities at the destination; and fast-paced tours in which the object of the trip is to cover as much ground as possible and to visit a maximum number of attractions.

In contrast, the Mexican-American concept of leisure seems to have Latin and Greek roots which stress leisure as a festive occasion. The Latin and Greek tradition views work as a necessary though temporary diversion from leisure, which plays a central role in life. Thus, travel for the Mexican-American would presumably be less constricted by the need to accomplish tasks or to achieve specific objectives.

In summary, it seems clear that a subculture will seek different benefits in travel and leisure than the dominant culture. One subcultural group may seek pleasure for the sake of pleasure. Other subcultural groups may place great value on cultural or educational benefits. Still others may place great value on social interaction or activities that contribute to one's physical well-being. Travel service firms have to be sensitive to ethnic and other subcultural differences because of the impact these differences have on leisure and travel preferences. This is particularly important in a travel market where catering to the special needs of specific groups is often the most viable way to earn profits.

Culture, Sport, and Travel.   Any discussion of how cultural values influence leisure and travel behavior would be incomplete without recognizing the increasing importance of sports as a primary consideration in pleasure travel. Sport is an intrinsic cultural value in most societies.[40] This is particularly so in the United States, where an active interest in sports and the desire to go somewhere to pursue them have become major motivational factors in the travel plans of millions of Americans.

In recent years, according to the Department of Transportation, the second largest increases in travel have been related to outdoor recreation. Outdoor recreation refers not just to fishing, hunting, and camping, but also to golf, tennis, skiing, scuba diving, and other sports. In 1976, *Sports Illustrated* conservatively estimated that one-third of all air travelers were sports travelers. In a study of business executives, the magazine found that 44 percent took at least one trip a year *primarily* to engage in golf, tennis, or skiing.[41]

That sport has become an important factor in the travel market should not be at all surprising when one examines the recent, phenomenal growth in the popularity of various participant sports in the U.S. From 1960 to

1975, for example, the number of active tennis players jumped from five million to 35 million. During the same period, the number of people who played golf at least 15 times a year more than doubled, and the number of people who skied more than 12 times a year increased from three million to more than 11 million.[42]

Many travel service firms have responded to the emergence of a new generation of travelers who attach great importance to sport and recreation. Airlines promote travel to destinations where one can find good weather and championship golf courses, ideal tennis facilities, or perfect skiing conditions. Major resorts are actively seeking the guest who wants to play golf or tennis, as opposed to the guest who would play tennis or golf simply because it is available. Some travel agencies are also capitalizing on the enormous growth of sports-related travel.[43]

It is important for the student of travel behavior to understand why sports have come to be a more significant cultural value not only in the United States, but in many other countries as well. We should keep in mind that from a historical perspective the increasing popularity of sport has happened rather suddenly. The explanations are rather simple:[44]

> People come to sports with the expectation of individual performance — they expect to do *some* thing and then see the results. They expect to perform superbly — once in a while — and to be impressed with their own performance. They expect a tangible result of their activity.
>
> Similarly, people come to sports *viewing* with the expectation of being awed, of being impressed by the craftsmanship and excellence of the players and the play. This is not terribly surprising — after all, how many people turn out on a Saturday afternoon to see my neighbors knock the ball around the course in the upper 90s? The ingredient here which is critical is *awe;* spectators want to say, figuratively, "Wow, look at that!"

Why is it important for an individual to be *awed,* or to do *some* thing and then see the results of his performance? Quite simply, because work styles have changed in industrialized countries like the United States. Two out of every three American workers are employed in service industries — education, health, advertising, accounting, research, and so forth — in which one does not *see* that which he produces. Moreover, most people are employed by organizations in which what is produced cannot be credited to any single person. Thus, one's contribution is difficult, if not impossible, to identify.

A hundred years ago, most Americans lived in rural areas. In those days, a person could easily see the fruits of his labor — tonnage of hay cut, number of horses shod, number of trees felled. Today, few workers create an entire product. It is difficult for the modern worker to say, "I made that!" Psychologically, however, it seems important that people be able to do so, to be able to look at their work and see that it is good. And so we use our leisure to find this satisfaction: to do something entirely by ourselves, to recognize it as such, and to exclaim with pride, "I did that!" Similarly, we identify with and delight in the spectacular performance of an individual in an athletic event.

It should not be surprising, then, that sports experiences are among the most vivid and memorable that we can have and that sport has become such an important value in the U.S. and other industrialized societies. An understanding of this cultural phenomenon can be very important, because sports offer a valuable way of segmenting the travel market and thereby more profitably serving the needs of consumer-travelers.

It's the Thought that Counts

In nearly all cultures gift giving is an important custom, although its functions and effects sometimes vary in interesting ways. In the United States, gifts are given on birthdays, at Christmas, as wedding presents, and on other special occasions. This custom concerns us here because it offers the travel industry one means of creating greater demand for travel services.

One of the key characteristics of a modern industrialized society like the U.S. is that consumers now spend more on services than they do on tangible goods. As a result, the giving of intangible services as gifts has become more popular. It is not uncommon today for people to give or to receive as gifts such intangible services as memberships to health spas, tickets to plays or concerts, gift certificates to restaurants, passes to ski resorts, and airline tickets.

The increasing popularity of giving *intangible* gifts seems due to more than just the fact that intangibles now play a larger role in our life-styles. To the recipient, the intangible gift represents an opportunity to shape the nature and character of the gift to suit his own preferences and needs. Consider, for example, someone who receives a gift certificate for a meal for two at an exclusive restaurant. This person will choose when the meal will be prepared and served, what it will consist of, and with whom it will be shared. Likewise, someone who is given an airline ticket to Hawaii will decide when he will go, what he will do while he is in Hawaii, how much time he will spend on Oahu and the outer islands, and perhaps even which airline he will fly on.

It becomes apparent, then, that a gift of an intangible service like travel is a particularly personal one. The recipient can tailor the gift to specific needs, preferences, or whims. This reduces the risk that the gift will not match the recipient's tastes, needs, or desires. Because of this, the recipient is likely to realize maximum enjoyment from the gift. For these reasons, travel is an attractive present. Nevertheless, while some travel organizations have made sporadic attempts to market travel as a gift, on the whole, the industry has not made significant and sustained efforts to develop this untapped market.

SUMMARY

People belong to numerous formal and informal groups. They do so because groups perform important functions for their members. Groups can also have a profound effect on the behavior of individual members, sometimes playing an important role in determining how leisure time is spent. The groups to which we belong and the roles we play within them influence what we do, with whom we do it, and where and when we do it. Moreover, the roles we play affect the goods and services we buy and consume.

A group defines the roles its members play and in this way influences individual behavior. Thus, role playing offers a useful perspective for understanding individual behavior in a travel setting. To one extent or another, a traveler's behavior is likely to be quite different from what it is at home — not just because different roles are played but also because the traveler is away from home. When he leaves home, the pleasure traveler can be said to enter a fantasy or play world in which he can choose and act out roles with greater flexibility. This makes it possible for the traveler to act more impulsively than he normally does, and to notice things that he would not otherwise see.

A social class is a large group of people who are approximately equal to each other in terms of social status. Members of the same social class also are similar in terms of their attitudes, values, and self-perceptions. A person from the lower social class, for example, generally perceives the world in somewhat limited and threatening terms. To him, travel is normally much less appealing than it is to someone from a higher social class, who is apt to be much more self-confident, adventuresome, and willing to take the risks associated with travel. Social classes tend to differ in parental attitudes toward children, husband-wife relationships, in attitudes toward and the use of credit, and in reactions to advertising and promotion. In one way or another, all of these differences affect individual travel behavior.

It is important to recognize that leisure and travel most often involve social activities. Moreover, we should not lose sight of the fact that the family unit is the single most important leisure group in western societies, and the most important source of group influence on individual behavior. Understanding how the family group influences individual travel and leisure behavior is greatly facilitated by the family life cycle concept. This concept is concerned with how the attitudes, needs, values, and interests of the family and its members change over time. These changes can help answer important questions about leisure and travel behavior.

A culture is another large group of people usually defined in terms of geography, language, religion, nationality, or some other factor. We can also speak in terms of subcultures. People who are part of the same culture or subculture share many common beliefs, values, attitudes, habits, customs, traditions, and norms of behavior. Culture is learned behavior, and it influences a person's aspirations in life, the roles he fills, how he relates to other people, the way he perceives things, the goods and services he needs, and the way he behaves as a consumer. Culture also influences an individual's leisure and travel behavior.

For a variety of reasons, the United States has, in recent years, experienced a considerable increase in the volume of travelers from other nations. It appears that this trend will continue and perhaps even accelerate. Some destination areas, in fact, will find that foreign travelers are a highly significant factor in their total tourism picture. This trend underscores the importance of understanding the cultural values, norms, traditions, and preferences held by travelers from other countries. Special types of travel services may be needed to best serve the needs of these individuals, just as their countries cater to the tastes of American visitors in certain ways. Travel organizations that are likely to benefit most from the growth of overseas travelers to the U.S. are those that genuinely understand cultural differences among visitor groups and serve their special preferences and needs.

REFERENCES

[1] Reuel Denney, "The Leisure Society," *Harvard Business Review*, Vol. 37 (May–June 1959).

[2] K. Roberts, *Leisure* (London: Longman, 1970), p. 41.

[3] Catherine J. Schmidt, "The Guided Tour: Insulated Adventure," a paper presented at the Sixth Annual Conference of the Travel Research Association, San Diego (1975).

[4] J.P. Spiegel, "Interpersonal Influences within the Family," in *Interpersonal Dynamics*, eds. W. Bennis et al. (Homewood, Illinois: Dorsey Press, Inc., 1964).

[5] See: Lyman E. Ostlund, "Role Theory and Group Dynamics," in *Consumer Behavior*, eds. S. Ward and T.S. Robertson (Englewood Cliffs, New Jersey: Prentice-Hall, Inc., 1973), p. 233.

[6] Erik Cohen, "Who is a Tourist? A Conceptual Clarification," *Sociological Review*, Vol. 22 (1974), pp. 527-55.

[7] William R. Burch, Jr., "The Play World of Camping: Research into the Social Meaning of Outdoor Recreation," *American Journal of Sociology*, Vol. 70 (March, 1965), pp. 604-12 at p. 605.

[8] Ibid., p. 606.

[9] Burch, "The Play World of Camping. . . ," p. 605. Much of the material in this section is drawn from this source.

[10] Peter D. Bennett and Harold H. Kassarjian, *Consumer Behavior* (Englewood Cliffs, New Jersey: Prentice-Hall, Inc., 1972), p. 110.

[11] Ibid., pp. 110-11.

[12] W. Lloyd Warner et al., *Social Class in America* (New York: Harper & Row, 1960).

[13] Thomas S. Robertson, *Consumer Behavior* (Glenview, Illinois: Scott, Foresman and Company, 1970), p. 119.

[14] H.J. Gans, *The Urban Villagers* (New York: The Free Press, 1962).

[15] Much of the discussion here is based on a number of sources, including the following: Bernard Berelson and Gary A. Steiner, *Human Behavior* (New York: Harcourt, Brace & World, Inc., 1967), chapter 5; Richard Coleman, "The Significance of Social Stratification in Selling," *Proceedings of the American Marketing Association* (Chicago: American Marketing Association, 1960), pp. 171-84; Sidney J. Levy, "Social Class and Consumer Behavior," in *On Knowing the Consumer*, ed. J.W. Newman (New York: John Wiley and Sons, Inc., 1966), pp. 146-60; Pierre Martineau, "Social Classes and Spending Behavior," *Journal of Marketing*, Vol. 23 (October, 1958), pp. 121-30.

[16] Bennett and Kassarjian, *Consumer Behavior*, p. 117.

[17] Bernard Barber, "Social Class Differences in Educational Life-Chances," *Teachers College Record*, Vol. 63 (1961), pp. 102-13.

[18] Bennett and Kassarjian, *Consumer Behavior*, p. 116.

[19] Levy, "Social Class and Consumer Behavior."

[20] Bennett and Kassarjian, *Consumer Behavior*, p. 116.

[21] Frederick D. Sturdivant, "Subculture Theory: Poverty, Minorities, and Marketing," in *Consumer Behavior: Theoretical Sources*, eds. S. Ward and T. Robertson (Englewood Cliffs, New Jersey: Prentice-Hall, Inc., 1973), pp. 469-520 at p. 483.

[22] H. Lee Mathews and John W. Slocum, Jr., "Social Class and Commercial Bank Credit Card Usage," *Journal of Marketing*, Vol. 33 (January, 1969), pp. 71-78.

[23] Raymond A. Bauer, "Consumer Behavior as Risk Taking," *Proceedings*, ed. R.S. Hancock (Chicago: American Marketing Association, 1960), pp. 389-98. Also see: Lyman E. Ostlund, "Role Theory and Group Dynamics," in *Consumer Behavior: Theoretical Sources*, p. 264.

[24] Stuart U. Rich and Subhash C. Jain, "Social Class and Life Cycle as Predictors of Shopping Behavior," *Journal of Marketing Research*, Vol. 5 (February, 1968), pp. 41-49.

[25] Bennett and Kassarjian, *Consumer Behavior*, p. 120.

[26] Donald R. Field and Joseph T. O'Leary, "Social Groups as a Basis for Assessing Participation in Selected Water Activities," *Journal of Leisure Research*, Vol. 5 (Spring, 1973), pp. 16-25 at pp. 24-25.

[27] This and other factors concerning the attitudes of children toward family vacation travel have been the subject of a research project, "Family Vacation Travel," conducted in 1980-81 at the University of Central Florida, Dick Pope Sr. Institute for Tourism Studies.

[28] Roberts, *Leisure*, p. 41.

[29] John R. Kelly, "Family Leisure in Three Communities," *Journal of Leisure Research*, Vol. 10 (Winter, 1978), pp. 47-60 at p. 47.

[30] Pitirim A. Sorokin, Carle C. Zimmerman, and Charles J. Galpin, *A Systematic Sourcebook in Rural Sociology*, Vol. 2 (Minneapolis: University of Minnesota Press, 1931).

[31] Roy H. Rodgers, "Proposed Modification of Duvall Family Life Cycle Stages," paper presented at the American Sociological Association meetings, New York City (1960).

[32] The discussion of the model that follows is based on: Patrick E. Murphy and William A. Staples, "A Modernized Family Life Cycle," *Journal of Consumer Research*, Vol. 6 (June 1, 1979), pp. 12-22.

[33] William C. Wells and George Gubar, "Life Cycle Concept in Marketing Research," *Journal of Marketing Research*, Vol. 3 (1966), pp. 355-63.

[34] Harrison Price, "The Ski Resort and Its Feasibility," *Journal of Travel Research*, Vol. 10 (Winter, 1972), pp. 1-4.

[35] Mary Lee Nolan, "A Qualitative Study of Family Travel Patterns," unpublished paper, Recreation and Parks Department, Texas A&M University (Spring, 1971).

[36] Joseph E. McGrath, *Social Psychology* (New York: Holt, Rinehart and Winston, 1964), pp. 119-20.

[37] Florence Kluckhohn and F.L. Strodtbeck, *Variations in Value Orientations* (New York: Harper & Row, Publishers, 1961).

[38] Royal G. Jackson, "A Preliminary Bicultural Study of Value Orientations and Leisure Attitudes," *Journal of Leisure Research*, Vol. 5 (Fall, 1973), pp. 1-22.

[39] See: William Madse, *Mexican-Americans of South Texas* (New York: Holt, Rinehart and Winston, 1964). Some authorities believe that certain of these values are really traits of the culture of poverty; see: Oscar Lewis, *A Study of Slum Culture* (New York: Random House, 1968).

[40] Gunther Luschen, "The Interdependence of Sport and Culture," in Committee on Sport Sociology of the International Council of Sport and Physical Education (UNESCO), *International Review of Sport Sociology*, Vol. 2 (1967), pp. 127-41.

[41] Robert J. Schreiber, "Sports Interest, A Travel Definition," *Marketing Travel and Tourism*, Proceedings of the Seventh Annual Conference (Salt Lake City: Travel Research Association, 1976), pp. 85-87.

[42] Ibid., p. 85.

[43] See: American Society of Travel Agents, *The Travel Agent's Guide to Sport and Travel*, a study sponsored by the Boeing Commercial Airplane Company and *Sports Illustrated* (1976).

[44] Schreiber, "Sports Interest . . . ," p. 86.

QUESTIONS FOR DISCUSSION

1. A person joins groups because they satisfy certain needs for him. Identify five needs that can be satisfied through membership in a group.
2. Identify and discuss five benefits that a guided tour group can provide to its members.
3. Ask a friend to spend a few minutes telling you about an ideal vacation trip he would like to take. Listen carefully and ask questions that will encourage him to describe the vacation in as much detail as possible. As you listen, note the extent to which your friend's ideal vacation would be directly or indirectly affected by the various group influences discussed in this chapter.
4. List all of the groups, both formal and informal, to which you belong. Which

one of these groups would probably have the greatest impact on what you would consider to be an ideal vacation. Why?

5. There are many different types of roles that a person may feel compelled to play. Pick someone you know and describe the role that he or she is forced to play by virture of his or her occupation. Does this person enjoy more or less freedom in acting out her occupational role when she is in a leisure or travel setting?

6. How does the role of a vacationer differ from the role of a tourist? Do you think these role differences influence the selection of a particular type of vacation?

7. Men tend to get involved in a greater variety of leisure activities than women. Why might this be so? Some physical leisure activities — like water-skiing and tennis — have begun to attract women in greater numbers. Why do activities like fishing and hunting remain primarily male-oriented — despite the fact that they are no more physically demanding than activities like skiing and tennis?

8. What are some of the reasons why a family's income may offer few hints as to how it will spend its leisure time?

9. Why will working-class people generally spend less money on travel than middle-class people? How might a working-class person be persuaded to spend more on travel?

10. Why is it that many of the members of an organized group are attracted to the same group tour package?

11. Why do the attitudes and behavior of a family and its members change over time?

12. Why is the empty nest stage of the family life cycle becoming longer than it used to be? What are the implications of this for those who market and sell travel services?

13. Five different travel strategies were identified in this chapter. Which of these strategies best describes your own preferred way of traveling? Why do you prefer this travel strategy?

14. Teenagers form a distinct subcultural group in U.S. society. One value that this subculture places great importance on is relationships with peers. What are some of the implications of this for those who market and sell travel services?

15. Why have sports become a valuable way of segmenting the market for travel?

16. Gift giving is an important factor in the marketing and selling of travel services. Why? Is it likely to be a more or less important factor in the future? Why?

POSTSCRIPT

The purpose of *The Psychology of Leisure Travel* parallels that of Stephen Daedalus in James Joyce's *Portrait of the Artist as a Young Man:* "I go to encounter for the millionth time the reality of experience. . . ." Drs. Mayo and Jarvis here have distilled the motivation underlying why people travel. Thus, they have encountered the reality of experience *via* research on travel, so that the reader can cull from that distilled experience knowledge of what have been, are, and may continue to be the motives for travel.

Much can be learned about travel motivation from its roots in myth. According to one renowned psychologist, Carl Jung, myth still affects us today. Jung suggested that, even as the human body has undergone an evolution, each part adapting to emerging environmental demands, so the human psyche may also have undergone evolution. Even as human bodies retain physical elements from eons past, Jung believed, the human unconscious retains remnants of the past which he called the *collective unconscious,* a universal awareness transcending time and embodied in *archetypes.* Archetypes are most often manifested in myths. Jung researched and catalogued thousands of myths and claimed that elements of myths from widely separated cultures and times were so similar that they should not be dismissed as accidental.

One of these similarities is travel, often an inextricable part of the mythological narrative. From myth, we can see that the earliest travel motivations were fear and the search for adventure. Two of the famous mythological examples are Hercules and Odysseus; for both, travel was the medium of heroism. Their travel was full of foreboding, but it allowed them to engage in superhuman adventures. Their actions were not possible or even feasible in their home setting. Only travel allowed such daring.

There is a sense in which the motivations of these ancient mythological characters parallel the motivations of contemporary travelers. Today, travel still means a release from the pedestrian and the familiar. That release has a price: fear of the unexpected, the unknown. But the foreboding and fear of travel may be balanced by the spirit of adventure. Further, many of the qualities currently ascribed to travel have been present for centuries. It is striking, for instance, that a present-day research technique, psychographics, categorizes travelers by how they view travel — from fearful on one extreme to adventuresome on the other. The traveler's characteristics are tied to destinations: from nearby amusement parks for the psychocentrics, to the outer reaches of Mongolia for the allocentrics. In effect, we have come full circle, beginning with the narrative of myths to sophisticated research techniques, both of which offer clues to individual traveler motivation.

The course of business — specifically marketing — has come full circle as well. It might be said that the history of tourism is the history of marketing. Marketing as a business activity is relatively new to the business scene. Merchants have exchanged goods for barter or money since time immemorial, but only in recent times have merchants begun to plan for the sale of their products. Time was if you had a product, the sale of that product was the culmination and end of business activity. Now, instead of designing a product and *hoping* it can be sold, business people ask questions: Who will buy this product? Why might they buy? How can we inform those who may be interested about the product?

Initially, marketing's interest was in groups, large masses of people who might be persuaded or influenced to buy a given product. However, the marketing view was almost exclusively "group think" — finding out what made groups of people think before a product was marketed. The first marketing research was conducted only after the product was produced. Then, at some point, a business person asked, "Why not find out what these groups want in a product before the product is developed?" From an analysis of group behavior, marketers moved to a more definitive examination of smaller segments. Life-style analysis, psychographics, Maslow's hierarchy of needs — all have enhanced the efforts to anticipate particular consumer needs. Modern marketing attempts to find out what the consumer needs by identifying as many of the peculiar characteristics of a consumer group. It then develops a product to fit those needs and offers that product to the consumer. As marketing research advances, a more precise statement of individual groups' needs will be in the offing. In fact, *The Psychology of Leisure Travel* will certainly lend considerable assistance to this process.

If marketing has progressed through a series of steps so that it can accurately fit a product to a need, the same can be said of tourism. From offering a product and hoping it would be purchased by an unknown group of consumers, tourism marketers have come to realize the importance of researching consumer needs and tailoring products to fulfill them. And so we come full circle: from the earliest inferred motivation of travelers to the growth of marketing, to the development of tourism, and so to this book. Drs. Mayo and Jarvis offer incisive insights into why people travel, who travels, and under what conditions travel decisions are made. For those who must employ the marketing process in tourism, *The Psychology of Leisure Travel* will help identify those decision-makers and those consumer needs, so that the tourism professional can better balance product developed and value exchanged.

We might well expect further research in these areas so that, at some indeterminate future time, there can be a perfect fit of people, product, and value. The invocation for future research will be the same as it was for Drs. Mayo and Jarvis: to distill from research the experience which makes for full understanding.

Edward M. Kelly
Institute of Certified
Travel Agents

APPENDIX

NOTE

The five cases in this appendix describe a wide range of problem situations in the travel and tourism industries. These cases are not intended to illustrate either effective or ineffective handling of an administrative situation by the firms or organizations involved. Rather, they provide an opportunity for readers to think through actual problem situations, using the concepts and principles developed throughout this book. The purpose of discussing cases like these is not to come up with the right answers; in fact, there are generally no right or wrong answers to the questions following each case. Instead, each case is an exercise in identifying, analyzing, and solving problems.

CASE 1: AIR FLORIDA

Founded in 1972, Air Florida operated for its first several years as an intrastate airline, flying passengers between Miami and Tampa, Gainesville, Daytona Beach, Orlando, and other cities in Florida. The carrier built up business by stressing frequency of service and by offering discounts at off-peak times. It was not until 1978, however, that the airline realized its first yearly profit.

In the fall of 1978, the Airline Deregulation Act passed Congress and provided Air Florida with the opportunity to grow into something more than an intrastate air carrier. By the spring of 1979, it had expanded its fleet to include two Boeing 737s and five McDonnell Douglas DC-9s, as well as a few piston engine planes. Also by this time, it flew from Miami and Fort Lauderdale to Washington's Dulles Airport and offered fares that attracted considerable publicity. Its $53 one-way weekday fare and $80 weekend fare contrasted with the $107 basic economy fare charged by the major airlines on the Miami-Fort Lauderdale/Washington route. Also in the spring of 1979, Air Florida flew to St. Croix in the Virgin Islands, the Bahamas, and Philadelphia. In addition, the carrier won the right to fly to New York's Kennedy Airport by pledging to offer sharply discounted fares, and to Houston's close-in Hobby Airport under the "automatic entry" provision of the deregulation act (which grants each airline one new route per year).

The impact of deregulation on Air Florida is illustrated by its dramatic increase in number of passengers carried after the deregulation act went into effect. During the first four months of 1979, the airline carried nearly 400,000 passengers, a 64 percent increase over the same time period in 1978. Meanwhile, revenue-passenger-miles increased by 192 percent — reflecting, of course, Air Florida's movement into interstate air transportation.

The carrier's growth and aspirations were perhaps best illustrated by its bid to acquire National Airlines. Actually, it sought only National's foreign routes and overseas jets, but its interest in these amazed some industry observers. Other carriers interested in acquiring National included Pan Am, Eastern, and Texas International.

The chairman and chief executive of Air Florida was C. Edward Acker, a former president of Braniff International. Acker headed a group that acquired control of Air Florida in 1977 for $2 million, a sum the carrier needed desperately for working capital. Under Acker's leadership, the carrier proposed the acquisition of National's four long-range DC–10s and rights to its routes from Miami to London, Paris, and Frankfurt, as well as a planned route to Tel Aviv.

According to the March 12, 1979, issue of *Business Week*, Acker insisted that the decision to bid for National

> was dictated by self-preservation. It goes back to the inroads Air Florida made with deep-discount fares on interstate markets dominated by Eastern. Eastern promptly retaliated by cutting intrastate fares in half on all flights between Miami and four Florida cities — Gainesville, Tampa, Daytona Beach, and Orlando. These were the markets that were the foundation of Air Florida, built by offering discounts at off-peak times. By cutting fares on all flights between those points, Eastern reduced Air Florida's traffic by 27 percent between October and December last year.

Acker publicly expressed his fear that if Eastern were allowed to take over

National it would become such a giant that Air Florida would be hard pressed to compete. Early in 1980, Air Florida charged in a formal complaint to the CAB that Eastern was engaging in various unfair and anticompetitive practices — including "predatory pricing" — and claimed the moves were designed to eliminate Air Florida as a competitor in Eastern's prime Florida markets. In its formal complaint to the CAB, Air Florida included copies of various internal Eastern documents. These included a memo stating that the answer to the "Air Florida problem" should be a low fare counter-offensive. This strategy, according to Air Florida, took the form of Eastern's intra-Florida "tag end" fares, which undercut Air Florida's low rates. Air Florida also complained that Eastern discriminated against it in several other ways.

Air Florida believed that it would have to continue its growth if it were to remain competitive. In the spring of 1980, the CAB gave the airline temporary authority to operate nonstop from Miami to Amsterdam, Brussels, and Zurich. The carrier proposed low discount fares for these routes, ranging up to 48 percent off rates charged by other carriers. The carrier also announced that it would begin daily service from Miami to Honduras, Haiti, and the Dominican Republic, and it also applied to the CAB for authority to fly to London beginning in 1981.

At this point, the reader is asked to assume that he is the director of sales and marketing for Air Florida. One of the key responsibilities of this position is the development of an overall advertising strategy for the airline. Further assume that you come across a reprint of an article in Air Transport World *which discusses divergent views of the role of airline advertising. A number of airline and advertising agency executives express their viewpoints and advertising philosophies in this article. Some of them are provided for you below.**

In advertising, as in so many other things the airlines do, many decisions are made on the basis of what the competition is doing. So today there is a flood of price advertising, embellished with what the airlines hope are catchy names — and with footnotes that often take away what the advertisements seem to offer. . . .

As Jonas Berger, head of the agency bearing his name, sees it, "The U.S. domestic carriers are all blending together in the public's mind, selling price and losing their individuality." Desmond Slattery of Tinker Campbell Ewald agrees: "Much price advertising is wasted. Despite the heavy advertising — maybe because of it — the public gets the idea that all the airlines match each other. So they pick their airline on another basis." Developing and exploiting this basis is the job of advertising, Slattery says.

Marvin Davis of Kelly Nason's LTD division sees things a little differently. Domestic airlines with very large budgets can probably get away with price advertising, he says, and bludgeon their message across. But international carriers, especially those with smaller budgets, must depend on finesse. "The product must be presented in the most appetizing way — call it imagery or magic. It can't be

---

*This section quotes from "Admen's Advice to Airlines: Make Sure You've Got It Before You Flaunt It," *Air Transport World* (July, 1978), pp. 41-44.

sold by price alone," he says. Unfortunately, he adds, much advertising tries to be different in order to catch this magic, but only ends up being a better carbon copy.

Davis believes, and John deGarmo of the deGarmo agency supports him, that airline advertising needs an injection of packaged-goods marketing expertise. Eastern gets high marks from deGarmo for hiring people with this kind of background.

"Travel is in the fashion business, just like liquor or clothes," Davis says. "You've got to create desire and demand for your product, and price isn't the best way to do it." That's why it is unwise to let sales management overshadow marketing management in an airline's operation, according to Davis. Sales wants to put bodies in seats, and thus tends to be price-oriented, whereas marketing tends to look for basic strengths that can be presented in a consistent and exciting program.

James Callaway of Holland & Callaway estimates that the airlines spend about 35% of their advertising dollars in newspapers and says that much of the money is wasted. "I don't see that they get their money's worth out of those big proud ads that list their schedules," he says. "Newspapers are for news."

To Callaway, "news" should be an easy-to-remember feature like "every hour on the hour" or "most flights to Podunk" or "we get you there for breakfast" or a new route, rather than listings that are better left to timetables.

A different view comes from Thomas Dunkerton of Compton Advertising, who says the consumer is basically lazy. Anything the airline can do to simplify his life — ease of travel, speed, convenience, comfort — will get his business if properly advertised. But the advertising has to stand for something real, not phony, Dunkerton says. What's more it has to be simple, specific, informative and relevant.

In Dunkerton's opinion, the airlines making the most money are those whose ads are not necessarily the most attractive but the most informative. "I never think of United anymore when flying between New York and Chicago," he says, "because I don't have a clear idea of their schedule."

Callaway's emphasis on news, however, is backed by other pros. Most of them see TWA's roundtrip check-in as the type of new feature that airlines can promote very profitably. Callaway also mentions Air Jamaica's inflight fashion show and Varig's "executive stewardess" as promotable features.

But "news" is just one of the ways to achieve uniqueness, the characteristic that inclines the traveler to think of one airline rather than another. Joe Berger criticizes the Asian airlines on this score: "They all seem to feature Oriental crews and service in their ads. Maybe it's time for someone to swim against the stream," he says. He took humorous advantage of this sameness for his client Varig's Los Angeles-Tokyo service by featuring a Japanese swinger-type male extolling Varig's excellent service.

John deGarmo disagrees. "I just love those Singapore Airlines color spreads, especially that slogan, 'Our wings have angels.' The ads get across the idea of the stability and credibility of this relatively new airline," he says.

. . . .The admen we talked to were unanimous in praise of British Airways' long-running campaign built around actor Robert Morley. The campaign meets three vital tests, they agreed: it establishes the identity of the airline, it sells the airline, and it sells the destination.

Questions

1. What specific factors, in your opinion, are most likely to influence travelers to choose to fly Air Florida? Why, in your view, are these the decisive factors?
2. If Air Florida continues to grow both as a domestic and international air carrier, what kind of advertising strategy should it use? Why?

CASE 2:   PANORAMA TRAVEL AGENCY

Marilyn Davis spent Saturday afternoon in her office at Panorama Travel clearing some paperwork off her desk and thinking about the decision she would have to make by the end of the month. Marilyn had started Panorama Travel four years earlier and had seen it grow to a point where it was now booking more than $1.2 million worth of travel business. She employed five full-time travel counselors, and two part-time agents were added during six months of the year.

During the last year, Panorama's business had increased by nearly 40 percent. Marilyn attributed most of this gain to her efforts to promote more cruise and group business. About 50 percent of Panorama's business had previously come from commercial accounts, but this source of business had decreased to less than 40 percent with the increase in cruise and group business.

Panorama Travel was located in a Northeastern city of close to 200,000 people. The economy of the city had for a long time depended primarily on heavy industry. Its blue-collar character had gradually become more balanced, however, as the city became an increasingly important commercial, banking, and medical center. In addition, two universities located nearby had doubled their enrollments during the preceding ten years, and this, too, helped to change the overall character of the resident work force in the city.

Some nine travel agencies operated in the city and the surrounding area. Panorama Travel was one of four agencies located in the downtown section of the city. As in many other cities, the downtown area had begun to deteriorate several years earlier, when many retail businesses moved out to the suburbs. The city, however, had begun a program of rejuvenating the downtown area, tearing down old buildings, turning two blocks of the main street into a mall, and attracting new businesses into the area. The numerous small retail shops that had once existed in the area began to be replaced by new office buildings, a couple of large banks, a new convention and civic center, several new restaurants, and a new 300-room hotel.

Panorama Travel operated in a street-level storefront location on the outer edge of the main 18-square-block downtown area. Marilyn Davis had selected this location for her new travel agency four years earlier in part because she was confident that the city fathers' plans for revitalizing the downtown area would work. She had also been able to negotiate what she considered a very favorable four-year lease.

By the end of the month, Marilyn would have to decide whether to renew the lease. Thinking it over, she realized that she had several options. She could renew the lease, although the landlord had already quoted her a rental figure that reflected the new economic vitality of the downtown area and would represent nearly a 60 percent increase in her rental expense. Marilyn thought that she might be able to negotiate a slightly lower rental figure. She also felt that if her business continued to grow, it would absorb the increased rental expense within a year or two.

Rather than remain in the same location, Marilyn recognized that there might be some good reasons to move Panorama Travel. One option was to move into the third-floor quarters of one of Panorama's competitors, a local bank travel agency that was going out of business. This new location would be situated directly in the center of the growing downtown area. Marilyn had already discussed the matter with bank officials and had been quoted a rental figure that was slightly higher than the rent she would have to begin paying if she kept Panorama Travel in its present location.

Another option was to move to a shopping center location. There were, in fact, two such locations at which Marilyn had looked. One was in a newly opened regional shopping center located northeast of the city, where most new residential growth was taking place. The rent at this location would be higher than at any other location Marilyn was considering. She was also aware of the additional overhead expenses she would incur at such a location.

The second shopping center location that Marilyn was considering was actually a small shopping plaza several miles away from the downtown area. This shopping plaza served one of the most exclusive residential sections in the area. It consisted of one medium-sized supermarket, a drug store, a variety store, a small restaurant, and a dry cleaning establishment. The space that Panorama Travel would occupy here had been used previously by a liquor store, and the rent would be only slightly more than Marilyn was now paying at her present location.

Marilyn realized that there were advantages and disadvantages to each location. There were many factors suggesting she should sign a new lease on her present location. One of these was that her present location could more easily accommodate expansion, which might be necessary in the future. At the same time, she worried about the added overhead expenses she could incur not only at her current location, but at some of the others as well. She recognized that if her rent expense rose sharply, she would have to reduce costs in other areas, at least for a period of time. For these reasons, Marilyn found herself leaning more and more toward the shopping plaza location.

Questions

1. What effect would a move from its present location have on Panorama Travel's present business? Can anything be done to ensure that none of this business is lost?
2. How can Panorama Travel manage to absorb an increased rental expense?
3. In your opinion, what decision should Marilyn Davis make? Why?

CASE 3: MATCH POINT TENNIS CLUB

A well-known resort in the southeastern U.S. hired Jim Wittenbach as its first tennis director. This was a newly created position, and Wittenbach's initial assignment was to make a comprehensive study of tennis operations at the resort followed by recommendations based on his analysis.

Development of the resort had begun in 1957, and it included residential subdivisions, parks, and utilities, as well as golf, tennis, pool, horseback riding, marina, and other recreational and resort facilities. The resort positioned itself as an "adult athletic playground" and heavily promoted its tennis facilities in the national media. Its principal business, however, was the sale and resale of homesites, houses, and villas. It also acted as agent and received fees for renting privately owned homes and villas. Nearly all of the company's sales were made to vacationers or visitors to the resort. The typical first-time visitor to the resort stayed seven days, while repeat visitors stayed twelve days. Research indicated that beach swimming was the most popular activity for both first-time and repeat visitors. Twenty-nine percent of repeat visitors listed golf as their primary leisure activity, while 17 percent listed tennis.

Jim Wittenbach discovered that tennis court usage had more than doubled during each of the previous three years. Even though the number of courts had increased from 8 to 23, utilization of the courts had increased from 18 percent to 47 percent. Wittenbach realized that the use of the tennis facilities would increase even more in the next few years for two reasons. First, the company estimated that the number of guests visiting the resort would double in the next two years. Second, the number of court hours per guest-night would continue to rise because of the rising popularity of tennis throughout the U.S.

It was clear to Wittenbach that he would need to recommend an expansion of tennis facilities at the resort. Any expansion beyond four new courts would create a serious problem, however, because there was not enough space for more than four additional courts at the site of the present tennis facility. Opening more than four new courts would require a duplication of facilities and staff at a new location. A second tennis pro shop, for example, would cost $100,000. In addition, each new court would cost $12,000.

The problem facing the company was that, in all probability, the demand for its tennis facilities would be very high during the summer months — higher than it had the capacity to serve. Extra courts could be built, but since they would only be used during the vacation months, they would cause a net loss to the company. Of course, limited court capacity during the summer months would not enhance the resort's image. Wittenbach had heard complaints about the unavailability of courts during the prime playing hours of 9–11 A.M. and 4–6 P.M. He was also concerned about comments that the combination of high temperatures and humidity from noon to 4 P.M. created very uncomfortable playing conditions during July and August.

Wittenbach concluded that the resort would need to double the number of courts if each guest who wanted to play tennis was to get the chance to play at least once a day for an hour. In a report to top management, he made several recommendations that would put off, for a time at least, the need to build an entirely new tennis facility. These recommendations included the following:

1. All promotional literature should warn prospective guests that the tennis courts will be crowded in the summer months.
2. Court time should be allocated through a reservation system that will steer demand to times when the courts are often not in use.

3. Court fees should be changed to increase the attractiveness of doubles play.
4. Set up tennis mixers and round robins and schedule them at the beginning of each week to enable a new group of vacationers to meet and size up each other's tennis game.
5. Promote activities that are not filled to capacity, such as surfing, sailing, and nature walks.
6. Add lights to a number of courts so that tennis could be played after dusk.
7. Open the courts at 6 A.M., two hours earlier than usual, and provide complimentary coffee and doughnuts to "early birds."
8. Build a few new courts, but neither a clubhouse nor a tennis shop, at a new site. Instead, set up a tent to house someone to check reservations, collect fees, and sell balls. The overflow tennis area would be opened only in the peak months and would be staffed mainly with college students on summer vacation.

Wittenbach concluded his report by stating that the recommendations he made would help to make tennis a profitable operation at the resort.

Questions

1. Evaluate each one of Wittenbach's recommendations.
2. How do you think visitors to the resort would react if all of Wittenbach's recommendations were implemented?

CASE 4: THE ANDREWS INN

In 1978, Mr. Frank Gasper joined with four other investors and purchased the Andrews Inn, a 125-room, full-service motor inn in South Bend, Indiana. Located less than a mile from Interstate 80, the Andrews Inn was one of four major lodging facilities located within a mile of each other. These four motels included a Holiday Inn, a Ramada Inn, a Howard Johnson Motor Lodge, and the Andrews Inn, the only independent among the four. The tourist and business travel markets were also served by a Quality Inn, an Albert Pick Motor Lodge, and two other Holiday Inns in the South Bend area. In addition, there were three budget motels and a number of small independent motels operating in the area.

The Andrews Inn had fared quite well in this market for several years. The predominant segment of the market it served was the business traveler. During much of the year, its weekday occupancy rate usually ran at 80 percent or better, and during the summer months the inn would often be completely full during the week. Weekend occupancy rates varied widely, however. During the summer months, tourist business would usually keep weekend occupancy rates above 50 percent. During the rest of the year, however, weekend occupancy rates would usually fall well below that figure, except on weekends when special events (such as football games and graduation exercises) at the nearby University of Notre Dame made hotel and motel rooms hard to come by in the South Bend area. The Andrews Inn had substantial repeat patronage, and even those customers who regularly patronized one of the competitive inns in the area often remarked how much they enjoyed the facilities at the Andrews Inn when it was necessary to stay there.

Since purchasing the Andrews Inn, Gasper and his fellow investors had become increasingly concerned with a number of developments. First, occupancy rates had gradually begun to fall off. Compared to figures of the year before, monthly occupancy rates had fallen an average of four percent for the past 12 months. This decrease had taken place despite the fact that room rates at the Andrews Inn had not been increased at all, while most competitors had raised their rates two to three dollars on average. The Andrews Inn had also been promoting weekend mini-vacations at special rates in an effort to increase weekend occupancy. It was generally agreed by the Andrews Inn owners that the fall-off in occupancy was the result of the rapid increase in the price of gasoline and a general slowdown of the economy.

A second factor that concerned Gasper and his fellow investors was that ground had recently been broken in downtown South Bend for a 300-room Marriott Hotel. This new hotel would operate directly across the street from a modern convention center that the city had constructed in the mid-1970s. In addition, it was known that an Ohio group was seeking zoning approval in preparation for constructing a 200-room Hilton Inn immediately adjacent to the Notre Dame campus. This new facility, if built, would be located less than three miles from the Andrews Inn.

At the most recent meeting of the investors, who served as the board of directors for the Andrews Inn, Gasper had listened to one of his colleagues, Mr. Ken Milani, propose that they affiliate with a major national lodging chain. Milani passed around some materials describing the Rodeway Inns organization, and after looking at this material the group discussed the matter briefly and then decided to devote their next meeting to a full discussion of the advantages and disadvantages of affiliating with a major national lodging chain. At the close of the meeting, Gasper remarked to one of his colleagues: "I'm not sure that this is going to be the answer to our problem. It seems to me that the $30,000 or so that it would cost to become part of an organization like Rodeway would not be the best way to try to solve our problem. We'll just have to study it closely, I guess."

A few days later, Gasper was in New York on other business. During the plane ride back to South Bend, he was reading a copy of *The New York Times* and happened to come across an article on the Best Western organization, titled "Best Western Passes Rivals, Revamps Image." This article is reproduced on the pages that follow.

PHOENIX — Best Western International, an association of more than 2,297 hoteliers in 50 states and 18 countries, is to lodging what the Sunkist cooperative is to oranges. A formidable marketer, Best Western exists only to serve its members. It has no shareholders, no company properties, and no corporate profits.

"We are the only nonprofit hotel chain in the world," said Robert C. Hazard Jr., the association's chief executive officer.

Best Western, which calls itself "the world's largest lodging chain," is growing faster than any other and has passed its major competitors, Holiday Inns, Quality Inns, and Travelodge. It increased its share of the market from 5 percent in 1975 to 11 percent last year, and Mr. Hazard predicts that, by the end of the decade,

Best Western will command one-third of the United States' $15 billion lodging business.

At a time when the lodging industry has become dominated by corporations, Best Western represents the organized effort of hundreds of independent hoteliers who want to remain independent while still enjoying the marketing and financial services offered by big chains.

Mr. Hazard, who joined the operation in 1974 when it was struggling, has convinced the members that the future of independent hoteliers lies in cooperating, sprucing up their image, and providing an elaborate computerized reservations network.

In five years, the 45-year-old former American Express executive has more than doubled the number of Best Western members. This month, he begins the long process of winning membership approval for a change from Best Western's image as a roadside motel and a change of name and symbol.

In the past, the quality and comfort of Best Western accommodations ranged widely, from four-star elegance in Colorado Springs to an occasional, somewhat scruffy roadside motel in an out-of-the-way town. The lack of standardization may have been Best Western's singular liability in competing with, say, Holiday Inns or Ramada Inns, which have offered a guaranteed level of comfort and service.

As part of Mr. Hazard's image-polishing campaign, the association instituted a quality-standards program complete with periodic checks of accommodations; in recent months, Best Western "terminated" 467 members for failure to meet the standards.

Even the association's familiar logo has come in for scrutiny.

"For our hotels in France, the Western image is not appropriate," he said. The yellow sign topped with a crown is unpopular with some members, so a search has begun for a new symbol. "What we need is a symbol that screams on the highways and whispers in the cities," said Mr. Hazard.

Through diplomacy and cajolery, Mr. Hazard has turned Best Western, initially organized in 1948 as a mutual referral association of independent motel owners in the western United States, into an aggressive hotel chain. A system that allows each member a voice has drawbacks, however, and Mr. Hazard, who cannot set policy or direct the company as most chief executives do, must answer to individual members and their elected board of directors.

Mr. Hazard tried and failed to get the members to drop individual names and use only the Best Western trademark. Such hotels as the Barbizon Plaza in New York flatly refused. He has also been in a long debate with members over quality categorization.

But he has been successful in demonstrating the benefit of a centralized "command post" in Phoenix. The first phase of Best Western's communications system cost $15 million. Using high-speed computers like those for airline reservations, it links the organization's hotels in 1,500 cities and employs 1,000 agents to handle the seven million calls that come in annually. But those calls generated about $175 million in room sales for members, or about 20 percent of their annual occupancy.

Mr. Hazard is intent on expanding and refining the system. Standing in an unfinished room at the new world headquarters here, he talked about the futuristic plan.

"We've got a designer from Disney World," he said. "We'll be able to pull in information from all over the world. Instantaneously, we'll be able to know how many rooms are filled on a given day in a given hotel anywhere."

Using the reservations system and support services including advertising and travel agency services, Best Western's members average pretax profit margins of up to 15 percent, about twice the industry average. Last year, Best Western members generated $225 million in net income and $1.5 billion in revenues.

Because Best Western's members are not responsible for providing profits for the parent, its affiliation costs and membership fees are about one-third lower than those for Howard Johnson's, Travelodge, and Holiday Inns, and half as expensive as those for Sheraton, Ramada, Rodeway, and Quality Inns. Mr. Hazard estimates that 25 percent of growth has come from franchise conversions.

The minimum fee for initial affiliation is $4,208 for 20 units or less plus $38 for each additional unit. Annual dues start at $610 for 20 units plus $21 a unit up to 50 and $7 a unit above that number. Other fees support the reservations center, the in-house advertising agency, and the training center for new members.

Best Western, like the franchisers, requires members to display the organization's symbol and use certain identifying products, such as soap and matches. Furniture and fixtures can be purchased through the headquarters at a discount, but that is not a membership requirement.

In the 1980s, Best Western will concentrate on what Mr. Hazard calls the "unique void" created by the moves by Holiday Inns, Hilton, and Ramada Inns into casino gambling; by Howard Johnson and Travelodge, which are both British-owned, into overseas markets, and by Marriott and Hyatt into the luxury segment of the business.

"Nobody has been caring for the average traveler, who wants variety in his lodging, ease of reservations, good service, and a medium-priced room," said Mr. Hazard. "That is our market."

Questions

1. What would be the primary advantages to Andrews Inn of affiliating with a national lodging chain organization? The disadvantages?
2. If the Andrews Inn owners decide to affiliate with a national lodging chain organization, what criteria should be established to help choose from among those chains with which it might be able to affiliate?
3. In your opinion, what should be done to deal with the problem of declining occupancy rates at the Andrews Inn?

CASE 5: THE FINNISH BUREAU OF TOURISM*

Until recently, Finland was a neglected area in the European travel market. It had been seen as too far away from the major tourist centers. Its climate had been

*Adapted, with permission of the author, from: Philip Kotler, *Marketing for Nonprofit Organizations* (Englewood Cliffs, New Jersey: Prentice-Hall, Inc., 1975).

regarded as too cold. Its language was unfamiliar. As a result, Finland attracted only a few thousand foreign tourists a year.

During the last ten years, however, there has been a major change in European tourism patterns and tastes. Many travelers have already visited traditional tourist countries such as England, France, Spain, Italy, and Greece. These areas are overcrowded in the summer months. Their prices have been rising constantly. Tourists have shown a growing interest in exploring other countries in search of new experiences.

All these factors led to the discovery of Finland by tourists. Perhaps the most important factor has been the intensive information and marketing activity of the Finnish Bureau of Tourism. The Bureau has directed very heavy advertising campaigns in several countries; and it has made loans to hotel chains and other enterprises working with tourism.

The Finnish Bureau of Tourism, located in the Ministry of Commerce, was created in February 1971. Its responsibilities cover the promotion of foreign tourism to Finland as well as domestic tourism, tourist enterprises and their financing, tourist information, vocational training for tourism, and the surveillance of government tourist property. To carry out its responsibilities, the Bureau has to work effectively with several different groups: airlines, hotel and motel chains, all media, foreign travel agencies, branch offices of Finnish travel organizations abroad, and foreign governments.

The tourist market "discovered" Finland in the late 1960s. The tourist-growth trend in recent years has been 30 to 40 percent annually, while in most other European countries it has been only about 20 percent. Tourism has become the third largest industry in Finland and has turned the Finnish balance of trade from a deficit of $31.3 million in 1963 to a surplus of better than $34 million in recent years.

Who are the tourists? Of the 2,300,000 foreign tourists, about half come from the other Scandanavian countries and the other half are non-Scandanavian. Of the non-Scandanavians, about 40 percent come from West Germany and the remainder are from America, England, Belgium, France, Switzerland, Italy, and so forth.

It would seem that the Finnish people would feel pleased with the country's success in attracting foreign tourists. On the contrary, the people have very mixed feelings. The rapid growth of tourism has been accompanied by several problems.

First, the tourist influx is highly seasonal. Nearly 50 percent of the tourists come in the three months of June, July, and August.

Second, most of the tourists have come from lower- or middle-income classes with small travel budgets; they live in tents or trailers; they bring their own food; in a word, they spend very little money in Finland. Furthermore, they crowd the Finnish vacation spots at a time when the Finnish people are also on vacation and seeking rest and relaxation. This has led to many complaints.

Third, Finnish environmental groups have complained that their scenic land, particularly the lake area and Lapland, is being threatened with ruin. The Lapps have complained about the litter and about tentfuls of tourists who camp next to their previously peaceful summer cottages.

The Finnish Bureau of Tourism recognizes that it has a new problem to solve. The earlier problem was to attract people to Finland. They succeeded but now are forced to adopt new objectives. Their major objectives must be to reshape the compositional and seasonal characteristics of the tourists. They seek to achieve the following specific objectives in the next few years:

1. They would like to attract fewer but wealthier tourists.
2. They would like to attract fewer tourists in the summer and more in the other seasons. This would leave more breathing space for the Finnish population during the summer.
3. They would like to attract more tourists who are motivated by wanderlust rather than sunlust. The sunlusting tourists want facilities like they have at home and this calls for much Finnish investment in new facilities. The wanderlust tourists, on the other hand, come to enjoy a different culture and live as people do in that culture.
4. They would like to attract tourists to areas in Finland that would not overtax or threaten Finland's best sites with pollution and ruin.

Questions

1. Are the new objectives of the Finnish Bureau of Tourism reasonable, consistent, and obtainable? Could you suggest any modifications of these objectives?
2. Outline a marketing plan for the Finnish Bureau of Tourism that will accomplish the set of objectives you believe are reasonable.

INDEX